CARTOONING

ROY PAUL NELSON

HENRY REGNERY COMPANY · CHICAGO

Library of Congress Cataloging in Publication Data

Nelson, Roy Paul.
    Cartooning.

    Bibliography: p.
    Includes index.
    1. Caricature. I. Title.
    NC1320.N38 1975   741.5   75-13236
    ISBN 0-8092-8212-7
    ISBN 0-8092-8211-9 pbk.

To Marie

Published by Henry Regnery Company
180 North Michigan Avenue, Chicago, Illinois 60601
Manufactured in the United States of America
Library of Congress Catalog Card Number: 75-13236
International Standard Book Number: 0-8092-8212-7 (cloth)
                                    0-8092-8211-9 (paper)

Published simultaneously in Canada by
Fitzhenry & Whiteside Limited
150 Lesmill Road
Don Mills, Ontario M3B 2T5
Canada

Contents

Preface

Cartooning evolves from a Caricature and Graphic Humor course I introduced at the University of Oregon in the Eisenhower years. Designed as an art appreciation as well as a how-to-do-it course, it has, over the years, attracted students not only from the school of journalism, which sponsors it, and the fine arts department, where you would expect to find a few cartoonists hiding out, but also from the political science department, the English department, and most other disciplines on campus. Cartoon lovers know no academic boundaries.

Like the course, the book serves two audiences: persons who "can't draw a straight line" but who enjoy cartoons and want to better understand the creative process behind them and persons with art ability who entertain the thought of putting it to professional use.

The course I teach dwells for some weeks on the birth of the cartoon and the stages it went through as it associated itself with the mass media. This book is not so broad in scope. Whatever appraisal the reader encounters here will be more contemporary than historical. To familiarize himself with cartooning's "Golden Age" he should turn to any of the numerous histories, biographies, and autobiographies cited in the bibliography.

Whatever drawing instruction the reader encounters will be more peripheral than literal. The teaching here is mainly by example. There are tidbits of advice, and most of the tricks and affectations of cartoonists are identified and explored, but the book, unlike the usual how-to-do-it, avoids a one-two-three, easy-steps approach. Cartooning is too lively an art to conform to any set of rules.

The book's chief value, I think, lies in its bringing together examples of the works of nearly 100 editorial cartoonists, caricaturists, comic-strip artists, gag cartoonists, illustrators, sculptors, and other artists, most from the present but some from the past. On these pages you will see drawings by some of the world's most honored cartoonists as well as drawings by some who are not well known but who should be.

That I have included examples of my own cartoons will not, I hope, seem too obviously a reaching out for recognition through association. Some points in the text that needed illustrating could not be handled very conveniently through negotiation with others. But no, I do not consider my cartoons as belonging in the same league with those produced by name cartoonists.

I am deeply grateful for the rights granted me by these cartoonists—and in some cases by their syndicates, publishers, and agents—to show their works. My most satisfying moment in gathering materials came a week after posting a letter to Gluyas Williams asking about a drawing of Robert Benchley I admired. Knowing Williams was born in 1888, I wasn't at all sure he was still around. But there it was: his note, written in his own hand (not quite as steady as in his great days with the original *Life* and *The New Yorker*) granting me the permission I needed. "I'm very happy to do anything to help perpetuate the memory of Benchley," he wrote. Cartoonists—many of them—are like that.

Start

1

Art on an Errand

The cartoon made something of a comeback in the 1970s after a decade or two of atrophy. Editorial cartoonists grew more vigorous in their attacks on public officials, one of the good things to come out of Watergate; gag cartoonists tackled subjects that, a few years earlier, editors would not have touched with a ten-foot pencil; comic strips became funny again; and advertising and public relations types seemed more willing in print to poke a little fun at their products or clients.

After the doldrums of the 1950s, the comic magazines came back strong in the 1960s and 1970s, some to subject their airborne heroes to introspection, some to espouse social causes. For those who liked their entertainment raw, there were the underground comics, or "comix" as aficionados called them.

Young people were drawing again, and not a few contemplated careers in what editorial cartoonist Don Hesse once called "The Ungentlemanly Art." Veteran gag cartoonist Bo Brown expressed what many thought when he said, "To

1

my mind, cartooning is one of the truly relaxing professions. If I'm tired, I draw."

The first issue of *The Mother Earth News* (January 1970), maybe because editor John Shuttleworth was a minor-league cartoonist for a time, devoted a large percentage of its space to freelance cartooning. As Shuttleworth explained: cartooning offers "a way out of the 9-to-5 rap for a certain number of talented and determined individuals. . . . It can be deliriously wonderful play that you just happen to get paid for." But, the magazine warned, "Cartooning, like most other endeavors, can be brutally hard work. . . ."

The colleges recognized the cartoon as a legitimate area for study. For fall semester 1974, Yale ran a course in political cartooning and hired Bill Mauldin to teach it. Out of 300 applicants for enrollment, the school selected a grateful· 18.

Museums displayed cartoons; dealers sold the originals (cartoonists had given them away in years past); gag cartoonists, dissatisfied with the 1930s prices they were getting for their work, organized into a guild, calling it at first the Magazine Cartoonists Guild and then, to broaden its base, the Cartoonists Guild.

Editorial cartoonists already had their Association of American Editorial Cartoonists and comic-strip artists their National Cartoonists Society. Even caricaturists had their own organization: Caricaturists Society of America.

By far the most important of the organizations was the NCC, with about 500 members, some of them coming from other than comic-strip ranks. Each year the Society awards a Reuben (named for Rube Goldberg) to the cartoonist voted by the members as best of the year.

But cartoonists do not take naturally to organizations, including this one. Rube Goldberg himself, although he served as the first president, once said: "Everything creative starts with disorganization. Most of the world's troubles have come from over-organization."

In 1974 the Museum of Cartoon Art opened at Greenwich, Connecticut, with Mort Walker, creator of *Beetle Bailey*, as president and Jack Tippit, the much-published gag cartoonist and creator of *Amy*, as director. In addition to the exhibits and collections, the museum houses a cartoon Hall of Fame.

Earlier, Bill Blackbeard, a writer and comics scholar in San Francisco, alarmed that libraries all over the country were destroying old newspapers with all their comics pages after microfilming them, started his San Francisco Academy of Comic Art to retrieve the papers, clip the comics, and store "runs" of them for scholars' use.

"The cartoon is a form which has a basic appeal that can't ever be done away with," Jules Feiffer has observed. "One of the reasons for the appeal is that it's extremely flexible. . . . It's a terrific form of shorthand, allowing one to express one's self in whichever way one chooses, without all sorts of excuses or embellishments or disguises. It's a direct, marvelous approach."

The word *cartoon* originally described the plan or drawing on heavy paper used as a guide for a painting, mosaic, tapestry, or other work of art. Today the word means a drawing, usually humorous, that stands by itself as a work of art, however crude its origin or humble its purpose. It is art destined for publication. Because, compared to other art, it is executed quickly and it is used, often enough, for commercial purposes, the cartoon has not enjoyed the serious attention other art has enjoyed.

In the plastic arts, the fine artists—the easel painters and the sculptors—enjoy the most prestige. So far as the critics are concerned, illustrators—the people who do art, no matter how fine, to accompany articles, stories, or advertisements—are hardly in the same class. They are lucky if the critics even notice their work.

"We're especially grateful to Jamie Wyeth for permission to use his drawings," *Harper's* says at the opening of a special issue on "American Character: Trial and Triumph" (October

1974). "Mr. Wyeth is a distinguished painter, not a magazine illustrator," *Harper's* explains apologetically. The truth of the matter is that when Mr. Wyeth allows his work to be published in connection with a series of magazine articles he becomes an illustrator, despite the disclaimer.

Lowest in the pecking order, of course, is the cartoonist. "Nothing more than a cartoon" is a term of reproach one hears applied to a piece of art or a literary work that fails to measure up to someone's arbitrary set of standards. Such use of the term reveals an ignorance of the role the cartoon has played in the mass media and even in the more select media of communications, including the galleries.

Defined broadly enough, the term *cartoon* can be applied to the work of some of the world's most honored painters and draftsmen, including Honoré Daumier in nineteenth-century France, William Hogarth in eighteenth-century England, and Francisco Goya in eighteenth- and nineteenth-century Spain.

The Cartoon's Purposes

There are those among cartoonists who are tied grimly to causes. Their art has bite but little comedy. So agitated over social injustice was Robert Minor, the *St. Louis Post-Dispatch* and *New York Evening Journal* editorial cartoonist who helped pioneer the stark, lithographic look in newspaper cartoons, that he became more and more involved first in socialist and later communist causes, drawing only for radical organs, like *The Masses* and *The Liberator*, capping his career not as a cartoonist, a calling for which he was eminently qualified, but as a worker for the Communist Party and an editor of *The Daily Worker*.

There are others who, like Virgil (Vip) Partch, are uncommitted but too sophisticated to place their faith in anyone's promise to right wrongs. They take seriously, however, their high calling to provide readers with what Partch describes as "a few yuks."

But even if the cartoonist means only to entertain, he

almost always does more than that. "You can't write or draw *anything* without making some comment on society," Al Capp, creator of *Li'l Abner*, said in a *Playboy* interview. "No cartoonist, no matter how talentless or obscure, has ever drawn a dog without having made a comment on the state of dogs. He's never drawn an outhouse without making some incidental comment about rustic life in America."

The Cartoon Solution

One of the many magazines failing to survive the Great Depression was *Open Road for Boys*, a not-very-distinguished publication but one remembered fondly by today's middle-aged cartoonists as the sponsor of a popular cartoon contest. Each month the magazine presented its readers a potential tragedy in cartoon form: for instance, a goat was shown about

to butt an unsuspecting nature lover over a high embankment. Or, as in Harold West's scene, a bandit was shown about to send a sheriff to his death. It was the job of the reader/cartoonist to come up with some solution: a follow-up panel. The more ingenious the rescue the better. Winning solutions were shown in a follow-up issue. There were two or three modest prizes, and, almost as exciting, a couple of honorable mentions along with some runners-up. The expectation of being among the elect saw many boys in the 1930s keeping close watch for the mailman each month. Among those who felt the thrill of national exposure for the first time in *Open Road for Boys* was Mort Walker.

What the young *Road* contributors did in that contest is what cartoonists have always done: They solved life's problems in ways not open to ordinary problem solvers. Where but in the cartoon world could a character fall hundreds of feet without so much as a hint of discomfort? Where else could someone like Beetle Bailey appear as a heap of rubble after a run-in with his sergeant and then show up fresh and alert the next day, with no signs of the earlier violence upon him?

Beetle Bailey is copyrighted by King Features Syndicate. This drawing is used by permission of Mort Walker.

Kinds of Cartoons
Editorial Cartoons

Editorial (sometimes called political) cartoons are cartoons with a message. They mean to sway public opinion. The weakest of them merely restate the news in graphic form. The strongest depict a political, social, or economic problem and, by implication, offer some solution.

In a *Time* essay, Stefan Kanfer in 1975 saw the editorial cartoon as "gaining influence. . . . The mood of the nation is skepticism, not credulity. The appetite for the cartoon is whetted. International and local tensions call for caricature, not portrait."

The strength of an editorial cartoon lies in its analogy. The best of the editorial cartoonists do not depict a problem in literal terms. They liken it to something else and invite the reader to stretch his imagination.

For a 1969 cartoon (p. 8) Bill Mauldin could have drawn a tired, overworked, or inefficient Nixon. People—and especially people like Richard Nixon—are more fun to draw than lightbulbs and wires. But that would have been taking the easy way out. Besides, Mauldin's point was not that the Nixon presidency experienced this difficulty; it was that the presidency in general was too much for one man.

Necessarily, the editorial cartoonist draws in a sort of shorthand, taking complex issues and reducing them to simple if not simplistic terms. Allan Nevins wrote of Hamilton Fish, a cabinet member in Grant's administration: "He sometimes chipped the cube of truth to make it roll." The same could be said of the editorial cartoonist.

"In satirizing events and event makers, the [editorial] cartoon refines material until only the ridiculous essence remains," Stephan Kanfer wrote in *Time*.

An effective editorial cartoon stirs the passions, causing readers to react vigorously against the message or nod their head in agreement.

"Most [editorial] cartoons are of a needling nature,"

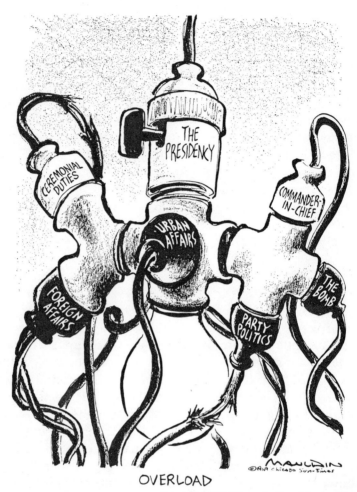

OVERLOAD

Herblock of the *Washington Post* said in *The Herblock Book.* "This
is a matter of much regret to me as it may be to some good
legislators who never get the recognition in pictures or in
words that is given to the hatchet brigade. . . . Cartoons don't
make up into lace valentines very well. . . . I could do pictures
every day of the week showing Uncle Sam resting his hand on

someone's shoulder and saying, 'Well done, Insertname,' and I think we'd all get pretty sick of them."

"On the face of it," David Low, the British cartoonist, adds in *Low's Autobiography*, "one would not say the attitude of political caricaturists was one of admiration or even goodwill. The traditional terms of their expression are perhaps better adapted to censure than to praise. Admiration is for the poets. A satirist perverted to hero-worship becomes pathetic and sickening. His approval can best be expressed by leaving its object alone."

The typical editorial cartoon attacks a bumbling if not devious public official. Or it deflates some stuffed shirt. To do either of these jobs, the cartoon resorts to *caricature,* the art of making people look like themselves, only more so. Caricature, which depends on distortion for its effects, is a high and dastardly art, eminently unfair, but necessary to make a character instantly recognizable and—usually—hated.

Some writers use *caricature* and *editorial* (or *political) cartooning* interchangeably, but, technically, caricature is only part of editorial cartooning. And not all editorial cartoons contain caricature.

Originally developed for magazines (Thomas Nast, for instance, the "father" of editorial cartooning in the United States, drew for a magazine called *Harper's Weekly*), editorial cartoons soon became more closely tied to newspapers, where they are found mostly on editorial pages, although the *Chicago Tribune* and the *Milwaukee Journal* have run them regularly on their front pages. Before the 1890s newspapers shied away from editorial cartoons because engraving time was too prolonged for daily deadlines. Besides, papers were divided into columns, and printers didn't like to break the vertical lines (called *rules*) and run material across columns. One-column cartoons would have been too small.

Editorial cartoonists are mostly a big-city phenomenon. The small and medium-sized dailies can't afford their own editorial cartoonists. The editorial cartoons they run come from feature syndicates, which pick up Bill Mauldin, Herblock, Paul Conrad, Pat Oliphant, and a few others from the big dailies and give them national audiences. And dominance of the field.

A few of the smaller papers have their own editorial cartoonists and so are able to make needed graphic comments on local matters. A lot of the work, unfortunately, is painfully amateurish. But then, so is the work of some of the big-city cartoonists, as the sampling gathered for *Today's Cartoon*, edited by John Chase, inadvertently shows.

Sometimes a small or medium-sized newspaper unable to afford a full-time editorial cartoonist and not satisfied to run only syndicated cartoons on national and international affairs will make an arrangement with a local cartoonist to submit work on a freelance basis.

When the big-time gag cartoon market began shriveling for him, Charles D. Pearson came up with an interesting idea for providing local cartoons to editors across the country who otherwise couldn't afford them. It worked like this: the editor would send him an idea, and Pearson, in his clean, simple style, would illustrate it. Compared to what he had been getting from the magazines for his gag cartoons, his fee was modest.

But Pearson no longer provides this service. "I ran into the problem of unrealistic weeklies with a circulation of two or three thousand who thought they could get original art drawn to size so it could be pasted up for five or fewer dollars per picture."

In the mid-1970s Pearson was self-syndicating a one-column feature called *Notes on the News*. Editors like such features—they're called *drop-in* cartoons—because they are handy to use as fillers when editorial columns don't quite reach the bottom of the page or when separation is needed between two one-column headlines. Such cartoons provide a little visual relief to a page without taking up much space. Often the drop-in cartoon is more a gag than an editorial comment, even though it goes on the editorial page.

One of the best of the drop-ins is Jerry Robinson's *Still Life*, a feature that defies categorization. Robinson uses dialogue between a couple of inanimate objects to put his point across. Asks a cannon in a sample *Still Life:* "What is a limited war?" Answers a cannon ball: "That's one where the casualties don't exceed the birth rate."

Usually, but not always, the point of view of the editorial cartoonist reflects that of the editor and publisher. The editor of a conservative editorial page, for instance, would not be comfortable running cartoons with a strong liberal bent. Where there are conflicts between editor and cartoonist, they are usually conflicts of taste or disagreements over the analogy the cartoonist has employed. Paul Conrad in the early 1970s came into conflict with his newspaper, the *Los Angeles Times,* and found his daily cartoon moved to the op-ed page (a page of special features opposite the editorial page) from its preferred position on the editorial page itself. Even Paul Szep, equally effective but less shrill, occasionally gets moved to op-ed on the *Boston Globe* when the point of view of the cartoon blatantly conflicts with the paper's view. But "I would say I have 99.9 percent freedom," Szep told *Cartoonist Profiles,* the magazine for professional cartoonists.

To keep readers of the *Miami News* from assuming that cartoonist Don Wright represents the editorial policy of the paper, the editors title his daily cartoon "As Don Wright Sees It."

When Herblock couldn't go along with the *Washington Post*'s endorsement of Eisenhower in the 1950s, he took a vacation before the election.

David Low, cartoonist for the *London Evening Standard,* attacked his own publisher, Lord Beaverbrook, in the publisher's newspaper. The cartoon showed "The Beaver" as a witch on a broomstick spreading "news for simple minds." A Conservative once asked Beaverbrook why he didn't fire the liberal Low. "I have often," Beaverbrook replied, "but he won't go."

While cartoonists tend to move in and out of various

cartoon categories, the editorial cartoonist, with his uncommon concern for history's surges, stays there on the editorial page, in most cases for the whole of his career. Some exceptions come to mind. The late Walt Kelly switched from editorial cartoonist for the *New York Star* to comic-stripper (*Pogo*), but that move may have been occasioned as much by the fragile health of the paper as by Kelly's desire to entertain rather than propagandize. At any rate, as the artist for one of the world's most popular comic strips, Kelly still managed to express some political views, much to the consternation of a few tradition-bound editors.

A less-known switch from the editorial page involves Fontaine Fox, who, before establishing his *Toonerville Folks* with a syndicate in 1913 (it later became *Toonerville Trolley*), did editorial cartoons for the *Chicago Post*. One of his editorial cartoons was drawn upon the occasion of Theodore Roosevelt's decision to enter the 1912 presidential race as the candidate of the Bull Moose Party. The caption: "Speaking of Hats and Rings!"

Alone among major American newspapers with a general readership, the *New York Times* does not employ an editorial cartoonist, although it does run outstanding cartoon art on the op-ed page and elsewhere, especially in the Sunday issues. Ed Marcus, who retired in 1958 after fifty years on the paper, was the last—and only the second—man to work as a *Times* editorial cartoonist. The other was Hy Mayer, better remembered as an editor of *Puck* and the writer/illustrator of numerous books.

Tom Wicker, the *Times* columnist, while not agreeing with the policy, explained that the paper did not employ an editorial cartoonist "on the grounds that, by their nature, editorial cartoons are overstated, oversimplified and therefore unfair. So they are, and more power to that in this cautious, double-talking world. . . ." Wicker wrote this on the occasion of introducing a collection of cartoons by Paul Szep. ". . . More power to Szep's bosses [on the *Boston Globe*] . . . for turning him loose on all the hypocrites, liars, dimwits, con men, parasites, fatcats and crooks that surround him and us."

"The editorial cartoon has become a welcome relief from some of the ponderous, elitist, overwritten poopery that typifies so many editorial pages today," puts in Don Wright, editorial cartoonist for the *Miami News*.

Comic Strips

A comic strip is a series of related panels, sometimes complete for one day, sometimes part of a continuing story. The story revolves around a main character and a cast of supporting characters. Some characters stay the same age throughout their comic-strip life, as Orphan Annie did; others grow up, marry, and have kids of their own, as Skeezix did in *Gasoline Alley*.

A popular strip survives its creator, thanks to the fact that the creator usually has an assistant—or several assistants—working with him. The carry-on version usually lacks the flair of the original, but most readers don't seem to mind. One strip that died with its creator, so unique was its style and story line, was George Herriman's *Krazy Kat*. And when Fontaine Fox retired, he retired his *Toonerville Trolley* with him.

We think of comic strips as an American invention, but they are really an outgrowth of illustrated stories that ran in publications in nineteenth-century Europe. They caught on in America at the turn of the century, playing a major role in the circulation wars of newspapers, particularly in New York. People actually bought papers to keep up on the antics of their favorite cartoon characters. When, years later, New York was paralyzed by one of its newspaper strikes, Mayor Fiorello LaGuardia appeared on a radio station (this was before television) not to reassure the citizens that the municipality remained inviolate but to read the comics to their anxious followers.

Rivalry between New York newspapers over the right to run Richard Outcault's pioneering *Hogan's Alley* starring The Yellow Kid led to coinage of the term "yellow journalism" for newspaper practices tending toward the garish and the sensational. The Yellow Kid was notable for his salty manner and the yellow ink used to fill in the long cloak he wore. He lives on as Alfred E. Neuman, the grinning symbol for *Mad* magazine.

All strips were "comic" at first (hence the name *funnies*), but a shift to illustrated adventure stories occurred just before and during the depression days of the 1930s. Some humorous strips, like *Blondie*, remained popular during this transition, and a few new ones appeared after World War II (*Beetle Bailey* and *Peanuts*), but it wasn't until the end of the 1960s that the strips became mostly "funnies" again.

Whether comic or adventurish, the comics were meant primarily to entertain, but countless examples of propagandizing can be cited, especially in the work of Harold Gray (*Little Orphan Annie*) and Al Capp (*Li'l Abner*). A number of comic artists today consider themselves commentators as well as entertainers.

Showing that, if anything, it is consistent, the *New York Times,* again alone among major newspapers, remains aloof from the comics. But the paper has a sense of humor about its stuffiness. In the December 15, 1974, issue of the *New York Times Magazine,* Jules Feiffer presented his version of "the kind of comic strip the *New York Times* might print if the *New York Times* printed comics." It was named *Hodgkins of State,* the "State" being Department, of course, and not College. You get an idea of the nature of the strip by the "Background" box in the first panel: "Bromley Hodgkins, Junior Foreign Service Officer, formerly with the World Bank, is mid-way through a debriefing session with his Department superior and reputed mentor, Hadley Wainwright. The following text is an interpretive re-creation and not intended to be factual."

Although developed originally by individual newspapers and run by them as exclusive features, comics have long since been taken over and distributed by feature syndicates. A single strip, like *Blondie,* can appear in more than 1,600 newspapers. Obviously, this is where the fortunes are made in cartooning. Way back in 1922, Sidney Smith negotiated a ten-year contract that gave him $100,000 a year for producing *Andy Gump.* Later cartoonists have done much better. The usual arrangement with a syndicate gives the cartoonist fifty percent of the take after expenses of promotion, production, and distribution are deducted.

Tom Peoples, director of comic art for Newspaper Enterprise Association, reports that his syndicate launches one or two new strips a year. At any syndicate, executives expect a strip to get off to a slow start, but if, at the end of a year, it does not show promise of substantially increasing its clientele, it may be dropped. *Peanuts,* syndicated by United Feature Syndicate, limped along for a whole year in the early 1950s with fewer than twenty papers before it really took hold.

Some newspapers conduct periodic readership studies of the strips they buy from syndicates to determine when a strip should be dropped in favor of another. Sometimes the survey takes the form of a contest asking for letters discussing the value of strips in general or telling why one strip is better than the others. Prizes consist of originals supplied by the syndicates.

In May of 1974 the *Los Angeles Times* dropped George Gately's *Heathcliff*, a syndicated cartoon panel involving a cat, and within a few days the editors were flooded with 900 letters, hundreds of phone calls, and several petitions. Within a month the feature was back on the pages of the newspaper. Never underestimate the power of cat lovers.

When the *San Francisco Chronicle* omitted a controversial *Doonesbury* episode, the switchboard handled 2,000 irate calls. It would appear that devotees of leftist satire are even more vocal than cat lovers.

One of the most successful comic-strip promotions was devised and staged by Al Capp and United Feature Syndicate in 1946 when *Li'l Abner* readers were invited to submit drawings of Lena the Hyena, the ugliest woman in Lower Slobbovia. About 1,000,000 entries came in. There were local and national prizes, and although Basil Wolverton, a former newspaper staff artist and a contributor to the comic magazines, placed only second in the Portland, Oregon, area contest, he placed first nationally, with Salvador Dali, Boris Karloff, and Frank Sinatra doing the judging. *Life* gave him a spread, and his career took a dramatic turn. His spaghetti-and-meatball style later was to be widely imitated, especially by cartoonists drawing underground comics.

In another comic-strip contest, Chic Young and King Features Syndicate for *Blondie* asked for names for the Bumstead's second child. More than 400,000 readers responded.

But considering the impact he has made, the most successful comic-strip artist of all time, no doubt, is Charles M. Schulz, creator of *Peanuts*. Unlike anyone on the comic pages before him, Schulz has been able to blend the intellectual with the comic. His strip manages to be both sophisticated and sentimental, appealing to adults as well as children, the well-educated as well as the person who moves his lips as he reads. The critics often compare him with George Herriman (*Krazy Kat*), but Herriman's appeal was only at the intellectual level, and at no time did as many as fifty newspapers subscribe. Schulz's subscribers number well over 1,600. And then there are all those spinoffs.

Charles Schulz's contributions to theological and psychological thought have been considerable (at least three books have analyzed these weighty aspects of his strips). And his popularization of the expression "Good Grief!" is no small achievement. The following strip shows another idea of Schulz's—one that deserves more attention than it got when it was introduced in early 1973.

© 1973 United Feature Syndicate, Inc. Used by permission.

Another strip in 1973 better represents his philosophical bent. As in the strip illustrated here, the characters are standing at a wall. This time Charlie Brown is talking to Lucy, of whom Schulz has said: "Beneath the surface there's something tender. But perhaps if you scratched deeper you'd find she's even worse than she seems." In the strip Charlie Brown is saying: "Someone has said that we should live each day as if it were the last day of our life . . ." In the next panel Lucy loses control of herself. She is all mouth and tears. She cries (in large, black letters): "AAUGH! THIS IS THE LAST DAY!! THIS IS IT!!!" And in the next panel: "I only have twenty-four hours left! Help me! Help me! This is the last day!! Aaugh!" In the final panel, with Lucy out of the picture, Charlie Brown, his head resting on his arm, a weary expression on his face, concludes: "Some philosophies aren't for all people . . ."

But for sheer artistry, the real genius in the business is Roy Crane, of whom Schulz has written: "My admiration for the work of Roy Crane knows no bounds. . . ." Schulz says *Wash Tubbs,* launched by Crane in 1924, was "the perfect comic strip because he [Crane] always stayed within the bounds of his medium. . . .

"He also had the comic artist's ability to create not only immortal lead characters but wonderful casts of supporting players, always including, of course, those marvelous galloping horses and little stray mongrels who stood around in the background observing the excitement."

And if any comic-strip artist created women more beautiful than Crane's women they have escaped the notice of this observer.

Probably Crane's most important contribution was to bridge the gap between the comic drawing typical of the early strips to the more serious, illustrative style of artists of the 1930s and thereafter.

He also experimented with several drawing mediums. At first his strip was all pen work with some occasional grease-crayon shading. Then, in the mid-1930s he introduced his widely admired Craftint doubletone technique, as seen in the following strip.

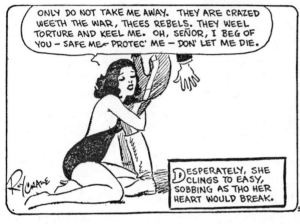

In both examples of Crane's work you see one of comicdom's arch villains: Bull Dawson. Dawson took center stage for a few weeks, disappeared, and then showed up months or years later.

Captain Easy, the hero, stole the spotlight from

diminutive Wash Tubbs, so that eventually the strip was renamed. But it was still *Wash Tubbs* when Roy Crane in 1943 left it to his assistant, Leslie Turner (now retired), and established a new strip, *Buz Sawyer*, with another syndicate. *Captain Easy* continues in about 500 newspapers under the direction of Bill Crooks (artist) and Jim Lawrence (writer). *Buz Sawyer*, with Crane still in charge, goes to about the same number.

Meanwhile, because of newsprint shortages and rising production costs, newspaper strips have fallen on lean years, despite the introduction recently of some bright new features. Nobody likes the new, smaller sizes. The first reductions in World War II nearly did in the adventure strips, which desperately needed their space to show all that scenic detail and action. Further size reductions have made it necessary to give over nearly half the space to the balloons if the lettering is to be at all legible. Even the nonadventure strips are hurting. Art Sansom (*The Born Loser*) said he would rather have a newspaper drop his strip than reduce it to a three-column width, a size some newspapers were considering. When Selby Kelly, who took over *Pogo* when her husband died, decided in 1975 to drop it, she gave as her reason the fact that the smaller sizes made impossible the inclusion of the necessary detail in drawing.

In putting together a comic strip the cartoonist has two choices. One is to show his panels from various vantage points, moving in and out, viewing from above, then from down below, etc. Occasionally he shows his characters in black silhouette only. He offers the reader plenty of variety. He dazzles him. Milton Caniff does this in *Steve Canyon*. Another way is to keep the vantage point fixed. Charles Schulz does this in *Peanuts*. And I have done it for the following editorial cartoon that happens to use a comic-strip format. The cartoonist would use such an approach if he wanted to build up to a point and didn't want variety to interfere with it. The strip proceeds relentlessly to the final panel.

TO MAKE AN OPINION COUNT...

The comic-strip artist keeps his cast of characters small so as not to confuse the reader. Even so, in a given strip all characters may look more or less alike. In most of the adventure strips, for example, all the young women look the same except for hair coloring. Some have blonde hair, some coal-black hair.

Often it is the clothing or a prop that differentiates the characters. When you look only at their builds and faces, for instance, there is not much to distinguish the cook from the sergeant in *Beetle Bailey*. Except this: the cook has folded-over ears, while most of the other characters in the strip, including the sergeant, have "S"s in their ears; the cook has a cigarette that sticks to his lower lip when he opens his mouth; and the cook has hair on his shoulders (he's usually in his undershirt).

One of the most interesting exercises in drawing is to dream up a character, get his features firmly established in your mind, and then show him in different poses: side view, three-quarters view, front view, and back view. Do all the sketches look like the same person? That's the test.

Comic strips are a daily and Sunday phenomenon. A problem peculiar to the adventure strips is what to do with the Sunday offering: should it be a continuation of the daily story—or should it be an entirely different story? Some dailies don't have Sunday issues. Roy Crane and Al Capp offer separate stories for Sunday; Milton Caniff continues his story, using Monday to do a little summarizing.

Another problem with the Sunday strips is to supply them in two versions: one for the editor with plenty of space, one for the editor whose space is cramped. Hence, many of the Sunday strips have throwaway panels so that the strips can be reassembled to take less space.

CARTOON PANELS. Included in the comic-strip category are cartoon panels like *Heathcliff* and Hank Ketcham's *Dennis the Menace*. Some of the most impressive cartooning in an earlier era could be found in the slice-of-life panels of T. A. Dorgan,

H. T. Webster, J. R. Williams, and Clare Briggs. Briggs is the only cartoonist to have a pipe tobacco named after him. Its slogan was "When a Feller Needs a Friend," a line from some of Briggs's panels. In the mid-1970s syndicates offered editors almost as many panels to choose from (204) as comic strips (225).

Before the photograph so dominated the visual part of the newspaper, one kind of cartoon panel was important enough to merit a category of its own: the sports cartoon. Typically, it consisted of a large, realistic drawing of a sports hero, done on a stipple-pattern paper that could take grease-crayon shading, surrounded by small, humorous drawings in ink alone. Tidbits of information were lettered into various parts of the cartoon.

Willard Mullin—the cartoonist who minimized head sizes so as to better concentrate on the action of the bodies—was probably the best of the latter-day sports cartoonists. ". . . When he hit his stride [in the mid-1930s] he brought to the pages of the [*New York*] *Telegram* a magnificently individual feature, artistically exciting and certainly, in the opinion of any editor, a circulation builder," Stephen Becker observed in *Comic Art in America*. "His drawing seems casual and almost ragged at first glance; but a closer look shows no line out of place, no unnecessary stroke of the pen, and an expressive-ness, a rakishness, an unbeatable, angular aggressiveness to the figures which make them models of emotion in action."

It was Mullin who gave the Brooklyn Dodgers the name "The Bums." The idea came to him following a conversation with a taxi driver. As reported by Lenora Williamson in *Editor & Publisher*, Mullin was asked by the driver when he got into a cab after a game, "How'd our bums do today?"

Mullin's biggest contribution was to introduce the *idea* to sports cartooning. In his hand the sports cartoon became either an independent feature of entertainment or a sort of editorial cartoon that dealt with a sports subject.

When the famous wife-swapping episode took place

among New York Yankees players, Bill Gallo, one of the nation's few remaining sports cartoonists, for the *New York Daily News* showed an office corridor with three doors; one with GENERAL MANAGER on it, one with FIELD MANAGER on it, and a third, with a sign painter moving away from the door, with MARRIAGE COUNSELOR on it.

COMIC BOOKS. Comic strips have also become part of the magazine world, first appearing in magazine form in the early 1930s. In badly cut-up versions, they also appeared as "Big Little Books."

The early comic magazines (from the first, everybody called them comic books) consisted of reprints of strips that had already appeared in newspapers. But the market even in those depression days seemed insatiable, and soon the magazines began to feature their own strips, most of high adventure, and most badly drawn. No wonder. As Nick Meglin says in *The Art of Humorous Illustration*, the comic magazines have always been "a notoriously ill-paying field." Because they pay by the page and the rates are pretty much standardized, only a fast-drawing cartoonist can make a living there.

Basil Wolverton, who freelanced to the comic magazines for many years, said in an interview in *Graphic Story Magazine* that for seven months in the early 1940s he worked seven days a week and still couldn't keep up with the demand for his strips. "The rates back then were so miserable that one couldn't afford time out. About the only time I saw my wife was when she came into the studio with a scoop shovel to clean out the deep accumulation of eraser particles." Later in the interview he said his income, with advertising work and other assignments, had grown enough so that "At long last I was able to afford . . . a real drawing board of my own. This was a happy event for my wife, who resented my working on her ironing board—especially when she was ironing."

Among those who graduated from comic magazines to

more lucrative and satisfying jobs are Mort Drucker and Jack Davis, standout satirists at *Mad*, itself an offshoot from the comic magazines. And what eventually became a newspaper strip, *Superman*, started out as a comic-magazine offering.

The golden age for comic books embraces the late 1930s, and books from that period command lofty prices today among collectors. One reason is that they are scarce; so many ended up in the paper drives of World War II.

Collector and comics scholar Bill Blackbeard praises *The Spirit* series of Will Eisner and the work of a few others. "But the overwhelming bulk of comic-book work in the non-humorous area has been abysmally underaccomplished, doggedly inane and lowbrow (the reader being considered a moron or worse by the editor and publisher combines involved, not without justification), derivative, imitative, and unimaginatively repetitive," Blackbeard heatedly observes. "The fascination this drek holds (aside from its apparent value as an investment) for its obsessed and monied latter-day devotees is only barely comprehensible in the light of the enormous popularity of similar schmaltz in other media, such as the Walton Family, Lawrence Welk, and Star Trek TV shows: i.e., the lowest level of consumer taste is involved, a level whose refusal point has never been ascertained, since the more appallingly dull, obvious and sloppy a work is, the more likely this lowest stratum of audience is to embrace and revere it."

An exception in latter-day nonhumorous comic-book work can be found in the *Vampirella* series of magazines put out by Warren Publishing Co. Much of the artwork here can be described as dazzling and innovative. Another exception can be found in the work of Frank Frazetta for E.C. Comics during the 1950s.

UNDERGROUND COMICS. The 1960s added a new breed: the underground comics. The drawing usually was painfully amateurish but adventurish, the themes reckless and outrageous. Some of the work was reminiscent of the "Tijuana Bibles" of the 1930s with their wallet-sized libels on newspaper comic characters. But underground comics characters were originals.

Underground comics evolved as a sort of protest against the Comics Code adopted by the big comic-magazine publishers. Whatever the straight comics avoided, the undergrounds reveled in: perverted sex, senseless violence, and drugs. But the strips could be read on two levels: for their scatalogical content or for their satire.

The first undergrounds were in black and white, but by the 1970s they were appearing in full color. The early underground cartoonists did not bother copyrighting their strips, assigning them "to the people." But with success came more businesslike practices. Although the pay was often negligible, cartoonists liked the new medium because, unlike cartoonists working for regular comic books, underground cartoonists took control of all aspects of their strips. There was no division of labor.

Mark James Estren in *A History of Underground Comics* traces the first underground cartooning to Texas but points out that the San Francisco-Berkeley area soon became the hub of the activity. New magazines constantly appeared—irregularly—and soon died.

Robert Crumb, who had to sell his wares at first from the back of his van, brought out *Zap Comix No. 1* in 1967. The following year Don Schenker brought out *Yellow Dog* comics, with its symbol of a dog with a back leg lifted. Published until 1973, *Yellow Dog* proved to be the most durable of the undergrounds.

The underground cartoonist with the most exposure is Robert Crumb. Crumb indulges himself in a luxury unknown to overground cartoonists: preoccupation in print with himself. Much of his work is autobiography. He freely airs his political and social prejudices and sexual preferences.

In *Dirty Laundry Comics,* he collaborates with A. Kominsky

(a woman), drawing himself while she draws herself. An opening panel shows the couple talking. For a change we have a page devoid of pornography. Crumb: "Aline, you say you're worried about what people will think. . . . Just what is it that worries you, Cutie-Pie??" Kominsky: "Well for one thing I'm afraid my drawing looks too crude and ugly next to yours." And in a second balloon: "People will make fun of me." In a final panel on the first page they are arguing. She: "P.S. I'm cuter in real life!" He: "No you're not!" She: "Yes I am!" That final balloon is at the bottom of the panel. Underneath the panel is a note lettered by Kominsky: "HA HA NO MORE ROOM."

About Crumb, Estren writes: ". . . no two people come away from him with the same impression—he seems to change his opinions of himself almost every hour." But: "If the underground comics have produced a Mozart, it is Robert Crumb."

Crumb does have his detractors, even among apologists for the undergrounds. Particularly galling to many is the sexism in his strips.

Trina Robbins, herself an underground cartoonist, objects to the way women are depicted in most underground comics. In her strips, women play a far different role from the roles they play in strips done by Crumb and other male cartoonists.

Some of Robbins's material is a bit rough by general-magazine standards, but "I really still do not feel that I do anything objectionable," she told Greg Weed, a comics buff and comic-book dealer, in a tape-recorded interview. "I would be very, very surprised if anybody busted my work. I don't think I'm censorable."

Robbins likes to draw beautiful women in a dated style. With a young daughter to watch over, she has to limit her output somewhat, but she manages to do a variety of things for the magazines. Probably her most admired feature is *Rosie the Riveter.*

In the preceding example, the second page of a two-page sequence called "Rip Van Rosie," Rosie has just awakened after thirty years of sleep at the war plant where she worked. (Someone had slipped a Mickey into her Coke.) On the first page (not shown) Rosie noted that the funny dress styles of the 1940s "don't seem to have changed much."

Trina Robbins and a few other underground cartoonists have done work for the overground, especially for the *National Lampoon*.

Gag Cartoons

These we can credit to the magazines, especially to one that emerged in 1925: *The New Yorker*.

Gag cartoons bear some relationship to the illustrated jokes that appeared in magazines before then, but they differ from these in that the caption consists of a single line of conversation. Caption and drawing work together to tickle the reader. Some gag cartoons work in pantomime.

You can see the interaction of gag line with drawing in a marvelous if disturbing *New Yorker* cartoon done in wash by the venerable Barney Tobey. Neither the gag line nor the superb drawing says much of itself, but together their effect is memorable.

"Isn't it nice, Harry, that we can sit here together for a <u>whole</u> evening and not feel we have to make conversation?"

Drawing by B. Tobey; © 1974 The New Yorker Magazine, Inc.

Army Medical Examiner: "At last a perfect soldier!"

There had been one-liners before *The New Yorker*, of course. One of Robert Minor's most reproduced cartoons, from a 1915 issue of *The Masses*, showed Anthony Comstock, the anti-pornography crusader, dragging a woman into court. He's saying: "Your Honor, this woman gave birth to a naked child!" Another Minor one-liner was an anti-military cartoon, from the July 1916 issue of the same magazine (above).

The two-liner appeared now and then after *The New Yorker*'s launching. Perhaps the most-remembered gag cartoon of the late Carl Rose was a two-liner in *The New Yorker* in the late 1920s. It showed a flapper mother at dinner arguing with her precocious daughter: "It's broccoli, dear." The daughter: "I say it's spinach, and I say the hell with it." A takeoff showed up in 1974 as a one-liner, again in *The New Yorker*, in a Mischa Richter cartoon showing a man at a party making a toast: "I say Happy New Year and to hell with it!"

The field of gag cartooning is broad enough to embrace aspects of both editorial cartooning and comic-strip making. Alan Dunn, *The New Yorker* cartoonist who died in 1974, was almost an editorial cartoonist in that his works were topical ("Often it seemed but a matter of minutes, and rarely was it more than a matter of hours, between the time Dunn read of an event in the newspapers and the time he turned in an acute pictorial comment on it," *The New Yorker* said in an obit), and he used a grease crayon on rough-surface paper, much as many editorial cartoonists do.

Although the casual observer may not have been aware of it, the late Peter Arno, with those powerful wash drawings dealing with high society and sexual mores, was also playing an editorial cartoonist's role, but with man and woman in general, not recognizable people, as his targets. "You don't do good work of this sort unless you're mad at something," Arno told a *New York Times* writer in 1937. "I've always rebelled against the social order—at least some aspects of it. As I grew up, I became dissatisfied with the life around me—the fatuous, ridiculous people. I had a really hot impulse to go and exaggerate their ridiculous aspects. That anger gave my stuff punch and made it live."

A gag cartoonist can make a telling observation about our way of life that would take a writer 2,500 words to cover in a magazine article. There is Everett Opie's *New Yorker* cartoon of a few years ago that shows a weary, middle-aged, guilt-ridden business executive and father (you can read all that in the man's face), at home after a hard day's work, martini in hand. His little boy walks by pulling a toy duck. The father asks: "How's your childhood going?"

And Whitney Darrow, Jr.'s, *New Yorker* commentary recently on modern marriage: a man asking a woman, "Allison, will you be my first wife?"

Saturday Review ran a cartoon in 1971 (unfortunately most of the cartoonist's name is cropped away, so I can't identify him) taking the public relations fraternity to task. It showed a board meeting in luxurious surroundings. The president stands at the head of the table, talking to other executives. He says: "Here's a letter from a stockholder who is profoundly impressed by our institutional image; but he wants to know what the hell we make."

Like comic-strip artists, many of the great gag cartoonists seem content merely to provide the reader with a bit of levity on what otherwise might be a dull or trying day. One of my favorite gags was a Reamer Keller: a cartoon of two old ladies sitting out on the porch of a house that could be reached only by climbing a mile-high (it seemed) flight of stairs. The mailman has just delivered their mail. One lady says to the other: "I've never seen him smile." Or maybe it was: "I never see him smile." I wrote to Keller for a copy and permission to show this gag in the book, but he wrote back: "I wouldn't know where to start looking for a clip of the two old ladies and the postman. Yep, I remember the gag. Think it appeared in *Collier's* or *The Saturday Evening Post*. I have more than 22,000 clips of cartoons [of mine] that have been published, but they're stored away in boxes."

He's been at it since 1935. The 1975 edition of *Writer's Market*, in a listing of cartoonists who are in the market for gags, reports that he buys 500 ideas a year!

Still, Keller thinks that "The magazine cartoon business is nothing to brag about these days. Most mags have dropped them or use just one or two. On the other hand, cartoonists are multiplying like McDonald hamburger stands!"

One of the joys in gag cartoons for the reader is that he can know more than the main character in the cartoon knows, and that can be satisfying. Lee Lorenz, cartoon editor of *The New Yorker* and frequent contributor, shows an older man on a sofa talking to a girl at a party. He is looking down at his hands, immersed in thought. "But enough about me," he says. He has failed to notice that the girl has moved across the sofa and is giving her attention to an appealing younger man hovering over her.

Gag cartoons are used mainly as filler material in magazines, to break up large areas of gray type or to fill out columns. They arrive at the magazine as freelance contributions in rough form, in batches of a half-dozen or more, each drawn on a sheet of 8½ × 11 paper, packed flat, and protected with a piece of cardboard. An editor looks them over, marks the one or ones he likes, and sends the batch back to the cartoonist with instructions to finish the okayed cartoons in a particular medium and size. Some roughs are bought "as is."

The important magazines, like *The New Yorker*, put favored cartoonists under a contract: the cartoonists give the magazine first look at roughs in exchange for a guaranteed monthly stipend, which is paid whether or not the magazine buys any of the cartoons. The cartoonists also stand by to take over gags submitted by gag writers or cartoonists who are less gifted as draftsmen than *New Yorker* regulars.

When the gag-cartoon market was big in New York, gag cartoonists used to make the rounds each Wednesday, starting with the first-class magazines and ending with the lesser ones. But many gag cartoonists then, as now, sold their work by mail.

The demise of so many general-circulation magazines has cut seriously into the gag-cartoon market. It's a discouraging business, despite the fact that there are still plenty of specialized magazines buying gag cartoons and several newsletters and Jack Markow's column in *Writer's Digest* handing out advice and listing the markets. When I used to submit gag cartoons to the magazines (I concentrated on the trade journals where I figured I had a fighting chance) my hope was to sell at least enough cartoons to pay for the postage I spent contributing them. I needed the money.

In effect, all gag cartoonists work "on speculation." Because acceptances are so infrequent and remuneration so inconsequential, many gag cartoonists eventually give up and move to more lucrative fields in advertising, magazine illustration, or, if they are lucky enough, comic strips.

Although originally a product of the magazines, gag cartoons have found their way into newspapers, too. The syndicates offer daily gag cartoons as well as comic strips and panels. One newspaper gag cartoon is Reamer Keller's daily *Medicare*, which concentrates on medical gags.

"YOU HAVE A STRONG HEART BEAT. I'M JUST WONDERING IF YOUR RIBS CAN TAKE IT."

Spot Drawings

Spot drawings depend usually on realism rather than on exaggeration. Some are abstractions. The best of them can be found—where else?—in *The New Yorker*, especially in the scratchboard drawings of Mario Micossi and the fine-line renderings of Judith Shahn. Some of the magazine's gag cartoonists do spots, too.

Unlike other cartoons, spot drawings—some of them— show up again and again in the magazine that first published them. How many times have you seen that *New Yorker* spot showing the screen closing in a theater with scattered patrons getting up to leave?

Spot drawings are mere vignettes, often decorative, designed to do nothing more than break the monotony of gray type area or act as fillers for columns that don't quite reach the bottom of the page. Occasionally they occupy space in the middle of an article or story, or they find a place up near a column heading.

Any drawing medium will do, but often the artist chooses to show solid areas of black to give the spots, which are always run small, some strength. Nicely composed, simplified scenes are a favorite with editors who use spots. Jack Markow has sold spots right out of his sketch pad. Walt Trag, who sells spots to trade journals and specialized magazines, submits them in batches of ten or twelve, just as he does his gag cartoons.

The following spot by Hugo Gellert was drawn for the June 1916 issue of *The Masses,* a journal that in its short life gave national exposure to numerous avant-garde writers, artists, and cartoonists.

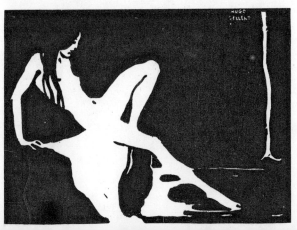

Illustrative Cartoons

Cartoons have always been popular as illustrations for stories and articles in newspapers and magazines, for humorous books, and for children's books.

Possibly the best cartoon drawing and painting to be found anywhere can be found on the pages of children's books. If you have the feeling that some of this great artistry is wasted on children, you should remember that it is the adult, not the child, who usually makes the book-buying decision.

One of the best of the children's book illustrators (it is difficult in this field to separate a cartoonist from an illustrator) is Maurice Sendak, a man of many styles, who now writes the books he illustrates. Nick Meglin devotes an instructive chapter to Sendak in *The Art of Humorous Illustration.* Another widely admired children's book illustrator is Tomi Ungerer, who also writes the books he illustrates. Ungerer is active in other art and cartoon areas as well. (See, for instance, *The Underground Sketchbook of Tomi Ungerer.*)

Sendak has recently ventured into television. The heroine of Maurice Sendak's *The Sign on Rosie's Door* made her television debut on CBS in 1975 in "Maurice Sendak's Really Rosie: Starring the Nutshell Kids," an animated musical special directed by Sendak and produced by Sheldon Riss of Sheriss Productions, Inc. Carole King wrote the music to Sendak's lyrics, did the singing, and provided the voice for Rosie.

The following piece of art is a scene from the show.

Courtesy of Maurice Sendak and Sheldon Riss.

Sendak, who did some comic-strip work before turning to children's books, did the rough sketches for the storyboard and supervised the details of animation.

ILLUSTRATIONS FOR EDITORS. Illustrative cartoons for articles or stories in newspapers and magazines often appear as a series. Sometimes they appear in print all about the same size, scattered throughout the text. Sometimes the editor chooses to run a large, inviting cartoon along with several smaller ones as follow-ups. Often the cartoonist gets the call because the article or story does not lend itself to photographic treatment.

A number of cartoonists have discovered that they can get into print as illustrators by writing humorous essays and providing their own drawings. They offer editors a package deal. Such an arrangement appeals to the harried editor, especially the one in charge of a small magazine, because it saves him the trouble of finding a cartoonist/illustrator and coordinating the art and copy. And the editor probably figures that he can get the package at a lower price than he would have to pay were he to buy the manuscript separately and then hire an illustrator.

ILLUSTRATIONS FOR ADVERTISERS. Cartoons are also used for advertisements prepared by advertising agencies or by advertisers themselves and for folders and other direct-mail pieces prepared by public relations people.

Like all illustrative cartoons, cartoons for advertisers do not stand by themselves. Their purpose is to catch the reader's eye and lure him into the copy.

"Hire him. He's got great legs," reads the headline for the ad of which the preceding drawing is a part. The copy goes on to say: "If women thought this way about men they would be awfully silly.

"When men think this way about women they're silly, too.

"Women should be judged for a job by whether or not they can do it."

The cartoonist is Jim Consor, and the sponsor is the NOW Legal Defense and Education Fund, New York.

Unlike illustrative cartoons used for editorial purposes, cartoons used for advertising purposes do not carry the signature of the cartoonist—unless he is a big name. Then the signature serves as a sort of testimonial.

Big-name cartoonists get assignments from agencies representing national advertisers, but occasionally a local advertiser will dip deep into his advertising budget and buy a name, as the U.S. National Bank of Oregon did when, for an institutional newspaper ad designed to boost Portland's Rose Festival, it went to Jack Davis, the *Mad* cartoonist and occasional *Time* cover artist. In this case, the cartoon is more than illustration; it is the entire ad.

Often an entire advertising campaign builds itself around a series of cartoons that, in various ways, illustrates a head-line that, so far as the advertiser is concerned, bears constant repeating. One of the longest cartoon campaigns is the one sponsored by the *Philadelphia Bulletin* to reach media buyers in agencies. Richard Decker, a *New Yorker* cartoonist, came up with countless ways to illustrate the line, "In Philadelphia, Nearly Everybody Reads the Bulletin." Always there was the little man jumping up and down, trying to call attention to some untoward happening, but everyone was too engrossed in his paper to hear. A more recent campaign was the one Roland B. Wilson illustrated in full color for an insurance company. Always there was a character about to be badly injured if not killed, usually by something falling. Only the

Hats off to the Rose Festival.

A salute to the 65th Rose Festival June 1st-10th.

companion was aware of what was happening. The potential victim was always saying: "My insurance company? New England Life, of course. Why?"

Last year the Germans, the English and the Italians made Renault their #1 import. Do they know something you should know?

You'll have to get out your magnifying glass to fully appreciate the crowd scene by Gene Calogero in an ad sponsored by Renault (the agency is Gilbert Advertising, New York). While at first the drawing may appear to be nothing but texture, upon close examination it reveals an amazing amount of exceptional draftsmanship.

Advertising illustration, at least at the brand-names level, pays more than story and article illustration; and advertising illustration of this magnitude pays—or should pay—most of all.

ILLUSTRATIONS FOR TV. Illustrative cartoons are not confined to the print media. Television provides a market, too. The ambitious cartoonist looking for a local market to crack might well put together a portfolio of his drawings and approach a TV station manager with the idea of providing spot drawings for cards and backdrops and drawings for local news items. A few stations have even experimented with locally drawn editorial cartoons.

Unfortunately, up to now television showings have consisted primarily of already-drawn cartoons. A cartoonist really sure of himself might want to try making drawings right in front of the viewer, as a chalk-talk artist would do. This would be taking full advantage of the medium.

Greeting Cards

Cartoons also play a vital part in the studio-card segment of the greeting-card industry. Studio cards are tall, humorous folders, printed on heavy paper, designed to fit a No. 10 envelope.

The typical card consists of a humorous drawing and teaser line on the cover, followed by a surprise ending line on the inside.

I have found that in my Caricature and Graphic Humor course at the University of Oregon, the most popular assignment of the term is the set of studio cards I ask each student to turn in for submission to card publishers. These go out as rough sketches. If he's interested, the publisher pays for the idea and either farms out the drawing to a professional or has a staff artist execute it.

Writer's Market and *Artist's Market* each year list greeting-card companies, their addresses, and their requirements.

While many of these companies have their own staffs, they still buy from freelancers. Some buy ideas only; some buy the art as well. The cartoonist who wants to do the whole card— the idea, the drawing, the lettering or type direction, the design—is probably happiest working with the smaller companies.

Like all markets, the greeting-card market forces some limitations on the cartoonist. For instance: Hallmark developed the neuter card idea, which insisted that the cartoon character be neither male nor female. The thought was that if it were one or the other, it would cut the buyers by half. Better that the card appeal to both male and female buyers.

The largest of the greeting-card companies—there are about two hundred in all—is Hallmark, which, at its Kansas City headquarters, maintains what must be one of the largest art departments anywhere: 350 men and women busily designing and drawing and fitting type.

A number of name cartoonists, including Mort Walker and Robert Crumb, worked for greeting-card companies.

Some of the comic-strip artists have lent their characters to the industry, including Charles Schulz (*Peanuts*), Marty Links (*Emmy Lou*), and Larry Katzman (*Nurse Nelly*).

Russell Myers, who does *Broom-Hilda,* also did a syndicated feature called *Honeybelle Hoopla's Greeting Cards!!* (the exclamation points are Myers's). Newspaper readers could clip them and send them to friends!!

Bill Harrison, who used to sell gag cartoons regularly to the major markets, discovered greeting cards in the early 1960s, but instead of freelancing to that market or joining an existing staff, he decided to set up his own company, the Harrison Publishing Company, Asheville, North Carolina. By 1974 he had fifteen employees. The Harrison line is designed primarily for businessmen. He told Jack Markow of *Writer's Digest:* "The idea of my cards is to promote goodwill between a businessman and his customers, using humor as the medium." For instance, one of his cards for salesmen shows a cowboy on a horse with an arrow through his hat. The cowboy is saying: "If I don't have any problems . . . I'll be riding into your territory soon!"

Another for-a-time celebrated small operation was set up at Eugene, Oregon, in the early 1970s to sell "un-greeting" cards designed to keep people from settling in the state. The line expanded to include similar cards for other states.

Ashleigh Brilliant, out of the Haight-Ashbury district of San Francisco, heads a firm, now located in Santa Barbara, with the happy name Brilliant Enterprises, that markets greeting postcards called "Pot Shots." One shows a line drawing of a cup of coffee and asks: "IS THERE LIFE BEFORE BREAKFAST?" Another shows a filled wastebasket accompanied by the legend: "BEFORE BURNING THESE PAPERS, LET ME MAKE SURE THEY'RE IN ALPHABETICAL ORDER." Still another shows a man lassoing a cloud. "I'M JUST MOVING CLOUDS TODAY—TOMORROW I'LL TRY MOUNTAINS."

Brilliant, who has a Ph.D in history, got his start in business by reading poems to the crowds in Golden Gate Park in 1967. He called his works "Unpoemed Titles." From the poems evolved the cards. By 1974 he had written, drawn, and produced some 500 different cards. He figured that from thirty to fifty million copies were in circulation in America and several foreign countries. The Chicago Tribune-New York News Syndicate began syndicating them as panel cartoons.

Animated Cartoons

✳ Winsor McCay (*Little Nemo*) was probably the first American cartoonist to produce an animated cartoon, but it took the genius of Walt Disney to perfect the medium. He and his artists made the first animated film with sound, the first with color, and the first that combined animated with live action.

So big did the Disney studios become that they set up

their own art school to train animators. A number of comic-strip artists, gag cartoonists, and editorial cartoonists benefited from early Disney training, including the late Walt Kelly (*Pogo*), Pete Hansen (*Lolly*), Hank Ketcham (*Dennis the Menace*), Brant Parker (*Wizard of Id*), the late George Baker (*Sad Sack*), gag cartoonists Virgil Partch and Eldon Dedini, and editorial cartoonist John Fischetti.

While animation can be achieved through the use of puppets and even unbaked, wet clay models that can be adjusted before each frame is photographed, the usual method is through cartoon drawing. Typically the background for a scene is drawn and painted separately from the figures. For a given film, thousands of drawings must be made on transparent sheets that, one by one, are placed over the basic scene and photographed.

✳ Hanna-Barbera Productions, calling itself "the world's largest producer of filmed animation," refers to animation as "the world's last remaining hand art." A single half-hour animated program (Hanna-Barbera in 1974 had thirty of them, syndicated or as first-runs, on the three television networks) takes several months to produce. At Hanna-Barbera that one program calls for 12,000 individual drawings by 150 artists: animators, layout men, background painters, inkers, and painters. Just to have Barney Rubble say, "Good morning; how are you?" to Fred Flintstone involves twenty-four drawings.

Quality animated films require innumerable subtle adjustments for each overlay. But cheap, crude animation can be achieved, as some Saturday morning showings on TV demonstrate, by changing only the mouth opening and by occasionally adjusting the eyes.

A different kind of animator is Ralph Bakshi, who, following an apprenticeship at Terrytoons, New York, in the early 1970s began producing X- and R-rated movies, including *Fritz the Cat*, based on Robert Crumb's underground comic strips; *Heavy Traffic*, largely autobiographical; and *Coonskin*, about blacks. Bakshi combines live action with animation, but in different ways from his predecessors.

He told a writer for the *New York Times* that when he was younger he "felt instinctively that the filmmakers were saying, 'Look how cute we are, combining these two media.' But it was a tremendous put-down of *both* media to do those things the way they did. I got the idea, even then, there might be a way of combining the two more effectively."

With film becoming increasingly a medium for the young to experiment with, animation has again captured the attention of amateur artists and cartoonists, just as it did early in the century when a number of cartoonists, even before Disney, produced their captivating if crude entertainments.

Advertisers have enough confidence in animated cartoons to use them to sell products, services, and ideas to all age groups. A consumer protection act passed in Quebec, Canada, regarded them as so effective that it outlawed their use in commercials aimed at children.

SLIDES. Somewhat related to films are slide presentations. The slide art that follows was prepared by Dan Mindolovich, staff

artist for Western Wood Products Association, Portland, to make some point about the parties—industry, the federal government, and the states—involved in land-use regulations. Using a Pentel and color felt markers, Mindolovich did the figures on separate sheets, cut them out, and mounted them on orange-colored board for a colorful cartoon that, unfortunately, we must view here in lowly black and white.

ChalkTalks

Chalk talks aren't as popular as they once were. Their novelty has been lost in the maze of more sophisticated film and electronic entertainment. The days of sell-out tours by the likes of Homer Davenport are over.

Still, when a cartoonist is called upon to make a talk, he often resorts to the practice of making chalk sketches, usually in color, on large pads of newsprint, standing to the side so the reader can see the drawing evolve, putting out what patter is necessary to help elicit the laughs. For the professional comic-stripper or gag cartoonist, the talk is usually nothing more than the showing of familiar characters or the redrawing of already published cartoons, an easy enough chore, especially if light guide-lines are sketched in ahead of time to help keep the cartoonist on target. The audience usually loves the show, especially those members up front who are able to retrieve the originals as the cartoonist rips them off the pad.

Harlan Tarbell, a professional chalk-talk artist, used to start drawing one thing, say a mouse, and end up drawing something else, say the face of a screaming woman. He also liked to do drawings that read one way rightside-up and another way upside-down. During his shows he would call members of the audience up to make circles, squares, and triangles anywhere on a page, and then he would convert them to a scene.

A few chalk-talk artists have been able to combine a bit of magic with their chalk talks. For instance, it is possible to plant a folded handkerchief in a pocket pasted on the back of a sheet, cut a slit through the paper (all ahead of time), and then in front of the audience draw a suit pocket over the spot where the handkerchief is, reach in, and pull out a real handkerchief.

Cartoon Creations

A final category of cartoons—a catch-all—defies naming. *Cartoon creations* comes as close as any term to covering the category.

Cartoon creations include sculptures, dolls, toys, etc.; wall murals painted in dens, playrooms, or offices or on buildings; one-shots; and spreads.

A one-shot is a single sheet, folder, poster, magazine, or booklet produced only once for sale or free distribution or showing.

Managing Director's Requirements for the AFPI District Manager

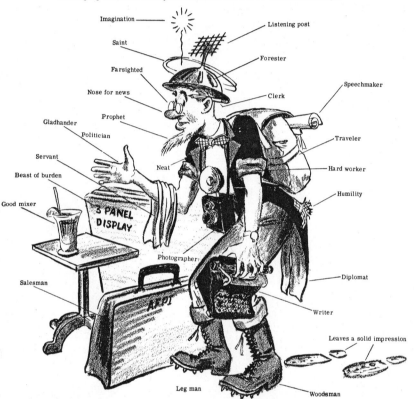

John Benneth, an executive for American Forest Institute and sometime cartoonist, did a one-shot for an annual meeting of that organization when it was known as American Forest Products Industries. The AFPI district manager—there were a number of them in various parts of the country answerable to the organization's Washington, D.C., head-quarters—was expected to be a man of many talents; but he was primarily a PR man. The three-panel display referred to in the drawing was something each district manager was expected to drag around with him as he made his various calls.

A cartoon spread features several cartoon comments on a given subject, such as kinds of drivers, students, teachers, eaters, and so on. Much of the material in *Mad* and *National Lampoon* takes the form of cartoon spreads.

Copyright © 1974 by E. C. Publications, Inc.
Used by permission.

"Remember what a big deal all the magazines made about the 'Gatsby Look'?" *Mad* magazine asks. Remember all those

Gatsby fashions? How come they didn't catch on? "What killed the 'Gatsby Look'? That's easy! The MOVIE came out!" Mort Drucker (with writer Stan Hart) presented *Mad*'s version of the movie in a feature called "The Great Gasbag." The opening panel, although this reproduction fails to hold all the detail, gives some indication of the great artistry of Mort Drucker and suggests why he is so widely admired—and copied—by other cartoonists.

. . . when they take the braces off
your teeth . . . and nobody notices.

This Paul Coker, Jr., panel—one of several—was drawn to illustrate a spread in *Mad* on "A Downer Is" (Lou Silverstone, writer). The panel carries the caption: "[A downer is] when they take the braces off your teeth . . . and nobody notices."

A cartoon spread is not the same thing as a collection of gag cartoons on a single subject. The drawings in a cartoon spread are not complete in themselves. Their effect is cumulative.

What Manner of Men?

Elsewhere in this book, especially where drawing advice is offered, the words *man, men, he,* and *his* should be read to include females as well as males. But *men* in the subtitle above probably has to be read in its narrow sense, for the truth of the matter is that cartooning has evolved largely as a man's profession. Only a paragraph's worth of cartoonists come to mind as exceptions: Helen Hokinson and Peggy Bacon from the early days at *The New Yorker,* Barbara Shermund, Martha Blanchard, Dorothy McKay, Mary Gibson, Mary Petty, Gladys Parker (*Mopsy*), Kate Osann, Hilda Terry, Irma Selz, Marty Links (*Emmy Lou*), Edwina Dumm (*Cap Stubbs and Tippie*), Marge Henderson (*Little Lulu*), Dale Messick (*Brenda Starr*), Margot Cook, Merrylen Townsend, Sara Black (*Pantomime Cartoons*), M. K. (for Mary Kay) Brown, Dorothy Bond (*The Ladies*), Luci Meighan, Betty Swords, Anne Mergen, Ruth Marcus, Nurit Karlin, Mary Gauerke (*Alumnae*), and, among the underground cartoonists, Trina Robbins and Aline Kominsky.

The only editorial cartoonists on the list are Anne Mergen, who worked for the *Atlanta Journal* in the 1930s and 1940s, and Edwina Dumm, who did editorial cartoons for a newspaper in Ohio before she launched her comic strip. I know of no women today doing editorial cartoons for a daily newspaper.

Obviously, there are a number of other women free-lancing and working for *local* publications and agencies, but there is no way of counting them, just as there is no way of counting their male counterparts. Even so, on the local as on the national level, male cartoonists no doubt greatly out-number female cartoonists.

Among women cartoonists known only locally is Louise Melton of Framingham, Massachusetts, who does editorial cartoons for a weekly newspaper. A good local woman cartoonist in my home town is Lynn Weed, who does cartoons for newspapers, direct-mail pieces, and posters. The following Lynn Weed drawing of a hippie couple (the woman is pregnant) appeared originally as a story illustration for a campus newspaper.

Courtesy of Lynn Weed.

One of the earliest women cartoonists was Gerda Wegener, who did sketches and caricatures for *Klods Hans,* a weekly published in Copenhagen, Denmark. "All Europe is showing admiration for Gerda Wegener. . . . In caricature she is making as high a mark as in her art of graceful figures, although she is only in her twenties," *Cartoons* magazine observed in 1912.

1—EVA, 2—THE BUDDING EVA, 3—THE BOLD EVA, 4—THE MODERN EVA, 5—THE MOTHERLY EVA, 6—THE MATURE EVA, 7—THE DISCOURAGED EVA.

In one pre-World War I feature, Miss Wegener in a decorative style shows the various stages in a woman's life, asking the reader to move down through the center of her drawing, then up to the upper left corner, then across, then diagonally to the lower left, then across and out of the panel.

By far the best-known woman cartoonist was Helen E. Hokinson. But it would be difficult, probably, in today's climate, for Helen Hokinson to market the cartoons about dowagers and club women that intrigued *New Yorker* readers from 1925 to her death in an airplane accident in 1949. Example: an overdressed, matronly woman, looking a bit worried, riding in the club car of a train, stops a steward and asks, "Isn't it about time for Massachusetts to begin?" (Most of the ideas were supplied by James Reid Parker and Richard McAllister.)

The Hokinson ladies "were a friendly breed," remembered John Mason Brown in a *Saturday Review of Literature* article. "This explains why they made so many friends. Miss Hokinson's fondness for them was transparent and contagious. Hers was the rarest of satiric gifts. She had no contempt for human failings. She approached foibles with affection. She could ridicule without wounding. . . ."

In strength of style, probably no women cartoonist matches Dorothy McKay, whose gag cartoons used to appear regularly in *Esquire*.

Another top woman cartoonist is Ruth Marcus, who for ten years produced "Small Wonders" for *Good Housekeeping* and for four years a syndicated panel, *Oh, Lady!* In 1974 the Chicago Tribune-News York News Syndicate launched her *G.P. Jones, M.D.* panel (a sample of which follows), but after

MR. SLADE, PLEASE TAKE EVERYTHING OFF AND STREAK OVER TO THAT EXAMINING TABLE.

9-21

about nine months dropped it when it became clear that not enough papers were going to subscribe.

Even with the militancy of some women's groups and the resulting infiltration of women into areas where previously they had only token representation, few women appear to be joining cartoonists' ranks.

Betty Swords thinks she knows why. In a letter to the editor of *Psychology Today,* responding to an article measuring sexism in *New Yorker* cartoons, Ms. Swords charges: "Woman cartoonists will find their ideas discriminated against if they don't follow sexist stereotypes. Just try to imagine a cartoon about a dumb *man* driver!—although the National Safety Council's statistics show them to be poorer drivers than women."

In an interview in *Cartoonist Profiles,* Ms. Swords admits turning out a few sexist cartoons herself in her less aware days (for instance: cartoons featuring dumb blondes). But in the 1970s Ms. Swords was furthering the cause of the National Organization for Women and creating feminist cartoons in which the female rather than the male emerged as the admirable character. For 1974 she illustrated the Male Chauvinist Pig Calendar.

Dorothy Bond, who once drew a syndicated feature called *The Ladies,* says only a few women become cartoonists "because in no other field are women so discriminated against." Miss Bond thinks the discrimination is especially prevalent "in the syndicate field . . . which is almost 100 percent male dominated." She feels that males do not know what kinds of cartoons interest women. She quotes from a letter from a syndicate editor responding to one of her contributions: "My wife and secretary like it, but I don't get it. . . ."

One of her most popular cartoons in *The Ladies* series—she got 4,000 letters on it, all from women—showed a young mother carrying a baby and holding the hand of a young child. The caption: "Meet the girl with the longest hours and the smallest pay in the world." It was not an angry cartoon—the mother was smiling—but it was a cartoon that women—many women—could identify with.

Another cartoon that brought enthusiastic response—she was told it was clipped and hung in many offices—showed a secretary (female) taking dictation from a boss (male). The secretary says: "Do you want I should the same exact your grammar use?"

In a short piece in *Cartoon World,* a monthly market newsletter for cartoonists, Luci Meighan lists "Ten Reasons Why No Girl in Her Right Mind Would Go into Cartooning." Among them: "It's fattening. Sitting at a drawing board for eight or more hours a day is fatal to the figure." And, referring to freelancing: "It's depressing. Females are neither sociologically nor biologically conditioned for being rejected." Further: "It's lonely. The only other people who could really understand you are other cartoonists. But since all cartoonists' wives are understandably suspicious, you'll never have a cartoonist friend."

In a more serious vein, Miss Meighan in a letter says that there are few women cartoonists because women are encouraged by parents and teachers to go into other activities. "Have you ever heard a parent encourage a daughter . . . to be a . . . cartoonist?"

Miss Meighan (or Mrs. Thomas), the mother of eight, somehow manages to spend ten hours a day freelancing. Her cartoons appear in *WomenSports, Genesis, Playgirl, Venus,* and *Sportswoman.* She reports: "Contrary to what one might believe, there's no editorial prejudice against female cartoonists; or if there is, I'm unaware of it. As a matter of fact, I get the feeling that . . . [editors would] *like* to support female artists."

Ironically, while women are underrepresented among cartoonists they are well represented among cartoon editors on magazines. The cartoon editors at *Playboy* and *Saturday Review,* for instance, are women.

Another underrepresented group among cartoonists are blacks. Among comic-strip artists we have Morrie Turner (*Wee Pals*) and Ted Shearer (*Quincy*) and one or two others; among gag cartoonists, the late E. Simms Campbell, who did gags regularly for *Esquire* and designed the Esky head that appeared with the logotype on the cover.

Possibly the only black man producing a daily editorial cartoon is Chester Commodore, working for the *Chicago Daily Defender*.

The Editor Draws the Line

Back in 1955, when paperback books sold for a quarter, Bantam Books brought out a little volume by Dave Breger, now deceased, called *But That's Unprintable*. It contained "135 hilarious cartoons they wouldn't dare publish!" Breger said that the cartoons, gathered from various cartoonists, violated taboos then in force, and for that reason they were rejected. But looking at them today one suspects that many of them were rejected by editors simply because they weren't very good.

His point about self-censorship, however, was well taken. The 1950s *were* an era of timidity, made that way partly by the specter of McCarthyism (a name coined by a cartoonist: Herblock) and also by a don't-rock-the-boat attitude among editors, especially where advertisers were involved. The 1950s were the years just after the advent of television when the magazines were fighting for their lives, amassing large circulations they could deliver to advertisers just as television was setting out to do. The newspapers ran scared, too. Breger quotes a letter from a syndicate editor to one of his cartoonists: "I feel that it is best to avoid gags that poke fun at advertising, promotion, publicity, and products that are advertised. Sometimes the advertising managers of client newspapers are sensitive about the possible effect of this type of gag on their customers."

The 1950s were a time, too, when America was awakening to its sorry treatment of minorities. It was a difficult time for cartoonists, who, earlier in the century, felt no qualms about portraying blacks as shuffling, silly characters, with shiny skin (a window patch on a solid black forehead), eating (what else?) watermelon.

The *Esquire Cartoon Album* (1957) carried a Dorothy McKay cartoon (it is impossible to tell in what year the cartoon ran because, typical of volumes like this, the cartoons don't carry publication dates, but it may have been run in the mid-1930s, shortly after *Esquire* was founded) showing a black woman in a black doctor's office. She's telling him: "I'se never been x-rayed, but I'se been ultra-violated!"

One of the cartoon instruction books of the 1920s, E. C. Matthews's *How to Draw Funny Pictures* (with illustrations by Zim), informed would-be cartoonists that "The colored people are good subjects for action pictures; they are natural born humorists and will often assume ridiculous attitudes or say side-splitting things with no apparent intention of being funny.

"The cartoonist usually plays on the colored man's love of loud clothes, watermelon, chicken, crap-shooting, fear of ghosts, etc."

And later: "The Jewish people are given to expressing themselves by hand. . . . Be careful not to offend the Jewish people in your cartoons, or you may be unable to get them published."

Still later: "[The Chinese] . . . have . . . [a] racial characteristic worth commenting on, and that is their honesty in financial affairs. Anyone who has business dealings with all classes and races will tell you that, as a race, John Chinaman is the most honest person you are likely to deal with."

Today's reader feels his blood pressure escalate or tugs at his collar in embarrassment as he reads such tribute to stereotype, but, in fairness, he must judge it in the context of its time. The same writer-and-artist team today would surely hold more enlightened views.

Zim, whose full name was Eugene Zimmerman, had been one of America's most-published comic artists, with several decades of exposure in *Puck* and *Judge* and more popular magazines. Thomas Craven in *Cartoon Cavalcade* said of Zim that he "was the spokesman of the humbler social orders whom he treated, not as inferiors nor as the underprivileged, but as self-sufficient Americans out of luck but very friendly and capable of laughter. The furniture was held together with pieces of wire; the rooms were sparse and disorderly; the inhabitants wore torn clothes and oversize shoes; but Zim made his shabby world affecting, and even attractive, by a fund of humor that came straight from the heart."

Making the transition to equal treatment of all races was difficult for cartoonists. The only way some could depict blacks was to draw them first as whites and then lay down some Zipatone on the faces. Among the important comic-strip artists, Mort Walker was the first to introduce a true black character in Lt. Flap. Walker dared to ridicule his new hip character in the same way he ridiculed other types in his strip.

Dave Breger tells of his problem making the transition in the 1950s: "It's fine when you make your usual cartoon characters look funny, but I found it was something else again when your cartoon characters are Negroes. I knew it wouldn't come off as intended. So, as the lesser of evils, I had no choice but to avoid the subject altogether. This was shying away from the problem, of course—not solving it."

Other sensitive areas in those days included religion, politics, death, infirmity, insanity—and sex.

Even belly buttons were touch and go. In what he described as a dry "Navel Maneuver," Mort Walker for years battled King Features over his right to put dots on his bathing beauties, but someone at the syndicate always took them off. As Walker tells it, the syndicate editor "has a box on his desk just for my old navels." Once, for his *Boner's Ark* feature, Walker drew a carload of oranges, all with navels prominently displayed. The panel slipped through unnoticed by the censor.

Compared to today's standards, the cartoons in Breger's book seem tame indeed. It is hard to imagine any of them causing a ripple. However, in the present social and political arena, some editors may be more timid than ever before. And understandably, especially on college campuses where trends become urgent. In the activist days of the late 1960s, the cartoon that offended any of several organized groups could result in anxious moments for its originator or the editor who published it. Even as this book was being written, in the relative quiet of the mid-1970s, the staff of the student news-paper at the university where I teach was "visited" by a surly delegation that dispersed only after a move was made by an editor to call campus security officers. The paper's offense: the publication of a Pat Oliphant cartoon showing Arab leader Yasir Arafat armed with a gun, addressing the United Nations. The protesters argued that the caricature was "racist." As a reporter later explained, the protestors "demanded that the . . . [paper] stop printing cartoons with racist overtones, citing other cartoons that had been published in the paper that they felt were equally offensive."

The new sensitivity extends to women's groups, who have succeeded on some publications in eliminating stereotypes of the woman as sex object and chorelady. And more. In a dramatic announcement in 1974, McGraw-Hill, the giant book publisher, announced it would no longer allow its writers of nonfiction to use such sexist terms as "the fair sex," "usherette," and "co-ed." And no mother-in-law jokes. The instructions to its 8,000 authors went on for eleven pages, the work of a twelve-person committee. Interestingly, the restrictions did not extend to fiction. Did the company feel that fiction does not build stereotypes?

Oddly, as the media yield to pressures from organized groups, they relax other taboos and even enter areas of bad taste involving other segments of the population. *Esquire* in one of its by now rare gag cartoons shows a blind man fishing at the edge of a river. The man's line does not reach the water; it just lies there in a tangled heap, and the poor blind man is unaware of the futility of his waiting.

Is it possible that we will live to see formation of the ultimate liberation group: the able-bodied organized against the infirm?

To illustrate how times have changed: the following cartoon, published in the *Chaparral*, a humor magazine at Stanford University, was considered risqué enough to be included under the heading "Select Subjects—in Naughty

College Papers" in the June 1912 issue of *Cartoons* magazine. The title, "A Rubber at Bridge," could be taken two ways, "rubber" meaning "look" as well as "a series of games." Cartoonist unknown, but he is a man with a clean style if a dirty mind.

Are Cartoonists People?

We get a picture of the cartoonist in Peter DeVries's comic novel *The Tunnel of Love*, the book that gave us that remarkable line, "Deep down, he's shallow" (a *bon mot* political commentators borrowed from DeVries, without proper credit, to use against Governor George Romney when Romney made moves to run for the presidency). In his novel, DeVries, with his background on *The New Yorker* working with cartoonists and gag writers to polish their gag lines, portrayed the cartoonist as a pitiable character, not very reliable, not up to facing life's complexities. Of course, this was only one cartoonist, and a fictional one at that.

From Malcolm Muggeridge, once the editor of *Punch*, England's equivalent of *The New Yorker* and, some say, its prototype, we get another picture of the cartoonist, this one nonfictional. In an introduction to David Levine's book of caricatures, *The Man from M.A.L.I.C.E.*, Muggeridge wrote that ". . . as a body of men, . . . [cartoonists] were, I discovered, inclined to be morose, abnormally sensitive, and surprisingly solemn, to the point that they seldom laughed even at their own jokes. Just as war was too serious to be left to soldiers, so, I used to reflect, humor was too serious to be left to cartoonists. On the other hand, they were kindly, gentle, and blessed with a curious kind of innocence that is seldom found in writers. I found them, by and large, lovable rather than likable."

Of course, Muggeridge was talking about gag cartoonists, a different breed from, say, editorial cartoonists, who might have impressed him differently.

In describing Duncan Macpherson, the editorial cartoonist of the Toronto *Star*, a friend suggested he is a combination of Mary Poppins, Mark Twain, and Attila the Hun.

Whatever his branch of the art, the cartoonist often surprises his reader when the two confront each other in person. The cartoonist who mercilessly attacks corruption with bold crayon strokes may well turn out to be a Caspar Milquetoast. Cartoonists don't any more look like what they draw than writers look like what they write. "Somehow I had expected you were shorter," a writer for the *Cornell Alumni News* blurted when he met the over-six-foot-tall Kurt Vonnegut. "I know," said Vonnegut. "I write small."

Look around you at any gathering of media people, and the moodiest fellow there is likely to be a gag cartoonist. Talk to him, and you may find his attention wandering as some improbable idea overtakes him. Put up with his staring, if you can; he's probably mentally tracing your outline for appearance in one of his upcoming pieces of hilarity.

A cartoonist draws pictures wherever he goes, regardless of whether he holds a drawing instrument in his hand. The whole world poses for him and is there for him to distort. "When I look at a scene in the country," says Saul Steinberg, *The New Yorker* cartoonist and cover artist, "I see a signature in the lower right-hand corner."

Cartoonists may take their art seriously, but not themselves. Johnny Hart *(B.C.)* in his autobiographical entry in *The National Cartoonists Society Album* writes: "While in the service I met and married my wife Bobby. I would have married my wife Fred but she was having an affair with my uncle Helen."

When told that Jules Feiffer was not impressed by his art, Basil Wolverton responded: "We have something in common, because sometimes I don't like it either." He added, with refreshing modesty: "A newspaper panel cartoonist once told me, 'You make all those little lines to cover up your lack of ability.' I was dazed. I had always hoped that viewers would regard it as shading, and didn't think that even another cartoonist would get wise to the awful truth."

Like any profession, cartooning has its share of oddballs. Hugh S. Fullerton in an article years ago in *Collier's* told of a cartoonist who used to lie nude in bed holding a sheet of paper against the wall with one foot while drawing with the other. The cartoonist was worried that he might someday lose both his arms in a railroad accident.

Charles Nelan, *New York Herald* cartoonist at the end of the 1900s, had trouble drawing the female form, so whenever a woman had to appear in one of his cartoons, he called his wife in to draw her.

George Lichty *(Grin and Bear It)* is said to have been ejected as a student at the Art Institute of Chicago for putting gag captions under master paintings.

In *The Country Boy,* Homer Davenport tells of how in his father's store he sold a customer a yard of gartering by taking ten inches and stretching it while he measured it. "I was big enough to help clerk in the store, but wasn't what you would call a safe clerk."

The late Harry Hershfield, who created *Abie the Agent,* as a newspaper artist was given a photo of a building to retouch. Hershfield noticed that the building appeared to be leaning to one side, so he carefully straightened it up, experiencing great pride in the result. It turned out, however, that the photograph was of the Leaning Tower of Pisa.

Alan Dunn had a phobia about fire. *The New Yorker* reported that he even went so far as to obtain blueprints of apartment buildings he visited so he could check out the fire escapes.

The art appears to run in families. Several father-and-son combinations have made their marks as editorial cartoonists. Clifford Berryman, who gave the Teddy bear its name, was succeeded on the *Washington Star* by his son Jim. J. P. Alley was succeeded by his son Cal on the *Memphis Commercial Appeal.* In the last century, Joseph Keppler, founder of *Puck,* was succeeded as editor by his son Joseph Jr.

At least three sets of brothers have made names for themselves as cartoonists. Frank Interlandi does *Below Olympus,* while his brother Phil does gag cartoons, especially for *Playboy,* and draws the syndicated *Queenie.* George Gately (his last name is Gallagher) does *Heathcliff,* while his brother John Gallagher does gag cartoons. The four Roth brothers— Ben Roth, Salo Roth, Al Ross, and Irving Roir—who came to America from Vienna, Austria, sold gag cartoons regularly to major magazines beginning in the early 1930s. Ben Roth founded the Ben Roth Agency, which, some years after his death, was renamed Rothco Cartoons. It acts as an agent for foreign as well as U.S. cartoonists.

In the comic strips, several family combinations can be cited. Of course, you might not want your daughter to marry a cartoonist. "Comic-strip artists do not make good husbands," wrote Don Herold, "and God knows they do not make good comic strips." "Who'd want to be married to me? I *draw* all the time," the animator Ralph Bakshi remarked to a *New York Times* writer.

Garry Trudeau, to whom *Doonesbury* brought acclaim at a tender age, plays a J. D. Salinger role. L. E. Sissman in a 1975 "Innocent Bystander" piece in *The Atlantic* saluting cartoonists, demonstrated that his column is appropriately named when he wrote: "I had hoped to tell you a little of how Trudeau thinks and works; my wish was stymied by the fact that he does not take phone calls or grant interviews. Good healthy sign, that."

Like most people, a cartoonist tends to grow more conservative as he gets older. A case in point is K. R. Chamberlain, who did cartoons for *The Masses* and *The Liberator* in the teens and 1920s and then, in the 1930s and 1940s, for William Randolph Hearst's King Features Syndicate, and finally, in the 1950s, for the National Association of Manufacturers. "As you get older you get more gentle," Chamberlain explained to writer Richard Fitzgerald, "you try to get more humor in . . . [your work], or you try to see a little of the other side sometimes. Everybody goes through that. I think Art Young was one of the few that stayed [socialist], and Bob Minor."

One cartoonist, reaching his sixties, went into politics. After a long career as a freelance cartoonist for major magazines, Dave Gerard, a Republican, ran for mayor of Crawfordsville, Indiana (population 14,000), and won. As mayor he also did a syndicated feature, *Citizen Smith,* that depicted encounters not far removed from those he had with residents of his hometown.

Charles Schulz suggests that "Cartooning is a *fairly* sort of proposition. You have to be fairly intelligent—if you were really intelligent you'd be doing something else; you have to draw fairly well—if you drew really well you'd be a painter; you have to write fairly well—if you wrote really well you'd be writing books. It's great for a fairly person like me." Al Capp underlines the indignity suffered by the comic-strip artist: he is not accepted by the writer because he draws, and he is not accepted by the artist because he writes.

Syndicate executives will tell you that the cartoonist can't spell. Not infrequently, a staff artist at the syndicate has to opaque out a word in the cartoonist's balloon and do some relettering to correct it. Rare is the cartoonist who knows the difference between "its" and "it's." And "all right" invariably shows up in a balloon as "alright."

It would be hard to think of an occupation in which the participant felt better about what he was doing. "I never knew anybody who so enjoyed his work," Franklin P. Adams wrote of Clare Briggs, the New York *Tribune* and *Herald Tribune* cartoonist. "Often while [he was] drawing a cartoon I have seen him laugh uproariously at it."

There is a little bit of the sentimental in cartoonists. Al Hirschfeld, who does the caricatures of show business personalities for the Sunday *New York Times,* works the name of his daughter Nina into all of his drawings. The name is buried in the hair or in the folds of the dress of the person he's caricaturing. The U.S. Air Force has used the drawings to help train cadets in instant map reading. Presumably, if they can find "Nina" quickly, they can spot targets better. Among editorial cartoonists, Hugh Haynie of the *Louisville Courier-Journal* used to work the name of his wife Lois into his cartoons. Paul Szep works in the name of his daughter Amy.

The cartoonist has his pride, too. "Had I found . . . [cartooning] to be merely a craft," David Low wrote, "I should have given it up long before as a boring business and gone in for something lively like stockbroking. I was like the pastry cook who believed that there weren't any arts worth considering except architecture and pastry-making, and considered that pastry-making came first. I was a caricaturist [editorial cartoonist] and I believed that caricature was the most important of the arts, if only because it clearly involved to a greater extent than any other the exercise of the two principles fundamental to all art in whatever medium of expression—selection and emphasis."

Tom Powers, an early editorial cartoonist, had his

contract written to guarantee that the byline over his daily feature would read: "By Tom Powers, the famous cartoonist." Dorothy Bond refers to herself on her letterhead as the "World's Leading Woman Cartoonist."

In an article in *The Liberator* (January 1920) Robert Minor told of his reaction to someone who "in a matter-of-fact conversation said that certain drawings that I made were his property. I flew into a rage. . . . He dares to say that he *owns* my drawing! My hand made that; my fingers—*my* fingers tingled to the joy of shaping those lines—and this impudent cannibal dares to put a claim upon it! This work is mine; it is a part of me."

As a group of professionals, cartoonists are a bit defensive about their status. Not counting the illustrators among them, their ranks are small: slightly more than 125 full-time editorial cartoonists working for American newspapers; only a few-score gag cartoonists selling regularly to magazines (although hundreds—perhaps thousands—try, settling for only an occasional sale); and perhaps only a couple of dozen cartoonists making really big money as comic-strip artists (with several hundred others making little more than skilled laborers make).

It was inevitable that cartoonists should organize their several professional organizations, launch newsletters and trade papers, establish museums for cartoon lovers and researchers (the two mentioned in this chapter aren't the only ones), and promote television specials and other events to call attention to a profession that takes art, combines it with journalism, and sends it on an errand to arouse and amuse a world of readers and viewers.

2

The Lightbulb over the Head

In his autobiography David Low, with some bitterness, noted that "No newspaper man gave a damn about Art; nor many newspaper readers either. . . ." When anyone complimented him on his work, Low wrote, that person really only complimented the idea.

"Was that why I sat up half the night fretting to get the right simper, frown or smirk on Baldwin's face? Was that the average response to the exercise of mind and imagination involved in playing with line values, as a musician plays with notes on the piano, to produce effects of farce, fantasy or tragedy? Was that why I strained my ingenuity inventing ways of drawing things that are undrawable, like an invisible man, say, or a couple of isosceles triangles having a fight, or a man chasing a dog on the blind side of a wall? Or why I strove to express emotions in familiar visual terms, to create—create was the word—pictorial symbols for ideas that have no shape or substance, like Freedom, War, Peace, Labour, Slump, Prosperity, Europe, Britain, and so on?"

Perhaps not. But all those remarkable effects were necessary to put the idea across. And to put an idea across, clearly and quickly, is what cartooning is all about.

A reader picks up a book for entertainment, information, or guidance—not to admire the beauty of the language. He sits through a speech not to freak out over the cadence or pear-shaped tones, however hypnotic they may be, but to learn something. Similarly, a reader, unless he is himself a cartoonist, usually notices a cartoon for what it says, not for how it's drawn. The drawing can be rather ordinary. In the words of Rollin Kirby, a three-time Pulitzer Prize winner, "A good idea has carried many an indifferent drawing to glory, but never has a good drawing rescued a bad idea from oblivion."

Of course, Low's ideas were as carefully worked out as his compositions, and if the compliments that he did get failed to encompass the full scope of his work, they did nevertheless point to a greatness that places him among the two or three greatest editorial cartoonists of the twentieth century. Low was widely reprinted, and not just in his adopted England. Perhaps his best-remembered cartoon is the one he drew in 1939 (after the Nazi-Soviet pact) showing Hitler and Stalin meeting in the smoking ruins of Poland. "The scum of the earth, I believe?" says a smiling Hitler, lifting his hat and bowing. "The bloody assassin of the workers, I presume?" answers Stalin, with the same gesture. The drawing is executed with great strength and economy, and the idea carries just enough of a tie to an earlier and very different meeting in history to give it a base and even a touch of irony.

Says Richard Rovere of this cartoon: "It took most of us more than 20 years to catch up with the truth captured by Low—that where ideology and national interest are in conflict, national interest prevails."

Coming up with an idea for a cartoon involves research and thought. But occasionally the idea comes from out of the blue. If he is observant enough, the cartoonist may find cartoons in what happens in real life. But it's easy to overlook some possibilities.

Before I went into teaching, it was necessary for me to finish a master's thesis. Researching, writing, and footnoting were chore enough; typing it in final form was, for me, an impossibility. (I use what has been referred to as the Columbus system of typing: hunt for it and then land on it.)

Fortunately, I had planned ahead by marrying one of the nation's celebrated typists, but at this stage in her life she was burdened by crawling infants. I couldn't be there to protect her from them, and we were up against a deadline. Showing an imagination I hadn't until then fully appreciated, my wife set herself and her typewriter inside a playpen, and there she stayed for three or four days until her job was completed.

I had forgotten all about the episode until 1974 when, reading the August 19 issue of *The New Yorker*, I stopped at an Ed Arno cartoon of an artist at work inside a playpen, his several clamoring kids with their clutter safely on the outside. When my wife invented this sanity saver, I was freelancing gag cartoons, but it never occurred to me, perhaps because I was too close to it, that right there was an idea for me, waiting to be drawn. And a *New Yorker*-level idea at that!

Ideas for Gag Cartoons

In analyzing the idea behind the cartoon, perhaps the best place to start is with the gag cartoon.[1] The newest of the cartoon forms, it is, at the same time, the most endangered of the species, not only because of the demise of the general-circulation magazine but also because of the emergence of the art director as a force in American journalism. Art directors, who on many magazines rank right up there with their editors, think in terms of unified pages, with title, art, and copy working together to do a communications job. To throw in an unrelated, self-contained gag cartoon to disrupt the flow is anathema to many art directors.

But as long as we have *The New Yorker, Saturday Review,*

---

1. Some of the material in this section appeared in a different form in "Back to the Old Drawing Board," a chapter in *The Fourth Estate* written by John L. Hulteng and the author and published by Harper & Row, New York, 1971.

Playboy (*Esquire* has practically dropped out of the cartoon picture), the women's service magazines, and trade and specialized magazines still giving gag cartoons prominent display, the art may yet survive.

To the cartoon connoisseur, gag cartoons represent the ultimate in the cartoon art. A gag cartoon is to be savored, not just looked at and read. The subtleties of the art are considerable.

Usually the whole point revolves around a single line printed underneath the cartoon, and everything within the drawing must substantiate that point. The gag cartoonist keeps his cast of characters down, his setting simple.

In most cases he has no particular ax to grind, but that does not mean he has nothing to say. If the editorial cartoonist is a political cartoonist, the gag cartoonist is a social cartoonist. The gag cartoonist is never happier than when, in the words of Stephen Becker in *Comic Art in America*, he is "jabbing away constantly at our shams and illusions," in the end touching upon some social truth.

Gag cartoonists come onto their gags in a number of ways. Sometimes they dream up a scene and then try to think of a gag line to fit. Sometimes they start with the line and then try to imagine a scene that will make it funny.

Asked by *Cartoonist Profiles* magazine how he gets his ideas, Eldon Dedini said: "To be truthful, it's still a mystery to me. And it's the mystery that makes it interesting. . . . Maybe if I knew more about it, I'd lose the touch.

"I find if I put enough stuff *in* me by reading and observing, something is bound to come out."

Chon Day finds thumbing through *Bartlett's Familiar Quotations* helpful—or even thumbing through his old roughs that didn't sell. "Strangely enough, I may be looking at one of these cartoons showing a policeman talking to a woman motorist, and, all of a sudden, an idea for a *boating* gag will flash into my mind—or a barroom idea—no connection at all, apparently, with the cartoon I've been looking at!"

Most gag cartoonists buy some of their ideas from outside sources. They pay the writer 25 percent of what the
cartoon earns and keep 75 percent for themselves. Only the
cartoonist signs the cartoon.

The alert reader may occasionally spot a gag cartoon with
a familiar ring, and, searching, find the original drawn by
another artist. This does not mean necessarily that the idea
was intentionally lifted. It may mean, rather, that the initial
cartoon was noticed by the later cartoonist and then forgotten, only to reappear in his consciousness years later. Or it
may be that the idea was really reinvented. "Damn those who
have made my remarks before me!" said Donatus way back in
the fourth century.

Certainly cartoon editors at the magazines can't
remember all the cartoons they and all the editors before
them, on all magazines, once bought and ran.

It has been said that the novelist has only a few basic
plots to work with. Similarly, the gag cartoonist has only a
few basic ideas. The setting, the props, the characters change;
the words in the gag lines vary; but the ideas persevere.

Perhaps you will recognize these "plots":

1. *The cliché.* Most journalists avoid the cliché. Not the
cartoonist. He can take a cliché and let a character act it out
literally and get a laugh. Virgil (Vip) Partch is a master of this
kind of gag. Vip shows a man lying dead on the sidewalk
while a companion, unaware of the tragedy, turns to watch a
cranky woman walk by. He says: "Boy! If looks could kill, eh,
Steve?" Dana Fradon makes a slight change in a cliché in a
New Yorker cartoon dealing with deteriorating telephone
service. An executive leads a caller to the door and says:
"Don't try to call me. I'll try to call you." In the same spirit, J.
B. Handelsman, also in *The New Yorker,* shows a middle-aged
man carrying a briefcase, raising his hat to the lady who has
answered the door. "Good day, Madam. I'm working my son's
way through college."

2. *That's life.* This includes any gag that depicts life as it is,

so that the reader will identify with it and say, in effect: "Ain't it the truth!" The late Tom Henderson, one of the most consistently funny men in the business, in the old *Saturday Evening Post* shows a lazy, unshaven man reading the paper, the phone on a table at his side. His wife has just picked up the receiver after rushing in from in front of the house where she's parked the car. She's dropped groceries all the way in and knocked over a chair in her rush to answer the phone. She's saying: "Yes, he's here." Orlando Busino in a recent *Ladies' Home Journal* shows a sign in a supermarket window: "FANTASTIC SALE! SAME PRICES AS YESTERDAY!"

Ed Sullivan's cartoon of a minister sitting in his well-stocked study, which turns out to be inadequate, could be

" I WISH I HAD THE ANSWER TO THAT, FRED!"
From *Stained Glass*, a syndicated feature for newspaper
church pages. Courtesy Ed Sullivan and Avant Features,
Canfield, Ohio.

considered an example of "that's life" humor, although with bookshelves like that it could also serve as an example of exaggeration.

3. *Ridiculous situation.* The opposite of "that's life." It just couldn't be that way! Jerry Marcus in *True* shows a worried woman driver with her husband sitting beside her. In back of her is a line of cars: a tow truck, a police car, and an ambulance. The husband says: "Relax, it's probably just a coincidence." Syd Hoff in *Esquire* shows a middle-aged couple being held up by a nonchalant robber. The woman says to the robber: "William, don't your own parents mean *anything* to you?" For the following cartoon, Dan Goldstein, a student having a first try at gag cartooning, comes up with a very different ridiculous situation.

"SHIKKELMAN STILL LOOKS SLUGGISH, IF YOU ASK ME."

Courtesy of Dan Goldstein.

4. *Out of character.* Sweet little old ladies act like gangsters. Kids talk like grownups. Ministers sit in bars with worldly women. Mulligan in *The New Yorker* shows a perplexed man and wife looking at a painting of a haggard, hungry woman holding a baby with a frightened child at her side. The scene is stark, desolate. The painting is signed "Norman Rockwell." The man says: "Well, there must be more than one Norman Rockwell in the world."

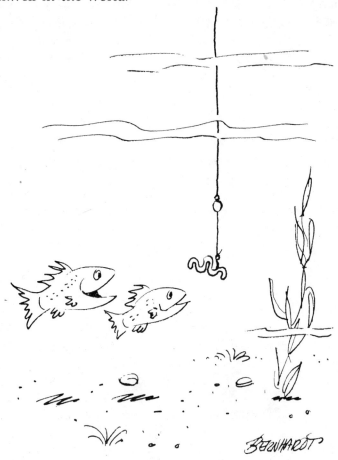

"The object of the game is to get the worm off the hook, then another one comes down automatically."

Another version of the out-of-character approach is Glenn Bernhardt's talking fish cartoon done for Industrial Press Service, a free syndicated service produced by the National Association of Manufacturers for weekly newspapers. The cartoon could also be an example of Plot Number 8: "ingenuity" (lower-species division).

5. *In character.* People act out their roles to the point of absurdity. Barney Tobey in *The New Yorker* shows a young man entwined with a girl on a park bench. With his free hand, and without looking, he's reaching into a bag of popcorn and feeding a flock of pigeons and squirrels. An older couple is walking by, and the man says to the woman: "Now, there's a warm human being for you!" Henry Martin in *Ladies' Home Journal* shows a man and wife visiting a cemetery. There are dogs barking at a grave. Says the wife: "Why, isn't that the final resting place of Ralph Morris, our late postman?"

6. *Understatement.* This is a favorite theme for the cartoonist; and British cartoonists have no corner on it. Jim Stevenson in *The New Yorker* shows an art expert examining a fine painting while the owner looks on. The expert has rubbed his finger across the painting; his finger is wet with paint. He says: "Well, this initial test suggests that the authenticity of your Rembrandt may be questionable." J. B. Handelsman shows a variation of understatement—underreacting, or failure to put first things first—in the *Playboy* cartoon shown on the following page.

7. *Exaggeration.* The opposite of understatement. Chon Day in the old *Saturday Evening Post* shows a tired, middle-aged man asleep on a couch. His wife—a little portly—and a lady visitor are talking. The wife says: "He's had a bad back ever since he carried me over the threshold." In a *New Yorker* cartoon, Dana Fradon shows two scientists in a lab. One startles the other with the comment: "My God! There are traces of tuna fish in this shipment of mercury." Fradon's is a gag cartoon in which the gag is everything; it could be run without a drawing. But the expressions on the faces of the scientists add considerably to the enjoyment.

"*Also, I know for a fact that you carry her picture around in your wallet.*"

8. *Ingenuity.* When man solves some problem in an unusual way, readers—even readers of gag cartoons—appreciate it. Rodrigues in the *Saturday Review* sets up a situation in which a father tries to tell his side of the story to a rebel generation. He's fat, balding, middle-aged, well dressed; he stands on stage at a run-down coffee house, strumming a guitar. Hippie types sit watching him, frowning. He's singing: ". . . Oh, my kid's twenty-three and he don't like to work/Oh, he don't like to work/When I was twenty-three I worked very hard/Oh, I worked very hard. . . ." (You could classify this gag as "out of character," too.) Dana Fradon again in a *New Yorker* cartoon shows a man walking along a street startled by a mechanical hand jutting out from a machine and holding a hat. A sign on the machine reads: "BEG-O-MATIC INC." Rea Avena in a *New York Times* travel section shows a Dutch boy with a hose plugged into the legendary hole in the dike; he is standing near a clump of tulips watering them.

9. *Stupidity.* In this kind of a gag the cartoonist lets the reader know something a chief character in the cartoon doesn't know. The reader feels superior. Jerry Marcus again, this time in *The Saturday Evening Post,* shows a middle-aged couple already in bed, looking bored. Another couple, obviously visitors, stands nearby. The man, hat in hand, says: "Well, we really must be going."

10. *The letdown.* Some definitions of humor suggest that this is the real core of humor. The reader is led to believe one thing, then finally disappointed. Jim Stevenson again, in *The New Yorker:* A guru sits in front of his high mountain cave. Around him are signs scrawled on the rock: "Smile and the world smiles with you, cry and you cry alone"; "Early to bed and early to rise makes a man healthy, wealthy and wise"; "A penny saved is a penny earned"; and so on. A disappointed, slightly hippie-ish couple has just arrived. The girl says to her male companion: "Something tells me we've come to the wrong guru." (Again, classification can never be exact. This gag could serve as an example of "understatement.")

Some of America's best wits use the gag-cartoon style of humor in real-life situations. Once when Franklin P. Adams escorted Mr. and Mrs. George Kaufman to a party, Mrs. Kaufman sat down on a cane-bottom chair and fell through and found herself stuck there. Adams's quick response was: "I've told you a hundred times, Beatrice, that's not funny!" And when Abe Burrows escorted some guests to the elevator in his apartment building, he told the operator: "Take these people wherever they want to go."

One way the cartoonist can stimulate his imagination to produce gags like the foregoing is to make lists of kinds of people, props, and places. For instance:

People	Props	Places
nun	umbrella	bedroom
teacher	bicycle	kitchen
baby	marbles	front lawn
mechanic	bowl of soup	desert
politician	typewriter	downtown
housewife	TV set	playground
cop	guitar	store
clerk	cat	inside of airplane
fat man	mailbox	voting booth
hitchhiker	statue	beach

Through a random selection, the cartoonist picks one item from each list and tries to connect them. Let's say he ends up with "housewife," "cat," and "front lawn." The combination doesn't sound very promising. But Martin Giuffre in *Good Housekeeping* used it, added additional cats, and mixed in some kids (nothing in the rules says you can't add something extra), and came up with this: The kids are leaving a party, each carrying a kitten, while a mother stands at the door and, with a kind of smug look on her face, waves at them. One of the kids says to another: "What a party! Everybody won a prize!"

Now I have no idea how Giuffre (or his gagwriter, if he had one) came up with that idea, but it *could* have come about in that way.

The longer each list is, the more possible combinations, of course.

An R. Hall of Liberal, Kansas, sells a set of three dial-a-gag wheels—one for people, one for places, and one for props—which, he says, can produce a total of 500,000 situations for which cartoonists can write gags.

To keep the professional cartoonist abreast of gags appearing in about sixty-five major and middle-level markets, Al Gottlieb of East Meadow, New York, brings out a monthly newsletter, *The Gag Re-Cap*. Included are addresses of markets and rates of pay. Gottlieb looks upon his publication as "a constant thought-stimulator, providing a never-ending source of gag bases. . . . There is no end to the number of saleable ideas that a nimble mind can come up with merely by making legitimate switches on the gags appearing in the *Re-Cap*."

An unintended function of *Re-Cap* is to demonstrate to the student how low the high art of gag cartooning can sink when it is directed to the tastes of readers of *Adam, Gallery, Genesis, Gent,* and similar magazines. Coming onto a whole column of "girlie" gaglines can be a sobering experience.

Ideas for Illustrative Cartoons

In some respects prose alone is more compelling than prose that is illustrated. A writer who encourages his reader to form his own picture doesn't need any help from an illustrator. For instance: Stephen Leacock with his marvelous line from the story, "Gertrude the Governess": ". . . he flung himself from the room, flung himself upon his horse and rode madly off in all directions." A cartoon could do nothing to improve this picture.

But there are times when cartoon art enhances humorous prose. When a great cartoonist collaborates with a great comic writer, the result can be eminently satisfying to the reader.

It can be satisfying to the writer as well. Perhaps among writers the most respected of the humorous illustrators is the meticulous Gluyas Williams with his beautifully designed, carefully controlled fine-line drawings. Among writers whose works were illustrated by Williams was David McCord, who has reported: "All of us who have written things, which Gluyas was willing to illustrate, openly agree that we were both fortunate and privileged. . . . If we have ever let him down, he has always held us up." Kenneth Bird, an editor at *Punch* who also did cartoons signed "Fougasse," called Williams "a superb noticer." Forrest Izard, a colleague of Williams's on the *Boston Evening Transcript*, said that for his sketches of theater personalities Williams would simply watch for a while, then return to his drawing board and work from memory. He never made sketches.

His admirable precision of line was most happily matched, perhaps, with the precision of words by Robert Benchley. (One of America's most productive writers of short, deadpan humor pieces, Benchley is remembered for a wire he sent friends in the States upon his arrival at Venice: "STREETS FLOODED. PLEASE ADVISE.")

Adding to the worth of the Williams illustrations for Benchley's writings was the fidelity of the caricature. Williams portrayed Benchley unerringly.

Here is an illustration Williams did for a Benchley essay on "Why I Am Pale." Benchley's problem, as the essay

Reproduced by courtesy of Gluyas Williams.

explained, was that an arthritic condition made it impossible for him to lie comfortably on the sand. ". . . Often I have to be assisted to my feet. . . ."

Another happy combination involved writer S. J. Perelman with caricaturist Al Hirschfeld. ". . . Signing him up to illustrate S. J. Perelman's prose was pure inspiration," Stephen Becker observed in *Comic Art in America.* "Perelman, incidentally, rejoices as much in describing Hirschfeld verbally as Hirschfeld does in adding his verbal [I think Becker means 'visual' here] thrusts to Perelman's literature."

Illustration that portrays a writer can also help in cases where the writer is less well known. One of my own ventures into this area involves an old friend, Embert Fossum, who writes of his return to college to get a master's degree. His article, "It's Back to School for an 'Old Geezer,' " appearing in *Old Oregon,* an alumni magazine, makes the point that an older man at first feels out of place among all those young students. I chose to illustrate these two climactic sentences: "I was positively elated one day when a dazzling young beauty came up to me during a break between classes and, after addressing me by my first name, borrowed a dime for a cup of coffee. Then I knew I had been accepted." The magazine editor gave me a mug shot (but not a side view) to work from, and I could remember the man's basic appearance; that was enough to bring off a caricature true enough that several readers, who knew the writer, recognized him without any difficulty.

A function of this illustration is to contrast the lithe lines of the fashionable woman student (the year is 1974) and the unpressed, over-the-hill figure that was the author (p. 84).

An editorial or advertising illustration differs from other cartoon forms in that it does not stand by itself. Its job is to enhance a piece of copy. But it would be a mistake to assume that there is no idea behind an illustrative cartoon. The idea is as crucial as for any other cartoon. The trick is to tell the reader enough to interest him in reading the copy but not so much that he will feel that, after taking in the cartoon, he can

ROY PAUL

move on to another page without stopping over.

 To come up with an acceptable idea for an illustration, the cartoonist has to read the story, article, or whatever and determine both its theme and its highlights. He may decide in his illustration to summarize; or he may decide to titillate.

 Peter Lippman faced the job of illustrating a semi-humorous article in the *New York Times* in which the writer, who did a lot of driving, told how important the car radio was to her. "Cars merely move me around; the radio keeps me in touch." Lippman's cartoon showed a head-on view of what at first glance was an ordinary car being driven down the road by a happy woman driver. But on closer inspection, the reader could see that the grille was really the face of a radio and the headlights were knobs for tuning and volume control.

Basil Wolverton put his awesome command of the pen to work to produce a series of haunting illustrations for *1975 in Prophecy* and *The Book of Revelation Unveiled at Last*, two Ambassador College publications produced in the mid-1960s. While admitting that his imagination was involved, Wolverton says that the drawings were "not based on my interpretations nor on those of anyone else, inasmuch as the Bible interprets itself to those who carefully look into it without prejudice." The three examples that follow were used to depict mass burials, famine, and the plague of boils in a post-

Courtesy of Ambassador College

nuclear war setting, part of the catastrophic events to accompany the end of the world.

Whether for a story, article, or advertisement, an illustration should restate or amplify the headline, never work against it. And almost never should the illustration add a dimension not present in the headline.

"Are You Reading Someone Else's *National Observer?*" asks a headline in an ad in that paper, an ad meant to appeal to potential subscribers. A cartoon shows a man on a bus or train with his face buried in the paper. He wears a slightly angry expression on his face because he is aware, apparently, that a second man two seats back of him is looking at the paper, too, through a pair of binoculars. On the lenses of the binoculars, way out in front of his face, are the eyes of the second man. This makes his eagerness to read the *Observer* all the more apparent.

To dramatize its slogan, "Never underestimate the power of a woman" (a registered trademark), *Ladies' Home Journal* in an ad in *Advertising Age* uses a comic-strip approach: a four-unit crosshatch drawing by Stan Mack. (Lawrence K. Grossman, Inc., is the agency.) Mack shows a Samson having an easy enough time, at first, holding up the world, but as trouble erupts all over. . . . In the final panel Samson seems mighty glad to have a woman around. Mack uses parallel structure— same-size units, same camera angle—to put his idea across clearly and quickly (p. 88).

How many wrong ways can there be for physicians to remove wax from their patients' ears? International Pharmaceutical Corporation turned the problem over to Virgil Partch. On page 88 are several solutions that Vip came up with to go with an advertising campaign directed to physicians. The headline for each ad read: "There's a Better Way to Remove Ear Wax." As the copy for each ad pointed out, the way was for the physician to recommend use of Debrox Drops by patients prior to their coming in for wax removal.

Never underestimate

How do you get a painter high on a pole? No, the answer isn't, "You have the pole pay for the drinks." The answer from a visual standpoint was provided by reporter/artist Richard Sept for the *Cottage Grove* (Oregon) *Sentinel*, a weekly newspaper. Sept's job was to show weekly progress in his

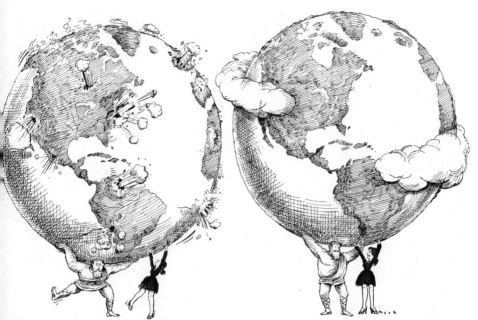

the power of a woman.

A Registered Trademark of Downe Publishing, Inc.

By permission of *Ladies' Home Journal*.

town's drive to reach the United Way goal. Asked to use the familiar thermometer, Sept decided to dress up his drawings with a cartoon character. Each week he came up with a new way to show the painter's progress. On page 90 are about half of his solutions published during the two-month campaign.

Courtesy of International Pharmaceutical Corporation and Virgil Partch.

Courtesy of Richard Sept.

Jack Barrett, staff artist for the *St. Petersburg* (Florida) *Times*, adds to the impact of a feature on alcoholism by playing with a bottle's shape and contents and by allowing the bottle to dominate several tragic and dependent figures that cling to it.

The illustrator, unlike other cartoonists tied to standard formats, faces a wide choice of mediums and shapes. The decisions he makes in this area are. almost as crucial as the decisions he makes about what in the story or article to illustrate. Illustrators in recent years have experimented with mixed mediums. Often several drawings and photographs are combined in a collage.

To produce a collage for a feature about actor Anthony Quinn in the *St. Petersburg Times*, Jack Barrett used pen and ink, Pentel, brush, Zipatone, and a spatter technique. Parts of the illustration were done on different papers and later pasted together (p. 92).

For a cover devoted to "The Anatomy of Rock: A Medical View," designer Bill King for *Physician's World* (December 1973), taking off from that famous Leonardo da Vinci sketch

of the man in a square inside a circle, showed a doctored photograph of a young man in mod clothes (high heels, long hair, brightly striped pants), one set of arms and legs extended to the square, another set to the circle. An example of a photograph used as a cartoon, it was an ideal symbol to use for the word "Anatomy" in the cover blurb.

Recently, the *New York Times, Writer's Digest,* and a few other publications have been experimenting with the use of gag cartoons as illustrations. Instead of tossing in any gag cartoon to provide a break in columns of gray type, the editors have chosen gag cartoons appropriate to the subject matter of the articles. *Writer's Digest* has even used them up front in its articles to accompany the article titles.

Ideas for Comic Strips

For a comic strip, there is, first, the basic idea—or concept—that sends the cartoonist to his drawing board to produce the six-weeks set of samples necessary to sell a syndicate on taking a new feature. And then there is the daily idea that keeps the strip alive.

Many of the successful strips have spawned imitation strips to serve the second or third newspaper in the area that didn't get the feature first. (A syndicate offers a strip to a newspaper with the promise that the syndicate won't sell the same strip to a competing newspaper.) But the best chance of selling a new strip to a syndicate is to devise a basic theme and cast of characters no one else has thought of. More often than not the new strip capitalizes on a new condition or interest that has taken hold.

Typically, a comic strip features an interesting hero—or anti-hero—and several carefully defined supporting characters. The cartoonist producing a comic strip becomes a one-man motion-picture organization: producer, director, writer, art director, cameraman, casting director, costume supervisor—and more.

Sometimes the strip represents a collaboration between a writer and an artist. And if the strip grows successful enough, the cartoonist hires a staff to help out. Some of the big-name cartoonists merely sketch in the strips in pencil, leaving the final inking to one assistant, the balloons to another. One of the things that has set Charles Schulz's strip apart from others is that he does it all himself. Nor is he receptive to ideas from outside. Of course, all the satellite activities—the television animation, the drawings for products, etc.—are handled by others, but Schulz oversees it all.

The daily ideas for established *adventure* strips evolve pretty much as ideas for novels evolve, or, more to the point, as scripts for radio and television soap operas evolve. Not much daily progress can be made in three or four panels.

The daily ideas for *comic* strips evolve pretty much as gag cartoon ideas evolve. Most of the popular comic strips today—*Beetle Bailey, Peanuts, B.C., Wizard of Id, Doonesbury*—are really gag cartoons stretched across three or four panels. *Beetle Bailey,* for instance, often makes use of the gag-cartoon approach in which a chief character has not been privy to information made available to the reader. The general in the strip sees one of his charges performing some act that, on the surface, seems unreasonable, but it is an act for which the reader has been prepared in earlier panels. The general's reaction is always: "Now what?"

If you think the gag-a-day strip is something new, consider this 1926 *Polly and Her Pals* offering of Cliff Sterrett's. Daily episodes like this went on from 1912 to 1958, when the great comic-strip stylist retired. (In case the term *foot-pads* throws you, it meant "holdup men who travel on foot.")

POLLY AND HER PALS

INTERFER

Ideas for Editorial Cartoons

The word *editorial* in the expression *editorial cartoonist* comes from the fact that the work most often appears on the editorial page of the newspaper, where, in America's system of journalism, the paper is expected to express opinion. Theoretically the other pages in the paper are reserved for objective reporting, where the writer's opinion does not intrude. Unfortunately, many editorial cartoons are not editorial at all; they are as objective as the news stories are supposed to be. What these cartoons do is merely dramatize the news.

Of course, that may be service enough. Just to make news understandable is a worthy goal. But the cartoon—the editorial cartoon—can do more. It can help people form opinions and may even inspire them to take action to solve some civic or social problem.

While the editorial cartoon belongs primarily to the newspapers, it has been used to a limited extent in magazines, too. The old *Saturday Evening Post* used them. So did *Collier's* (Rollin Kirby, after a distinguished career on the *New York World*, the *New York World-Telegram*, and the *New York Post*, did cartoons for *Collier's* as did Ding Darling) and, in its last days, *Life*. *Time*, *Newsweek*, and *U.S. News & World Report* all reprint editorial cartoons, as do opinion magazines like *The New Republic* and *The Progressive*. The underground newspapers featured editorial cartoons, too.

The most influential underground editorial cartoonist was probably Ron Cobb, once an apprentice at Walt Disney studios. *Avant Garde* called him the "Daumier of the New Left." His best-known cartoon, probably, was one that might just as well have appeared overground. It showed a mesmerized middle-class man roaming around with his portable television set amid the ruins of what was probably an atomic bomb attack; he's looking for an outlet to plug into. A Cobb cartoon more likely to stay underground was the one showing a faith healer with his hands on the stomach of a pregnant woman. The faith healer is saying: "In the name of Jesus Christ! Abort! Abort!!"

What does it take to be an editorial cartoonist?

Ranan Lurie, the Israeli-born cartoonist and caricaturist brought to America to be *Life*'s cartoonist and now syndicated, says you have to be a political analyst, an artist, a caricaturist, a humorist, and a journalist—all five. He says the only difference between James Reston (the *New York Times* columnist) and an editorial cartoonist is that Reston doesn't know how to draw.

Some of today's editorial cartoonists think there may be too much emphasis on humor. "I see a trend among young cartoonists to draw something very funny rather than to have something worthwhile to say in a cartoon," says Bill Sanders, editorial cartoonist for the *Milwaukee Journal*. Don Wright of the *Miami News* thinks "there's a tendency of too many cartoonists to use humor as the sole means of getting a point across—and I'm sad to see this. . . . Many young cartoonists lock themselves into this light, humorous style but can't do the very heavy, dramatic cartoon when an issue calling for it arises."

One of the younger cartoonists who relies mostly on humor is the *Richmond News Leader*'s Jeff MacNelly, who at twenty-four, just two years into daily editorial cartooning, won a Pulitzer Prize. He says, "What I look for is the humorous, entertaining angle in expressing my opinion. . . . I know that many cartoonists don't feel that this is the function of an editorial cartoon, but I believe that it's a very important part of my cartoons. I think that you can get the reader's attention and hold it better through humor than with a hatchet. This is not to say that I avoid the serious issues and the serious approach to many issues. I simply feel that my more successful cartoons have been the ones that provoke a good laugh."

He adds: "I'm not trying to change any minds. If I wanted to do that, I wouldn't be doing funny cartoons. . . . I'm not a big dogmatic, doctrinaire type. I've never been a crusader. . . . People get turned off by that kind of thing. . . ."

With his art MacNelly prefers to settle for "little truths here and there," as Art Buchwald does with his writing. He would rather kid his victims than attack them. The reader does not have to be hit over the head with the idea. "I let the characters in my cartoon say that something is bad or that something should be done . . . , rather than preaching to . . . [the reader] in the form of my own words in a caption," says Ed Valtman, editorial cartoonist for the *Hartford* (Connecticut) *Times*. "And I try to leave it for the reader to discover the final meaning himself. I attempt to direct him so he'll come to his own conclusions."

There is always the danger the reader won't get it.

N. Wylie Jones, in an article in *Richmond,* a city magazine, tells a story about a phone call received by Jeff MacNelly. It was from a woman who had purchased a MacNelly original at a fund-raising auction.

"Who does the squirrel represent?" she asked.

"That's not a squirrel."

"What is it?"

"A beaver."

"Is it supposed to be somebody?"

"Yes. George McGovern."

"Well, is that all there is?"

"Yes."

"Then it's not a very deep cartoon?"

"No. It's very shallow like all my work."

When you have to explain a cartoon, MacNelly says, it kills it. It's like trying to explain a joke. So he doesn't try.

One of the biggest problems an editorial cartoonist faces is the visit or phone call from a relative or friendly reader who has come up with an idea. Noncartoonists simply do not think in cartoon terms; seldom is a suggested idea of any use to the cartoonist. The cartoonist must develop a facility for dealing with these people without offending them.

Also adding to the cartoonist's frustrations is the fact that real life often outdoes the cartoon in its extravagances. In a talk to a religious gathering in Lausanne in 1974 Malcolm Muggeridge told of a problem as editor of *Punch:* "In trying to ridicule those . . . set in authority over us, one was constantly frustrated because, as it turned out, they were themselves infinitely more absurd in what they did and said than in one's wildest inventions."

Watergate seemed made to order for the nation's editorial cartoonists, but actually, as Jeff MacNelly explains, it was difficult to come up with ideas. "It's impossible to parody something that has already become a parody."

Steps in the Process

The process for coming up with editorial cartoon ideas for many papers works like this:

1. The editorial cartoonist sits in on a daily conference of editorial writers, meeting with the managing editor, who briefs them on the news that's breaking. Subjects for editorials are discussed and assigned; the cartoonist makes notes. Knowing what editorials the newspaper will be running—what topics will be covered—the cartoonist returns to his desk to see what he can come up with. Perhaps he will work on an idea that will complement the main editorial for the next day. Or perhaps he will tackle a subject that won't be covered by the editorial writers. What he does, essentially, is isolate one news item from among the many available. He asks himself two questions: (1) is the news item significant? and (2) will most people have seen it?

2. Then he *reacts* to it. He takes a stand.

3. When he knows what he wants to say, he writes what amounts to a one-sentence editorial. He develops his theme.

4. Then the cartoonist looks for an analogy he can apply to the situation. He avoids as much as possible depicting his idea literally. If he does a cartoon on a sewer-bond election he does not necessarily draw sewers. Or bonds.

It may be that a simple scene or stage prop is all that's needed for the analogy. Thumbing through picture books or catalogs may provide the necessary inspiration. But the cartoonist avoids looking through other cartoons at this stage. Noticing and admiring other cartoons in his leisure time undoubtedly influences him later when he is working on his own cartoons. This can't be helped. But the cartoonist does not want to deliberately flirt with plagiarism.

He may find his analogy in a well-known story, fable, play, or movie. Or in a proverb. Or a cliché, song title, even an advertising slogan. In a cartoon I did for local consumption that brought more comments than any I can remember (two phone calls) I used a cigarette advertising slogan then popular: "You can't take the country out of Salem." A rural group interested in maintaining the right to burn off their fields after harvest had tied up the legislature with its demands. So I showed a giant (bigger than the capitol), dressed in typical farmer's clothes, puffing on a cigarette, squatting on the steps, blocking entry for urban legislators. The caption was the ad slogan. (If you're not very good in geography, I should tell you that Oregon's capital is Salem.)

Occasionally the editorial cartoonist resorts to a pun. Charles B. Slackman in *New York,* soon after Gerald Ford was confirmed as vice president, showed the Fisk Tire symbol, but with Nixon, rather than the familiar child, holding a candle and a tire. The tire upon close inspection turned out to be a tape spool. The caption, of course, was: "TIME TO RETIRE."

Paul Szep (another Pulitzer Prize winner), in one of his lighter moments for the *Boston Globe,* used the analogy of *Bonnie and Clyde* to express his feelings about the Bobby Riggs-Billie Jean King tennis match—"the biggest heist since the Brinks job," as Tom Wicker called it. A bonus laugh in the cartoon (p. 100) involves a live piggy bank also about to enter the car (Szep's interest in sports comes naturally enough; he's an ex-professional hockey player).

BONNIE AND CLYDE

In a cartoon for the *Richmond News Leader,* Jeff MacNelly drew on a familiar scene from Winnie-the-Pooh to show Teddy (Bear) Kennedy losing interest in going after the honey of the presidency in 1976. The bees of Chappaquiddick and family illnesses were too persistent; Kennedy made his 1974 announcement, and MacNelly drew his cartoon. A cartoonist with a lower energy level would have been content to merely reproduce one of Ernest H. Shepard's lovable illustrations and apply appropriate labels. MacNelly only borrows enough of the Shepard effects to place the cartoon in context. Not the

TEDDY-THE-POOH

Reprinted by permission of Jeff MacNelly.

least of the accomplishments here is the Kennedy likeness MacNelly is able to achieve, despite the fact that what he is really drawing is a bear.

Sometimes the cartoonist wants the idea to take hold gradually. Perhaps what he's after is a double take. In "We want the soap operas back on," a cartoon about the Watergate hearings, Paul Szep shows a bunch of angry old women, swinging umbrellas, descending on a television network executive. They've had enough of Watergate coverage. It takes a little study of the cartoon to discover Richard Nixon in the onrushing crowd.

In a provocative editorial cartoon by Tony Auth of the *Philadelphia Inquirer*, the idea takes the form of a puzzle. The

Pick the draft dodger.

HE FEIGNED ILLNESS.

HE TOOK DRUGS THAT RAISED HIS BLOOD PRESSURE.

HE STAYED IN SCHOOL 12 YR

HE GOT MARRIED.

HE PRETENDED TO BE GAY.

HE OBJECTED TO THE WA ON MORAL GROUNDS A WENT TO CANADA

©1974, PHILADELPHIA
AUTH

cartoonist gets the reader to participate. As a result, the reader considers an aspect of the escape-to-Canada phenomenon that he might not have considered if he had been preached at by Auth.

But usually, the idea comes over at once, with great force. One of Herblock's most remembered cartoons in the *Washington Post* was one he drew during Nixon's campaigning for Republican Congressional candidates in 1954. Nixon had made some wild charges about Democrats. Herblock showed a welcoming committee meeting Nixon, who was emerging from a sewer manhole, carrying a suitcase. One man yells to the crowd: "Here he comes now."

To show that a mayor had a closed mind on open housing, Bill Sanders of the *Milwaukee Journal* showed him with a boarded-up house for a head.

To show that the city council in Charlotte, North Carolina, was not really solving mass transit needs, Doug Marlette, editorial cartoonist for the *Charlotte Observer*, showed the council as a Neanderthal man, chipping away at a big stone wheel, with a map showing "MASS TRANSIT NEEDS" in front of him. There was no caption. (One of the youngest of the editorial cartoonists, Marlette joined the *Observer* staff in 1972, only a year after graduating from Florida State University.)

Often other media enter into the newspaper cartoon. Paul Szep parodied *Time*'s "Man of the Year" annual issue by showing, on the occasion of Clifford Irving's Howard Hughes hoax, a *Time* cover featuring two businessmen with their pants down. The men represented *Life* and McGraw-Hill, the two publishers affected. Running diagonally across a corner of the cover was the familiar cover banner, but with the words "CONNED MEN OF THE YEAR."

Editorial cartoonists have even used other cartoons as the basis for their ideas. Charles Schulz's characters often show up in an editorial cartoon, badly drawn but recognizable, bearing labels to help the cartoonist make his point. There is always an "apologies to . . ." line, but still, such use of characters is unfair to the characters' creators. As Schulz points out, the unsuspecting reader may think the original cartoonist is making the point, and it may be a point the original cartoonist does not agree with.

A more acceptable version of this kind of editorial idea was presented in 1973 by Mike Peters of the *Dayton* (Ohio) *Daily News*. He showed a cartoon that looked a lot like R. Ripley's "Believe It or Not!" panel. But it was "R. Nixon's Believe It or Not!" One of the items showed seven reels of tape. The legend read: "OPTICAL ILLUSION (THERE ARE NINE TAPES HERE)."

Sometimes the analogy is best when it directly relates to the subject. When it appeared that the American Medical Association had lost its fight against Medicare, I did a cartoon showing a worried doctor, representing the A.M.A., placing his stethoscope on the chest of a man in a casket, the dead man representing the anti-Medicare campaign. An undertaker tries to comfort the doctor by saying, "There's nothing more you can do for him now, Doctor. . . ."

What kind of an analogy would you come up with if you wanted to show that a particular politician or world leader was trying to be all things to all people, that he plays too many roles? Bill Mauldin of the *Chicago Sun-Times* handled that problem with the analogy of the paper doll. The character stood there in the middle of the cartoon in his underclothes, a cutout on a paper stand marked "FOLD." Surrounding him were several items of apparel, all signifying different occupations or roles, and each of the garments had those familiar little paper tabs that are to be folded back to hold them onto the figure.

Of course, editorial cartoonists have no corner on metaphors and similes. Every good writer uses them. Here's Malcolm Muggeridge, for instance, in the second volume of his autobiography, *Chronicles of Wasted Time,* using words to draw a cartoon of two very different editors he worked for in England: "Working for [C.P.] Scott was like waltzing with some dowager at a mayoral reception in Manchester; for [Lord] Beaverbrook, like taking the floor in a night-club in the early hours of the morning, when everyone is more or less drunk."

And James Reston describing Nelson Rockefeller before his confirmation as vice president: "He feels like a beached whale, eager to help President Ford . . . but unable to do anything until sworn into office." A cartoon in words.

"Holy" Hubert Lindsey, the Don Rickles of the evangelical set, who travels to West Coast campuses to argue Christ and trade insults with agnostics and militants, once issued a "proclamation" to some anti-Vietnam war clergymen. He was suggesting they abandon politics and devote their attention instead to matters of the spirit. He used this analogy: "You remind me of the old woman who is mopping the water from the floor while the bathtub is full of water and running over because both faucets are open." Another verbal picture, just waiting for some editorial cartoonist to come along with the proper labels to attach to the woman, the tub, and the faucets. The cartoonist might well file such verbal pictures away under "idea possibilities" whenever he stumbles onto them in his reading.

For a writer, a figure of speech can change a dull paragraph to a sprightly one. For an editorial cartoonist, a figure of speech (visually portrayed) can make a mere illustration on the editorial page into a genuine editorial cartoon.

5. The analogy, once chosen, becomes the stage. What the editorial cartoonist needs then are actors. They may be real people in caricature. Or they may be familiar symbols like Uncle Sam, John Bull, the Democratic donkey, or the Republican elephant.

Once a symbol is established in the public's mind, an editorial cartoonist almost has to use it. "Through repetition the various devices become worn and threadbare; yet there is no escape from them for they have become established in the public's mind, and any variant would change or obscure the meaning of the message the cartoonist wishes to express," observed Rollin Kirby.

One of the real satisfactions for the editorial cartoonist is to create a symbol where none existed before, as Herblock did with his Mr. Atom, and then watch other cartoonists pick it up. A lesser-known Herblock symbol (the artist hasn't used it much) is the dog with a checkerboard pattern on his body. The dog represents a Checkers speech—any politician's attempt to explain away his financial affairs.

The cartoonist who got here early had the best opportunity for symbol creating. Thomas Nast in the nineteenth century not only revived the donkey for the Democrats; he was the one who invented the elephant for the newly formed

Republican party and the tiger for Tammany Hall, the corrupt Democratic organization that ruled New York City. And it was Nast who worked out the figure and costume for Santa Claus as we know him.

KING DEATH'S DISTRIBUTION OF PRIZES.
BACCHUS TAKES THE FIRST PREMIUM.

In a cartoon pointing out the evils of drink, you can see Nast's symbols for Death and Drunkenness. "Although wine was served on occasion in the Nast household in the manner of the artist's native Germany," wrote his grandson, Thomas Nast St. Hill, "Nast abhorred the misuse of alcohol. . . ." Nast's moral crusades are not so well remembered as the political ones.

One of the most firmly rooted symbols is Uncle Sam: tall, bewhiskered, wearing rather formal clothes, including spats, but still looking more rural than urban. His origin, though cloudy, clearly goes back to a time before Nast. Sam's face and uniform have changed gradually over the years, and cartoonists have tended to modify his dress and features to comply to their particular styles.

Lately the cartoonists have debated the appropriateness of this symbol for modern America. Bill Mauldin refuses to use him, preferring instead to deal with real personalities.

In a cartoon for the *Toronto Star*, Duncan Macpherson uses an eagle symbol and combines it with an Uncle Sam hat to depict the United States. "The man in the cartoon is Canada's energy minister Donald MacDonald," he writes. ". . . The Federal government which MacDonald represents is determined to conserve Canada's energy for Canadian use. This approach is repudiated by the oil operators (mostly American) and the Provinces in which they work.

"Donald MacDonald's many-faceted problems are depicted in this cartoon of him wading through the Athabasca Tar Sands with the American symbol overhead, threatening a takeover" (p. 108).

If the symbol for the United States is meant to represent the common man rather than officialdom, the cartoonist is more likely to use a short, bewildered, maybe even henpecked middle-aged gentleman wearing glasses and a mustache and smoking a cigar. Typically, he is labeled "taxpayer" or "John Q. Public" (the Q was supplied by Vaughn Shoemaker); and he may be shown with his pockets turned

inside out. His suit, not particularly fashionable, could stand pressing.

Herbert Johnson's version of the common man is shown protecting Theodore Roosevelt from abuse by reactionaries of 1912. Johnson, who did this cartoon (p. 109) for the *Philadelphia North American*, later moved over to *The Saturday Evening Post*, where his editorial cartoons more often than not supported conservative causes.

One of the most telling cartoon symbols was the one invented in the 1920s by Rollin Kirby for Prohibition: a tall, skinny, dark-suited, tall-hatted character carrying an umbrella.

Symbols can have different meanings for different people, and they can change their meanings over the years. The umbrella is a good case in point. You can see its intended meaning in the Kirby symbol. But in the late 1930s, because Neville Chamberlain, prime minister, carried one with him when he returned from a meeting with Hitler to report to his people that all was well, the umbrella became a symbol of appeasement for the British. In more recent times an American insurance company has used the opened umbrella as a symbol of protection.

6. The normal procedure for the editorial cartoonist is to write the caption after the analogy is worked out and the symbol or symbols are selected. But sometimes the caption

comes first. The advantage of writing the caption early is that it forces the cartoonist to pinpoint his theme.

The caption may be a direct quote coming from someone within the cartoon who has his mouth open, in which case it has quotation marks around it. Or it may be the cartoonist's own comment, a sort of title, in which case it would not be enclosed in quotation marks. Some editorial cartoons can get by without captions.

Holiday Cartoons

Of all his assignments, doing a holiday cartoon probably gives the cartoonist the least satisfaction. What is there to say about Christmas or Easter or Thanksgiving Day that hasn't already been said? Too often the cartoonist settles for a well-meaning if innocuous illustration for those days. But occasionally he comes up with a telling observation, as Bill Schorr of the *Kansas City Star* does in the following cartoon.

Courtesy *Kansas City Star* and Bi

President Ford has reason to be concerned on this Thanksgiving Day, as this captionless cartoon points out. (Schorr, another young editorial cartoonist, joined the *Star* staff in 1973 after Dan Dowling retired. He had only recently graduated from California State University at Long Beach.)

If the cartoonist has no idea, he may be able to get by on drawing alone. The preceding cartoon, titled "Armistice," is a good example of that kind of cartoon. It does nothing but remind readers that a lot of persons were killed in World War I. There is no *idea* here, as such. The cartoon merits the space it took in the *Morning Oregonian* back before the depression only because it is well drawn: the scene is pleasantly composed, the texture bold, and the perspective dramatic. Tige Reynolds, the cartoonist, left out his customary tiger symbol (he was one of the first cartoonists to use a symbol with his signature) because the playful character would have been inappropriate in this setting.

Obit Cartoons

Perhaps the hardest idea to come up with is the idea for an obit cartoon. What is there to say, really, except that we all mourn good ol' Charlie's passing? Only rarely is the deceased so hateful that one dares to attack him in an obit cartoon as he was attacked while he lived.

A few obit cartoons stand out, like J. N. "Ding" Darling's cartoon drawn upon the death of ex-President Theodore Roosevelt, the "Rough Rider." "The Long, Long Trail" was first discarded by Ding as unworthy, but because he couldn't get another cartoon done in time to make the *Des Moines Register*'s deadline that day in 1919, Ding let the editor run it in the first edition. He did a second cartoon for later editions of the paper but forgot to notify his syndicate of the change, and the earlier cartoon went out to more than one hundred other papers. It became immensely popular. *The World of Comic Art,* a now-defunct quarterly, estimated in 1966 that the cartoon, through various reprints, reached a circulation of 25,000,000, ". . . quite a record for a cartoon that almost ended up in the wastebasket." In addition, the cartoon was reproduced in bronze for the Roosevelt Hotel in New York and a high school in Des Moines.

When Ding himself died, fellow cartoonist Frank Miller showed him in front of that famous cartoon, also waving, but clutching drawing board and pencils. Incidentally, Ding was one of the few cartoonists who drew their own obits. His was a cartoon captioned "Bye now—it's been wonderful knowing you" and showing a cluttered studio with a ghostlike figure waving while rushing out the door. On one wall, small but recognizable, was the famous Roosevelt cartoon. Ding drew his own obit cartoon at the age of eighty-two while seriously ill in a hospital.

"THE LONG LONG TRAIL"   ·   ·   ·   *By Ding*

Another great obit cartoon, much reproduced, is Bill Mauldin's commentary on the John Kennedy assassination: a drawing of the Lincoln Memorial statue with head in hands, crying. Interestingly, it took Mauldin an hour to do that cartoon, whereas it ordinarily takes him up to five hours to make a drawing. You can see how others handled this death—but you won't be much impressed, unless you like to see Uncle Sam with his head bowed from different angles or empty rocking chairs with flags draped over the backs—in a collection put together by Captain Raymond B. Rajski in *A Nation Grieved* (1967).

When Walt Disney died in 1966, *Paris Match* and at least one U.S. cartoonist showed a picture of Mickey Mouse crying.

When Picasso died in 1973, Paul Szep, deciding he had no real obit message for *Boston Globe* readers, simply drew the great artist's portrait, but in a most appropriate style.

PICASSO 73

Reprinted by permission of Paul Szep.

When I was assigned an obit cartoon on Winston Churchill, I drew the figure of death holding up two fingers in the "V for Victory" salute Churchill made famous in World War II. But I didn't submit the cartoon because it wasn't exactly what I wanted to say about the great leader. Another idea has occurred to me for Richard Nixon's obit cartoon (cartoonists tend toward necrophilia): a picture of God telling a group of reporters: "You won't have Richard Nixon to kick around any more."

Local Cartoons

A newspaper not quite large enough to support a full-time editorial cartoonist can supplement syndicate offerings by buying occasional cartoons from a local freelancer. The local cartoonist in such an arrangement would be expected to concentrate on local affairs. At least, he would present a local slant on national affairs.

But once he's established, the local freelancer can branch out. He still has an advantage over the syndicated artist on national issues in that, living nearby, he can beat cross-country mail delivery. News of national importance may break in the late afternoon; the local cartoonist can have a cartoon on the editor's desk the next morning.

Such a cartoon was one in which I commented on a *Ramparts* magazine disclosure of CIA involvement in youth organizations (p. 116).

Presumably, a young woman would be cautious about letting a stranger pay for her drink, especially if he looked like a lecher. The implication: he's not buying her a drink for nothing. The idea was prompted by the then shocking disclosure that youth groups in some colleges were being underwritten by the CIA.

Another local cartoon was a gentle jibe against the affectations of dress of the hippies just as they were beginning to flower on the campus where I teach. Called on to do a Halloween cartoon, it struck me and my collaborator (a

"The gentleman has taken care of the check"

"How did you guys do tonight?"

teaching colleague helped me with this one) that what the
youngsters wear when they go out trick-or-treating was
closely related to what some of the college students were
wearing as everyday attire.

"Afghanistanism" is a disease in American journalism
that allows communicators, including cartoonists, to speak
out forcefully on evils back in Washington or in some other
part of the world but that paralyzes them when it comes to
attacking local cupidity. One tends to be a little more cir-
cumspect with an official subject when he lives within walking distance or when he may appear at the local coffee shop—
which might explain why my editorial cartoons freelanced
over a twelve-year period to the *Eugene* (Oregon) *Register-Guard*
(circulation 60,000) were not quite the blunt instruments one
would hope for. Certainly I cannot blame the *Guard* itself,
which is admirably free of the disease. But I think my problem
was more a case of low threshold for boredom. I simply found
local issues less engrossing than national issues. I became
what a colleague, Professor Roy Halverson, refers to as "a
knee-jerk middle-of-the-roader." That a blandness had crept
into my work was never more apparent to me than when I
received from one of my readers a contribution labeled
"Typical Roy Paul Cartoon." Two persons, indifferently
drawn, were shown talking. One was saying: "I think Eugene
is nice." The other was saying, "I think everything is nice."

The Impact of Cartoons

Today's editorial cartoonists may view with amusement
and some envy the *New York Journal*'s enthusiastic but
unrealistic appraisal of one of their brothers from an earlier
era: Homer Davenport. "HANNA FORCED OUT OF
POWER/AND THE MAN THAT DID IT!" read the headlines. The copy running above a photograph of Davenport
says, "Pierced by Homer Davenport's pregnant pen, the
dollar-marked personality of Mark Hanna has fallen from its
political pedestal. The *Journal* cartoonist has forced the Cleve-

land millionaire to take his position in the lists of giant Trusts
and abandon political leadership." Copy inside the cartoon

says, "This Masterpiece . . . Scared Hanna Out of Power."
Would that it were true that a cartoonist could affect so
dramatically the course of political affairs.

Shortly before his death, Ding Darling wrote: "Looking
back over the whole history of picture-making intended to
accomplish any major diversion of the trend of thought of
nations or the world in general, I find few, if any, political or
social or religious trends which have been materially affected
by the use of cartoons or pictures.

"I don't remember any political campaigns which have
been either won or lost because of cartoons or cartoonists. . . .
I know of no General who won a war, no heathen who
became a Christian, and no candidate whose success or failure
was seriously altered by the use of cartoons.

". . . [Cartoons] may have added to the ardor of the
reader with like beliefs, but I don't think they ever moved any
mountains or changed the course of history."

His words were typical of the introspection of an old
man, his energies no longer driven by ambition, his mind no
longer clouded by arrogance. But that is not to say that an
editorial cartoonist can't expect to exert *some* influence on local
and even national affairs. First, though, the editorial cartoonist must face an inescapable and perhaps surprising fact
of life.

"Maybe the strongest thing political cartoonists have
going for them is their reputation for influence on public
opinion," observes James B. Lemert, associate professor of
journalism at the University of Oregon and an expert in
communication research. "If so, it might be in their interest to
suppress communication research findings on popular understanding of political cartoons. These results are about as
balloon-pricking as some cartoonists are. Only a small segment of the population even understands the point of political
cartoons, let alone agrees with them."

LeRoy M. Carl, a journalism professor at Temple University, testing readers in three cities in the late 1960s in order to

determine how well editorial cartoons communicate, found that only a small percentage of readers understood what the cartoonists were trying to say. For example, a cartoon showing Jim Crow blackbirds flying north (which meant, so far as the cartoonist was concerned, that racial bigotry was becoming an increasing problem in the North), meant "northern migration of Negroes" to most readers.

Lemert's and Carl's warnings underline how important it is for the cartoonist to subject his work to sample reader reaction, or something close to it, before turning the work over to the photoengraver or offset cameraman. When there were junior high school students around as part of my family, I almost always called one in to my studio to explain the idea in my drawing as he saw it. If he read a wrong meaning into the cartoon, I was reasonably sure the typical reader of the newspaper would, too. So it was back to the old drawing board for me.

Not only must the editorial cartoonist satisfy himself that what he says is understood, but he must carefully examine the logic of his cartoon to see that it does not disintegrate as its implications are followed to their conclusion.

These are considerations that need not concern the gag cartoonist, the comic stripper, the illustrator, and the animator. The goals here are more modest: to entertain. Whether these cartoons succeed in their more attainable goals is almost immediately evident.

Although there is not much controlled research to support the thesis, it may not be unreasonable to suggest that, in the final analysis, it is not the editorial cartoon, with all its agonizing over important political affairs, or the gag cartoon, with all its sophistication, but the lowly comic strip that has made the biggest impact on our lives. It has always appealed to the largest audience in the mass media, and to the young, the impressionable, and the ignorant. It has brought us the theology and psychology of Charles Schulz, yes, but also the pornography and ideology of the underground. It brought on some self-censorship in the 1950s. In the 1960s it fostered a whole new movement in the fine arts: Pop Art. It has launched holidays, started fads, promoted foods, coined words, introduced toys, and inspired songs, plays, and movies. All the sociological studies of the cartoon focus on the strips.

In 1948 British anthropologist Geoffrey Gorer wrote that the comics are "one of the few important bonds . . . uniting all Americans in a common experience." In 1963, assessing the strips with children in them, Professor George Newton Gordon of New York University wrote: "In an adult culture that is pretty much out of touch with the world of childhood, the comics have had the guts—and the brains, probably—to stick with the unvarnished truth." "Compared to some other popular art forms the comics are still rudimentary and simplistic," David Manning White and Robert H. Abel wrote in *The Funnies: An American Idiom.* "Yet they have succeeded in imparting to the national consciousness a sense of identification and belonging exceeded by no other art form." Pierre Couperie and Maurice C. Horn in *A History of the Comic Strip* cited "the realization that the American comic strip is not an incoherent series of pictures, but the most authentic form of the dreams, hopes, splendors, and miseries of our century."

3

Visual Hyperbole

What sets the cartoon apart from other art forms is exaggeration. A cartoon screams, while an ordinary drawing or painting whispers. The exaggeration involves the idea as well as the drawing. In a gag cartoon in *The New Yorker* commenting on fast-rising food prices in the mid-1970s, George Price suggested that changes could occur between the moment you threw an item in your shopping cart and the moment you plunked it on the counter in front of the cashier. He showed a grocer with a price stamper in his hand chasing a woman with a full cart who is racing for the checkout stand. The cartoon needed no caption. In a 1975 *Beetle Bailey* sequence, the general asks, "Where's Miss Buxley?" "I don't think she's here yet," answers the older secretary. Feeling the seat of Miss Buxley's chair, the general responds: "She must be—her chair is warm." Answers the older secretary: "That's from yesterday."

Not that cartoonists have a monopoly on exaggeration. Some in the fine arts out-exaggerate the cartoonists. Part of the appeal of Modigliani's portraits and nudes comes from the elegantly elongated faces and necks. Modigliani did not let the facts of anatomy interfere with his work as an artist.

Sculptor Lou Rankin uses exaggeration when he casts animals in concrete for sale by carriage-trade houses like Gump's of San Francisco. These pleasantly distorted fine-arts pieces bring on the same kind of chuckles cartoonists get with the animals they create. You see a Rankin lion here in two shots taken from slightly different angles to demonstrate how the ingeniously designed glass eyes follow the viewer as he moves past the wary and winsome creature.

From the author's collection. (The stand is by Kn

In the world of illustration, Roy Carruthers shocks readers with what *Print* magazine calls "art . . . based . . . on

Courtesy of Collins, Miller & Hutchings.

the use of discordant elements to create graphic tensions. . . . Carruthers' art has leaped over the precipice of the surreal and landed both feet square in the realm of the fantastic, just this side of the bizarre." To create the disproportionate figures in his paintings, Carruthers first makes meticulous drawings. His work is carefully polished. "Otherwise it would merely appear badly conceived," he says. "Everything has been deliberately considered and planned." The preceding Carruthers cartoon appeared in an ad sponsored by Collins, Miller & Hutchings, a Chicago photoengraving concern. The art director for this ad was Bruce Griffith, the agency Hurvis, Binzer & Churchill.

Surprisingly few serious artists, however, have the facility to produce cartoons. Cartooning requires a talent apart from mere art ability. Drawing is part of it. A sense of design is another part. But most important is an inventive mind.

In drawing a cartoon it is not enough to cross a character's eyes and stick his tongue out. That is strain, not exaggeration. That is the drunk putting on a lampshade at a party. The laughs, when they come, are only polite or embarrassed. The cartoonist is not a showoff. He does not exaggerate for the sake of exaggeration. He exaggerates to make a point or, to use the self-conscious language of the photographer, "to make a statement."

To show someone walking fast, the cartoonist spreads that person's legs farther apart than normal. It is obvious that the boy in the following drawing is trying to get past some bad news.

The exaggeration often involves some oversizing—to call attention to a prop. In this drawing showing a youthful photographer understandably incensed because the school editor has "improved" one of his photographs by cutting it into an "interesting" shape, you can see the offending pair of scissors drawn much larger than normal size.

Of course, some things can't be exaggerated. They are exaggerations to begin with. "What do you suppose God thinks of man (created in His own image) putting on his pants in an upper berth?" asked Don Herold, an advertising cartoonist. God upstaged the cartoonist when He gave us feet, fat people running, and anteaters. Even with Andrew Wyeth-like realism, these things would be funny.

On the man-made level, consider the monsters with tail fins that Detroit was turning out in the 1950s. There is not much a cartoonist can do to improve on the piece of machinery depicted on page 128. About all he can do is show it as it is.

The cartoonist wastes his reader's time if he depicts a scene with complete fidelity. If that's what the cartoonist wants, he might better turn the assignment over to an illustrator or photographer.

The cartoonist needs to overstate his case, as in an editorial cartoon in which I commented on the lack of effectiveness of sign ordinances in the city of Eugene. A real estate agent is shown trying to sell a house (the wooden floor immediately suggests "empty house") by stressing the picture-window feature. The prospective buyers appear far less enthusiastic about this feature than the real estate agent does. No wonder. See what the view offers: only signs and more signs. Ugliness all around. Now, the city was never this bad, but how else to make the point?

"Notice the large picture window..."

For *Pele Mele* in Paris, Mauryce Motet uses two panels to make a similar point. And the year was—1912. In case the reproduction here does not make the captions clear enough, the first one reads: "You wish to make a landscape painter of your son and yet you teach him to draw letters?" The second one: "Why, certainly. They are the most prominent parts of the modern landscape."

"You wish to make a landscape painter of your son and yet you teach him to draw letters?"

"Why, certainly. They are the most prominent parts of the modern landscape."

Called on to show a busy secretary, it would not be enough for the cartoonist to simply draw her typing—or even typing furiously. A better solution would be to show her with more than the usual number of arms, one holding a phone receiver against her ear, one typing, one filing, one handing a letter to the boss.

Which brings to mind an old Charles Addams cartoon showing a husband, waiting to be fed, and a housewife at the stove. She has three fully developed arms. (From the cartoon's setting you assume she is probably a freak who works for the circus.) She's using one arm to hold the baby, another to hold a frying pan, and the third to stir whatever it is she's cooking. She's saying: "Wait a minute, can't you? I've only got three hands."

In one of his gag cartoons in *The New Yorker*, Barney Tobey through exaggeration does a remarkable job of depicting laziness, decay brought on by riches, and contempt for the arts—all in one cartoon. He shows a servant at an easel working on a paint-by-the-numbers canvas. An obviously well-off gentleman sits nearby directing him, saying: "Now Sections Nine and Fourteen with turquoise blue."

It is unlikely that so haughty a man would receive a Mickey Mouse doll for Christmas or that an old lady would receive a barbell set, but in a cartoon (p. 131) giving recognition to the back-to-the-stores-after-Christmas crowd, it seemed appropriate to stretch a point. Even if the old lady *did* get a barbell set, surely she would keep it in its box, the better to make an exchange. But it was more important to communicate quickly with the reader than to stick close to real life. So there she is with her ridiculous gift, obstructing the aisle.

Despite the exaggeration, the details within the bus are authentic (for instance, the slant of the windows). As an out-of-towner contributing this cartoon to a Portland newspaper, I had to phone the bus company for literature showing the inside of one of its buses. Had I slanted the windows the

"As a matter of fact, I'm going downtown to exchange one of my gifts, too"

wrong way or committed some other grievous error, some eagle-eyed reader would have noticed—and complained.

Where There's Smoke

Jack Roberts, a principal in the Los Angeles office of Ogilvy & Mather Inc., the advertising agency, is also a cartoonist—and a good one, with a clean, almost George Price-like quality to his work. Yet the style is distinctively Jack Roberts's. In an illustration taken from the book *So You're Going to Take Tennis Seriously?*, which he both wrote and illustrated, you can see the importance of action in the Roberts style.

The "poacher," described as a player who intercepts a ball at the net before it reaches his partner, is helped in his flight across court by the expected swish lines (but oddly no puffs of

Courtesy of Jack Roberts. From *So You're Going to Take Tennis Seriously?* Workman Publishing Company, Inc., New York, 1974.

smoke) and wind-blown hair, normal enough signs of action. But notice the added touches: the curled shoe toe on the left foot and the pull of the man's trunks, exposing his belly button. The unreal straightness of the man's back and of his left arm helps, too. And so does the fact that the flesh of the face seems pulled forward by the force of the wind.

The handling of the ball is worth mention. The swish lines show its rapid movement before the poacher gets to it; the dotted line and two little arc lines next to the ball suggest that after it hits the racket its speed is arrested. Nor is the poacher's partner very happy about what has happened.

Remarkably, Roberts succeeds in lifting the woman player off the ground without drawing a shadow under her.

To give the action full attention and to adequately silhouette the figures, Roberts avoids drawing the pattern of the netting.

One of the joys of drawing is that there is no limit to the possible ways of depicting a given action. In my Caricature and Graphic Humor class one term I gave the students this problem: Show an angry old or middle-aged woman striking out at a student with her purse. Not one drawing in the nearly thirty turned in resembled another in "camera angle," facial expression, nature of attack. Following are five samples (all drawn hurriedly in class on ordinary newsprint paper with ordinary pencils or ballpoint pens).

In the first, the lady is made old, perhaps accidentally, by the feebleness of her swing. The artist helps the action along by swish lines, but still, the student pictured is in no immediate danger. (Notice that his eyes are both on the right side of his face, a bit of cartoonists' license that no one is likely to object to.)

Courtesy of Don Nelson.

In the second example, the student is in a little more danger, mostly because his antagonist is built along sturdier lines. Note the force with which she wields her purse, depicted not only by swish lines but also by "nervous lines." The "FWAP" may be the artist's own noise invention. Our sympathies are directed to the student by the poverty of his dress. We know he is poor because of the patches. Never mind that the patch on his jacket is more the kind we'd expect on bare skin.

Courtesy of Peter Finch.

In the third example, the victim seems more inclined to defend himself. And it's a good thing: this purse swinger uses both hands. The artist further communicates to us an anti-teacher bias. (In giving the assignment, I didn't specify what the woman should be.)

Courtesy of Richard Sept.

The fourth example gives us a swing with a little more action because the artist has widened the arc. One can imagine that the purse, despite the absence of many swish

Courtesy of Lucinda Jonsson.

lines, really whizzed by the student's head. The student, with his sweet and worried expression, looks innocent enough. The books falling to the ground add to the impact.

The fifth example comes from a student with more drawing experience than the other students. Through the use of contrasting arcs, he gets maximum action in both figures. The little explosion in the middle of the swish lines is a nice touch. And so is the fact that the purse, having done its damage, hangs loose in contrast to the stiffness of the arm.

A cartoonist can help his action along by lettering words right near where it takes place. Early in his career in the 1930s and 1940s, Roy Crane, the patron saint of action in the comics, delighted in the art of onomatopoeia. Captain Easy slugged it out with Bull Dawson to such sounds as "KLOP!" "LICKETY WHAP!" "UNK!" "SPLAT!" "KLAM!" "KONK!" and "WUMP!"

From the author's collection. Reproduced by special permission
of Newspaper Enterprise Association (NEA).

It's easy enough to work some action into a sports scene
or fight; it is not so easy to work it into a simple scene
showing two characters talking. Here Roy Crane, in a panel
from his *Wash Tubbs* in 1941, shows how it is done. Observe
Easy's stance: a slight crouch. You can almost feel Easy
working his right arm into his coat sleeve. Vicki's holding on
to her hat is a typical Crane subtle touch. What otherwise
could be a dull panel sparkles under Crane's handling. (The
shading results from Crane's use of Craftint Doubletone No.
214 paper and does not require halftone reproduction. You
see the panel here close to actual size.)

The cartoonist can best express action in a cartoon by showing it at its beginning or at its conclusion. He makes his character stretch. Had this bully been shown with his arm only partially completing the swing, it would not look as though he were really striking the boy. No "SPLAT" is needed here; the fact that the boy is crumpling is evidence enough that the bully has hit his target.

Courtesy of Jim Redden.

To show a figure running the cartoonist bends it far forward, puts a determined look on the face, spreads the arms and legs (if it's the left leg that's forward, it's the right—not the left—arm that also goes forward), and puts in the expected sweat marks, swish lines, and puffs of smoke. You'll notice in the following cartoon that all these effects still are not enough.

You have to lower the ground and get the man up in the air to really show him moving.

Never mind if the action does not accurately depict what would happen in real life. This logger looks more like a slugger taking a cut at a low, fast one than a man doing his job in the woods. But at least he's trying hard, and that's the point.

Incidentally, not many cartoonists seem able to depict what a tree trunk looks like once a tree is felled. While readers will applaud exaggerated action, they will not forgive a cartoonist for getting technical detail wrong. The stump of a felled tree does not look like the one on the left; it looks more like the one on the right.

The reason is that the sawing goes on above the point where the notch is chopped; the notch controls where the tree falls, and as it falls, it tears the interior fibers.

Generally, the more action you want to convey, the less detail you bother with. Fast-moving objects turn into a sort of blur. Action is also enhanced by the setting up of a series of diagonals. Diagonal lines suggest action.

Another secret is to show your character off balance. That's what gives this bowling father (he couldn't find a baby sitter) the movement he seems to have.

You can suggest action without showing the person or animal performing the action. In one of its advertisements, headlined "Where to Find a Frog," Rand McNally showed a rock at the left of the picture, a clump of grass at the right, and in between and joining them was a dotted line that rose up and down in two or three arches before settling behind the clump of grass. You could sense the frog moving from left to right in the ad even if you couldn't actually see it.

For this illustrative cartoon to accompany an article on hay fever, I did not show the woman sneezing. I showed the aftereffects.

This kind of action invites reader participation in the cartoon. Using his own imagination to figure out what went on before, the reader experiences some of the joy of creativity.

Come Hell or Hiawatha

One thing the cartoonist soon learns is that he cannot exaggerate what he does not understand. He picks up an understanding of figures, props, and settings by observation—while standing in lines, waiting in offices, sitting in crowded auditoriums. Much of what he sees he files away in his mind.

He can readily visualize most of what he is called upon to produce. But sometimes an assignment comes along that stops him: the depicting of the devil, for instance. Or a drawing of an Indian maid in full regalia.

Even though it's a cartoon, a certain amount of accurate detail, enough to make the figure instantly recognizable, is necessary. So the cartoonist turns to his "morgue," a file drawer of clippings taken from all kinds of magazines. (More than most persons, cartoonists mourn the passing of *Life;* it was the ideal magazine for a morgue builder. *National Geographic* is good, too; but who cuts up back copies of that magazine?) The morgue covers every conceivable subject, with separate folders for each.[1] For instance: there would be one on "aircraft," another on "costume," another on "legendary figures," another on "nationalities and races."

But a good morgue takes years to build. And the cartoonist continually adds to it. He learns to date each entry, for although at first it may be contemporary, it soon becomes a period piece.

A good illustrated set of encyclopedias and a collection of Sears catalogs are invaluable as supplements to the morgue.

Chrysler Motors Corporation each year offers a free collection of printed photographs of its cars, both current and classic, to illustrators and cartoonists, with the hope that these cars will show up in art supplied to editors. To make the collection really useful, the corporation offers a number of photographs taken from odd angles.

Whatever fidelity to period costume the drawing at the top of page 144 enjoys comes from my referral to an illustrated history of dress. Detail even in this kind of drawing need not be extensive.

Whether he uses a morgue or printed works for reference, the cartoonist makes an effort to refer to photographs rather than art work. Art work has already gone through the process of interpretation. Such visual facts as are there are no longer objective. And when the cartoonist works

---

1. My *Fell's Guide to the Art of Cartooning,* Frederick Fell, New York, 1962, carries a list of morgue headings.

from another's art he flirts with the danger of lifting style and technique as well as fact.

A Zoo in a Folder

The folders getting the most use in my morgue and the morgues of many other cartoonists are those filled with printed photographs of animals.

I wish I could say I dashed off these drawings of animals without referring to pictures, as I would dash off drawings of the human face and figure. But I do not draw animals often. I am not so familiar with their anatomy.

The cartoonist can utilize his drawing ability to reproduce photographs literally, staying close to the detail in them, as I have done in this series of animal sketches. Or he can simplify and improvise, using photographs only as starting points.

"Dachshunds are ideal dogs for small children," Benchley wrote, "as they are already stretched and pulled to such a length that the child cannot do much harm one way or the other." The cartoonist called upon to draw one of these unfortunate beasts can be expected to go well beyond any restrictions set up by the American Kennel Club.

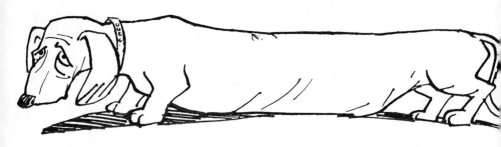

Bill Schorr of the *Kansas City Star* takes liberties with a cow's anatomy (p. 147) to make the point that it wasn't just the Republicans who in the early 1970s had drawn monetary support from the milk producers.

Perhaps cartooning's most peculiar animals right now are the formless, silly-looking cats and dogs in the amusing work of George Booth in *The New Yorker*. It is unlikely that Booth has been putting in a lot of overtime researching those animals.

But often research can be beneficial. For an end-of-the-summer cartoon drawn for a feature that echoed Robert Benchley's thought that "A dog teaches a boy fidelity, per-

Courtesy of Bill Schorr and the *Kansas City Star*

severance, and to turn around three times before lying down," I looked at several photographs of dogs from my morgue. Then, satisfied that I had the details of a dog's con-

struction mastered for the moment, I drew from memory, letting my imagination help out. This way I was able to achieve more of a cartoon look, bringing to the dog some of the character I would bring to the human figure.

Bill Schorr stood an elephant upright and put clothes on him in a cartoon commenting on the plight of the Republicans in that eventful year of 1974.

Courtesy of Bill Schorr and the *Kansas City Star*.

Cartoon animals are funnier when the cartoonist contorts the animal's limbs to make them conform to arms and legs and when he puts human expressions on their faces. Dogs may not laugh or cry in real life, but they do in the cartoon world.

A cartoonist raised on a farm with lots of animals around may not have to consult his morgue for animal poses as often as a city-bred cartoonist does. Homer Davenport, born and reared outside of Silverton, Oregon, before the turn of the century, was surrounded by farm animals and found them more agreeable models than human beings. His editorial cartoons, drawn for newspapers in Portland, San Francisco, New York, and finally, thanks to chain ownerships and syndication, for newspapers all over the country, often reflected his love and understanding of animals. Davenport didn't invent the tiger symbol that represented Tammany Hall, but he drew it as well as Thomas Nast did and added a light touch as well.[2]

2. Much of the information about Homer Davenport in this book comes from Reed Havens, a retired insurance executive, who was related to the Davenport family by marriage.

When Accuracy Counts

Even when the cartoonist's morgue is complete enough, he has to exercise care in using it. Once I had the job of illustrating a historical article on a trip down the West Coast taken by President Warren Harding while he was mortally ill. At one station, as the article pointed out, the president was unable to come out on the observation car platform to greet the crowd that had assembled. In my cartoon, I decided to show an aide trying to explain the president's condition to a surly crowd.

That's what hurts. It can't be a helpful personal call from the reader who is a stickler for accuracy. It has to be a published letter, for all to see.

I found what I thought was an appropriate but uncaptioned clipping in my "trains" folder and made my drawing, adding a portrait and some bunting to the car, feeling rather pleased with the way the drawing came out. Until that letter-to-the-editor from a railroad buff. It seems I had drawn a caboose or some kind of a car in which no traveler, much less a president, would spend any time.

"I kept learning over and over that real life experiences were necessary to my drawings," Bill Mauldin wrote in *The Brass Ring*. "If a drawing lacked authenticity, the idea behind it became ineffectual, too. This was especially true in the infantry, where a man lived intimately with a few pieces of equipment and resented seeing it pictured inaccurately. Once I drew the safety ring on the wrong side of a hand grenade hanging from a man's belt. It was a tiny thing, and I couldn't find a razor blade to scratch out the detail for a correction, so I was tempted to let it go. In the end, though, I signed my name backward and asked the engraver to reverse [flop] the whole drawing. I never regretted it."

"I figure there's bound to be someone reading my cartoons who knows the technical aspects of whatever I'm drawing, so I might as well be right," adds George Price, who likes to make on-the-spot drawings of the props he puts in his cartoons.

"Look, Ma—No Hands!"

It is interesting to study a cartoon to see how a cartoonist sidesteps some drawing inadequacy or lack of research. For instance, an editorial cartoonist who has trouble with caricature often shows a politician either from a distance or from the back of his head and lets the label do the identifying.

The trend toward simplified backgrounds came about primarily as a result of cartoonists' desire to speed up the reading of their work—necessary these days in the mass media—but also partly from the fact that houses, furniture, and trees are hard to draw.

Some cartoonists have trouble with hands and feet. If you are one of them, take heart. This sketch shows you how to get around that handicap.

4

"It Looks Just Like Him!"

In the words of a Peter DeVries character, "Winter sports leave me cold." In spite of this, some years ago a colleague talked me into accompanying him and several of his friends on a February fishing trip. Following a miserable day in the rain in leaky boats, with little to show for it, we met in a dingy café before adjournment to our various homes. Because I had failed to impress anyone with my fishing dexterity, and, worse, because I couldn't speak the language common to sportsmen, my friend felt it necessary to shed some light on the not-so-obvious aspects of my character that made me a friend worth having.

"You should see the way he can draw," he offered. "Here." Handing me a ballpoint pen and a paper napkin, he instructed me to capture the likeness of a buddy of his sitting across the table from us. I looked over in horror, for the subject was one of God's own caricatures: one of those persons with a face meant to reassure people, when they look at themselves in the mirror, that they aren't so bad after all.

This fellow had no chin; his badly spaced teeth protruded; his nose headed in several directions; and the bags under his eyes were enough to send me home packing.

I protested, but to no avail. So I began to sketch, determined to do a caricature in reverse. Maybe by understating his features I could come up with an acceptable likeness.

Unfortunately, I was *on* that day. Within a few minutes I had produced one of the most telling and hilarious sketches of my career. Experiencing a sense both of pride and terror, I passed the sketch over to my impresario. His face paled. Crumpling the sheet angrily, he growled: "You can do better than that." I tried again. If anything, the new sketch was even more on target. Again my friend, usually composed but by now badly flustered, crumpled it and then hastily turned the conversation to other matters, leaving my reputation both as a sportsman and as an artist sorely scarred.

Dreams and Nightmares

To the cartoonist the world is divided into three classes of people: the ugly, the handsome, and the nondescript. Only the uglies or near-uglies are easy to draw. Say what you want about Richard Nixon: The press hounded him for his duplicity and the public grew weary of his platitudes, but it was a sad day for editorial cartoonists when Nixon for the final time flew away to San Clemente. Even writers hated to see him go. This from Nora Ephron, writing in *New York:* "The depression that I feel—and that all the other journalists I have seen in the days since the abdication feel—is palpable. If there was one thing the Nixon administration was right about, it was that there is indeed an East Coast liberal press establishment, and right now it feels lousy that it doesn't have Richard Nixon to kick around anymore."

With his ski-slope nose and wide jowls, Nixon bowed to no major political figure as a subject fit for caricature. And during his short-lived second term, Nixon was everywhere in the public prints.

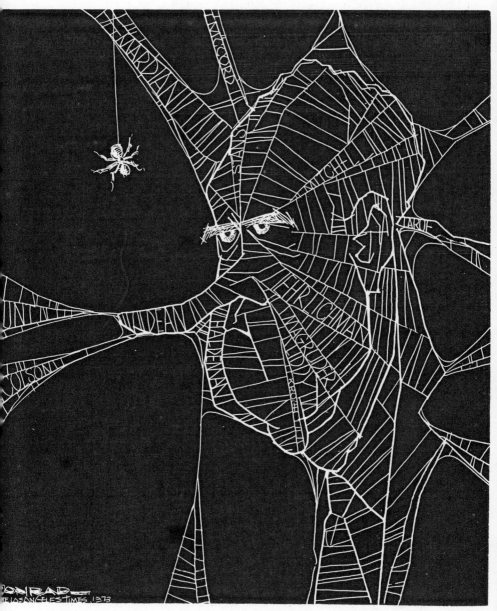

Editorial cartoon by Paul Conrad. Copyright, *Los Angeles Times*.
Reprinted with permission.

As the web of Watergate began to include more names, the very important central figure began to emerge. In a 1973 cartoon, Paul Conrad of the *Los Angeles Times* caricatured the beleaguered president in a unique way. The cartoon ran without a caption (p. 155).

Editors looked for every conceivable way of showing Nixon. *Time* found Nixon troublesome as a cover subject because he was so easy to caricature. Despite what the magazine did to Nixon inside, it didn't want to be cruel to him on the cover, according to a report in *The New Yorker*. *Newsweek* on its May 20, 1974, cover ran one of the most effective caricatures: a side view in solid black showing only part of his face. The brow, nose, upper lip, and part of the chin—these were sufficient to clearly establish identity. It was a commercial application of the ancient art of using scissors to cut side-view silhouettes out of black paper.

"Anything you say, Lyndon..."

Almost as easy to draw was Nixon's predecessor, Lyndon Johnson, with his big ears and nose, squinty eyes, and indented mouth. The preceding cartoon was reprinted in *U.S. News & World Report* shortly after Johnson succeeded the fallen John Kennedy, when Congress was in a mood to pass almost any law to support his domestic program.

Another easy-to-draw politician was Johnson's vice president, Hubert Humphrey, with his arched brows, hole-in-the-snow mouth, jutting chin, and head too big for his facial features.

So was Spiro Agnew, with his bullet-shaped head, the squinty eyes, and the nose that seemed to start at the top of the forehead. Agnew had the added advantage for cartoonists of having been ridiculed early in his vice presidency with the line, "Mickey Mouse wears a Spiro Agnew wristwatch." You may remember that Agnew wristwatches were actually marketed. When income-tax and other troubles forced Agnew to resign his office, Bill Schorr for the *Kansas City Star* drew one of the wristwatches exploding, with wheels, wires and other interior parts, along with the face, flying off in all directions. Duncan Macpherson of the *Toronto Star* as part of a cartoon showed a pair of forearms with a Mickey Mouse wristwatch on one wrist: it was enough to say "Spiro Agnew," although there was no face shown and no label.

And Henry Kissinger was an easy subject. One of the best of the Kissinger cartoons—by Duncan Macpherson—shows the much-traveled secretary of state standing in front of a group of nine men with their suitcases and briefcases. Standing next to a globe and holding a long sheet of paper, Kissinger is saying: "O.K. men—here is my itinerary." Every face in the cartoon was Kissinger's. In another great Kissinger cartoon—by Doug Marlette for the *Charlotte Observer*—the man is shown as a spoiled rich child, holding a globe in his hands. He's dressed preciously in short pants and ruffles. Only the face is old: unmistakenly Kissinger's. It was at a time when the indefatigable and awesome secretary, was, for the first time, really, enduring some harsh criticism. Marlette had him crying, saying: "Leave me alone or I'll take my ball and go home!"

Even good-looking John Kennedy, with his cowlick and puffy eyes, presented no big problem to cartoonists.

No wonder, then, after years of easy going, cartoonists viewed with alarm the ascension of square-faced, nondescript Gerald Ford. "There may be something he as President can do to curb inflation," said cartoonist James Trelease of the Springfield (Mass.) *Daily News*, "but there is nothing he can do to curb the cartoonists' growing wrath—short of having his face altered.

"He is what we call a 'nobody.' That is, there is nothing distinguished about his face. If he robbed a bank the teller would be hard-pressed to come up with a description. . . .

"By comparison with our three previous presidents, Ford is a cartoonist's nightmare."

In one of his editorial cartoons, Draper Hill of the *Memphis Commercial Appeal* drew himself as "Poison Q. Brush, Esq., Editorial Cartoonist" in his office looking at the "Help Wanted" ads. On his desk was a bust of a bland Ford labeled "MR. NICE GUY."

'FILE THIS UNDER "OPEN ADMINISTRATION"!'

Editorial cartoon by Pat Oliphant. Copyright, *The Denver Post.* Reprinted by permission of the Los Angeles Times Syndicate.

Still Ford, with his high forehead, short nose, long upper lip, long chin (at least as Pat Oliphant portrayed him), thinning hair, and weak eyebrows offered more possibilities to the cartoonist than, say, Harry S Truman. *There* was a president without a handle. He didn't even have a period after his middle initial.

The vice president Ford picked, Nelson Rockefeller, was much easier to draw. Cartoonists had played around with him for years. The only change involved the horn-rimmed glasses.

Dick Wallmeyer's caricature of Nelson Rockefeller was made during the Congressional hearings over his confirmation as vice president. Rockefeller, you will remember, had a lot of explaining to do over the gifts and loans he had given to friends and subordinates. Wallmeyer nicely combines a suitable prop and a good likeness. He achieves his likeness by concentrating on the slanted, squinty eyes and the mouth that dips low in the center during a smile.

"I'D LIKE TO END THE MYTH THAT I WIELD GREAT ECONOMIC POWER."

Courtesy of Dick Wallmeyer, editorial cartoonist for the *Long Beach* (California) *Independent Press-Telegram*.

Eyeglasses can be an important prop in caricature.
In the 1970s he became something of a folk hero, but in

the early 1960s, when he was a presidential candidate, Republican Senator Barry Goldwater was something of a joke, at least to most intellectuals and much of the press. When before in our history had most newspapers supported a Democratic candidate for president?

Pretend Spectacles

FOR THE EUGENE REGISTER-GUARD

His black, heavy (for their time) horn-rimmed glasses became his trademark. By altering the symbol slightly, I was able to make my thoughts clear on his qualifications to be president. The caption may be redundant, but I wanted to make sure that readers wouldn't get the wrong impression from the upward-pointing thumb.

To get his likeness of Senator Edmund Muskie in the following cartoon, Paul Szep of the *Boston Globe* uses powerful

"IT ONLY HURTS WHEN I RUN"

Used by permission of Paul Szep.

lines, solid blacks, and strong washes. And he moves in close, eliminating all but the most essential detail. This editorial cartoon was prompted by Muskie's faltering bid in 1972 for the Democratic nomination for president. "Florida" and "N.H." represent Muskie's showing in the primaries of those two states.

Ivan Chermayeff, a big name among graphic designers, has shown that he can draw caricatures, too. He did one for an ad announcing a second series of the widely praised "Upstairs, Downstairs" program on Masterpiece Theater, a

Upstairs, Downstairs

series underwritten by Mobil. Three observations here: Chermayeff shows that it is possible to caricature a woman— and one with a pretty face. In this case he emphasizes Rose's (Jean Marsh's) arched brows and her thin, wide mouth. Second: he does his sketch with an unrelenting thick line, a sophisticated and demanding approach not recommended for the beginner. Third: he exhibits his fine sense of design by setting up obvious relationships among the various elements that go into his drawing. Note that the lettering at the top takes on the same character as Rose's hat and hair. The bowlike shape of the background is appropriate to the subject and to the Edwardian period, which the series represented.

Used by permission of Jack Barrett.

For his caricature of Art Buchwald, Jack Barrett, staff artist for the *St. Petersburg* (Florida) *Times*, used tightly controlled, decorative lines. The hair isn't merely drawn; it is *designed*.

To draw Groucho Marx it wasn't necessary for Emilio A. Grossi to show all the features. Just the prominent ones were enough. The caricature was used in various ads and posters to announce that *You Bet Your Life*, a classic quiz series, was back

Courtesy of WNEW-TV, Metromedia Television.

on the air at WNEW-TV, New York. Grossi is an art director as well as an illustrator.

Local Likenesses

At the local level, cartoonists have their peculiar crosses to bear. Mine has been that good-looking figure of some national prominence: Mark Hatfield. During all the time that he was governor and then U.S. senator, he gave me trouble.

The trouble with Hatfield was that he was one of those persons whose features are better in the aggregate than individually. Hatfield's nose, for instance, is not one we ordinarily associate with the all-American look.

One little trick I learned with Hatfield and with all good-looking men: give them long eyelashes. Never mind whether or not they really have long eyelashes.

"Hey, everybody—meet my buddy Mark!"

A much more likely subject for caricature was the late Senator Wayne Morse. The eyebrows alone could do the job. The preceding cartoon shows Wayne Morse with Hatfield after Hatfield was elected senator to serve with Morse. Earlier Morse had feuded with Hatfield. The slightly embarrassed look on Hatfield's face is accomplished by the weak smile and the tugging at his collar.

An unmentioned hazard of caricature is that your subject,

when you're not looking, changes. Most obviously, he grows old. His face fills out. He lets his hair grow out, or he goes bald.

I finally mastered Hatfield to the point where I wasn't ashamed to put my signature to a cartoon in which he starred, but it has been several years since I have had occasion to draw him, and I notice that his most recent mug shots in the papers portray a man quite different from the one I drew over the years.

Cartoonists should enjoy the luxury of Salvador Dali, who says he doesn't paint a portrait to look like the subject; rather, the person he paints grows to look like his portrait.

Portraits vs. Caricatures

Following are line portraits of columnists to go with their columns on the *Eugene Register-Guard* editorial page: James Reston, Mary McGrory, James J. Kilpatrick, Tom Wicker, Russell Baker, Anthony Lewis, Carl T. Rowan, Ralph McGill, James Marlowe. The editor wanted them small and light so

that they would not be intrusive on the page.

To better control the detail, I did them considerably larger than they were to appear in print. The large size presented a difficulty: to maintain enough strength in the lines to take the big reduction.

The editor preferred realistic portraits to caricatures because they were to run frequently over a period of several years. A caricature may say more with greater flair, but its lifespan is shorter. Its novelty soon wears off, and the piece of art becomes intrusive. Further, caricature might not fit the mood of many of the columns. Some of these writers deal with weighty matters.

"Accomplishment will prove to be a journey, not a destination."

Dwight D. Eisenhower 1890-1969

I see that the old flagpole still stands. Have your troops hoist the colors to its peak, and let no enemy ever haul them down.

DOUGLAS MacARTHUR
1880-1964

These two pieces ran on the occasion of the subjects' deaths. Again, caricature would not have been appropriate. Realism—or something close to it—seemed called for.

Even in an editorial cartoon, realistic handling may be more appropriate at times than caricature. And not just for obit cartoons. Regular editorial cartoons that praise living officials or those trying to sell voters on a candidate might best be done with realism.

Perhaps the most famous cartoon Homer Davenport ever did was the one showing Uncle Sam standing behind Theodore Roosevelt, Sam's hand on Roosevelt's shoulder.

Sam is saying: "He's good enough for me!" (Davenport, at least in 1904, switched from the Democrats to the Republicans.) The candidate's face did not get Davenport's usual comic treatment. The Republicans liked the cartoon so much that they reprinted it everywhere: not only in many newspapers but also on posters and campaign literature.

Oddly enough, the cartoon resurfaced twenty-eight years later, twenty years after Davenport's death, to help elect another Roosevelt, this one a Democrat. Shown here, it was basically the same cartoon, but a staff artist for the Hearst newspapers (papers that were to disown FDR by the time of the next election) had changed Teddy's face to FDR's and slimmed down the body a bit. It may be the only example in American history where a deceased cartoonist helped elect a president.

'He's Good Enough for Me!'

But in the typical editorial cartoon of attack in which a public official plays a villainous role, that official must be immediately recognized and, often, despised. Then caricature is the answer.

Like a shark in warm waters, the cartoonist stalks his victim, looking for any excuse to attack: eyes too heavily lidded, brows too bushy, nose too bulbous, mouth too wide, chin too indecisive.

Not that the cartoonist has the waters all to himself. The writer is there, too. Columnist James J. Kilpatrick, for instance, in assessing Governor George Wallace's political future when it appeared that Wallace had found a way to live with the paralysis that resulted from the assassination attempt, used physical description to better explain the man to readers. "He has the same sort of catfish mouth that William Jennings Bryan had," Kilpatrick wrote, "an orator's mouth, stretched by the rigors of stump speaking." A cartoonist could almost take up his pen and follow the directions supplied by Kilpatrick.

And here is Timothy Crouse in *The Boys on the Bus* describing Vice President Agnew's press secretary: "If Victor Gold had been a character in a Broadway play, he would have been played by Martin Gabel. He was a short man on a short fuse, with a high forehead, a drill instructor's bearing, and eyes sufficiently full of fire to suggest that smoke would momentarily shoot out from his nostrils."

From a writer at *Newsweek:* "No one has ever accused Gene Shalit of being just another pretty face. His lumpy visage is crowned by an aureole of bushy black hair and slashed with quizzical eyebrows and a 5-inch-wide mustache, conjuring up a cross between Jerry Colonna and a startled bullfrog."

Or, here's P. G. Wodehouse describing one of his fictional characters: "She looked as if she had been poured into her clothes and had forgotten to say 'when.' "

The following caricature of two southern governors

engaged in some early 1960s anti-integration activities shows
how contrast can set off two faces in caricature: the lean, old,
wrinkled one on the left (Ross Barnett) and the rounder,
fatter one on the right (George Wallace, before the attempt
on his life). See how different two faces can be: tired, puffy,
weak eyes; thinning hair; big ears; a neck too small for the
collar for one. Heavy brows, pug nose, an overbite, and
swept-back hair for the other.

To ridicule these men, I gave their sign-painting technique an awkwardness not to be found in the most inept
student in a high school art class. Notice how the man in the
foreground holds his brush: firmly enough, but without any
evidence of skill.

In some uses caricature stands by itself, not needing the
support of a full editorial cartoon. The artist becomes not a
cartoonist but even more of a specialist: he becomes a
caricaturist.

Interest in caricature runs in cycles. It was especially
popular in the 1920s and 1930s when caricaturists like Al
Frueh and William Auerbach-Levy were important partici-
pants in the art. It made a comeback in the late 1960s and
1970s.

If a newspaper without access to a local caricaturist wants
to run caricatures of persons in the news, and those persons
enjoy national prominence, the paper can subscribe to a
caricature service, like the one the Los Angeles Times
Syndicate offers. The caricaturist, Dick Wright, former
editorial cartoonist with the *Sacramento Union*, provides editors
with a starting package of 100 well-known personalities and
then mails at least two additional caricatures to subscribers
each week.

In the 1930s the trick was to use as few lines as possible
to achieve a telling likeness. In the 1970s the art became more
detailed.

The most celebrated caricaturist in America in the 1970s
was David Levine, whose work first gained national attention
in *Esquire*. He drew many of the world's literary figures for *The
New York Review of Books*. Once both *Time* and *Newsweek* featured
Levine caricatures on their covers the same week.

His best-remembered caricature, perhaps, was the one of
Lyndon Johnson after Johnson's gallbladder operation. In a
let-it-all-hang-out age, a famous news picture had shown the
president, his shirt pulled up, pointing to his scar. Levine's
cartoon showed Johnson pointing to a scar, but the scar was
in the shape of the map of Vietnam.

Levine's intricate cross-hatch style is widely imitated,
notably by artists appearing on the op-ed page and elsewhere
in the *New York Times*, but never quite duplicated. Still, it is not
exactly an invention of Levine's. It is a style derived to some
extent from the work of Thomas Nast; Nast's great admirer,

Homer Davenport; and others of the pre-lithographic crayon school.

"David has the wit, taste and genius to sense exactly how far to sink his teeth into the essence of a subject without losing credibility or lapsing into polemical farce. Moreover, his work invariably serves to expand our knowledge of the subject, not simply as to features but to something of the person beneath," Dugald Stermer wrote in *Communication Arts* magazine. Stermer labeled Levine "the finest caricaturist of our century, and deserving of mention along with Hogarth and Daumier."

Levine's devastating portrayal of William F. Buckley, Jr., editor of the conservative *National Review*, columnist, and television personality, ran in *The New York Review of Books*.

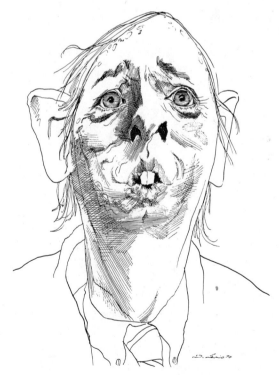

Less well-known now but clearly one of the world's best caricaturists is Sam Berman, now residing in Spain. His caricatures of Nazi leaders drawn for *Collier's* during World War II won him wide praise. Later, as head of his own map-making firm, he created the largest global relief map ever made. More than sixty-five museums and colleges ordered copies.

Some of his caricatures have been done as sculptures. For a series of caricatures of the presidents completed for *Lithopinion,* one of which is shown here, Berman used Magic Marker grays on newsprint and finished them up with a Mars No. 2 pen. He rendered them directly. No penciling.

By permission of *Lithopinion* No. 27, the graphic arts and public affairs journal of Local One, Amalgamated Lithographers of America and lithographic employers, New York. © 1972 by Local One, A. L. A.

Berman himself thinks the caricatures in this series were as successful as any he's done because "they are free and relaxed."

The following *cartoonist's* version of President Woodrow Wilson, shown with his secretary of state, William Jennings Bryan, before Bryan resigned, was done by Art Young, whose woodcut-like drawing style belied his radical political stance. The cartoon, entitled "Not Harmonious," appeared in *Metropolitan.*

The Self-Caricature

In learning to do caricatures, a good place for the cartoonist to start is with his own portrait. We know our own faces only too well, having studied them in the mirror each morning. Without advertising the fact, most cartoonists pull an Alfred Hitchcock from time to time, putting themselves into their cartoons when the role calls for such typecasting.

From the biography, *The Story of Hendrik Willem van Loon*, written by his son, Gerald Willem van Loon, and published by J. B. Lippincott Co., Philadelphia, 1972. Reprinted by permission of the author.

Hendrik Willem van Loon, the late author/illustrator of *The Story of Mankind, The Story of the Bible,* and other popular books of the 1920s and 1930s, drew with scratchy lines in a quaint style. He was a man of enormous bulk, as the preceding sketch on an envelope addressed to his son suggests. See how he dwarfs his typewriter.

Homer Davenport did a sketch of himself (p. 177) not long after arriving in New York. You can compare it to a photograph taken at about the same period of his life. Davenport was in his late twenties at the time and not bad looking. In fact, he looked a little like actor Errol Flynn of a later era. Yet Davenport, through the art of caricature, was able to make a drawing that looked like himself and ridiculed his looks at the same time.

How It's Done

Homer Davenport's favorite victim for caricature was Mark Hanna, the power behind President William McKinley.

The photograph is reproduced through the
courtesy of the Oregon Historical Society.

Davenport, who worked for the Hearst papers when they
were Democratic, gave Hanna, the wealthy Republican, a suit
with a dollar-sign check.

In the *New York Journal* for November 8, 1896, following
the election of McKinley, Davenport, in an illustrated article,
told how he had distorted Hanna's features during the
campaign. It was as if a magician had taken his audience into
his confidence to explain his tricks.

It was clear that Davenport had spent a lot of time
studying Hanna. For instance, Davenport wrote: "His eye
shifts like the eye of a parrot, and you can't make a move he
does not follow. You have seen the elephant in a circus parade

keeping step with the band, his trunk extended toward one side of the street, pleading for popcorn, and his beady eyes scanning the other side of the street in hope of peanuts. Mr. Hanna's roving optics remind me of those of that noble beast."

The following art accompanied Davenport's article. Unfortunately, because it is taken from a yellowed newspaper it is not as clear as it should be, but you can still see how the famous cartoonist did his distorting. In the center he shows Hanna in a reasonably realistic pose, to the right in a pose that is pure caricature. Around the edges you see realistic drawings of Hanna's hand, eye, nose, ear, sideburn, mouth, and neck along with distorted drawings for comparison.

MARK HANNA AS HE IS AND AS DAVENPORT MADE HIM.

In most cases, a cartoonist would work from a photograph to do a caricature. But a perfectionist might prefer to sketch from life, arguing that a photograph, like a painting, carries its own interpretation. Doing a caricature from a photograph, David Low said, was a little like doing a biography from *Who's Who* (the British equivalent of *Who's Who in America*). Low didn't even settle for a real-life pose. He used to follow his subjects around to catch them in their unguarded moments.

Rather than work directly from a photograph or even from life, the cartoonist may find that he can produce a better caricature by studying the face for a while, noting the shape of the head, amount of hair, and any outstanding facial features, then drawing from memory. Such practice may help the cartoonist break away from realistic sketches.

If the cartoonist runs out of faces to caricature, he can turn to a singular volume brought out by Dover Publications in 1967: *Dictionary of American Portraits.* There he'll find 4,045 generous-sized mug shots of important Americans, most of them from the last century. A remarkable gallery of facial expressions and features!

More Than Just Another Ugly Face

The impersonator we saw often on television in the 1970s, Rich Little, could screw up his face to make it look just like the character he was imitating. More than that, he could sit, stand, and walk like any of his victims. Rich Little had the mannerisms down cold. His Johnny Carson turned around stiffly and always fidgeted with a pencil; his Ed Sullivan humped his shoulders and cracked his knuckles; his Richard Nixon shook his sagging jowls and held up his arms in the victory salute.

Similarly, the caricaturist deals with more than just the face. Any oddities—or even deformities—of figure might appear in the total picture. You know how important such details are. From a half block away you can pick out a friend without seeing his face; you can recognize him by his walk.

MR. DAVENPORT AT WORK.

In a caricature of Homer Davenport drawn in 1897 by an admiring fellow cartoonist, Frederick Earle Johnston of the *Pittsburgh Times,* we see something we do not see in the self-portrait; Davenport was a long, lean, lanky fellow.

In the following caricature Davenport tried his hand at depicting his boss: the then youngish William Randolph Hearst, who, not many years before, had been expelled from Harvard for perpetrating a practical joke on his professors. Two years after this caricature was drawn, Hearst was to send his famous telegram to Frederic Remington in Cuba, in answer to the artist's complaint that the promised military skirmishes he was to sketch weren't to be found. "PLEASE REMAIN," Hearst wired. "YOU FURNISH THE PICTURES AND I'LL FURNISH THE WAR."

Davenport's high-chair effect in this sketch helps define Hearst's playful, even childish nature. The *Examiner,* which Hearst had previously edited in San Francisco, and the *New York Journal,* which he had just acquired, were playthings for Hearst.

Were this book more a history of cartooning, Hearst would be much mentioned, for he provided audiences for many of America's best cartoonists. King Features Syndicate traces its origins to him. Hearst and another publisher, Robert Patterson of the *Chicago Tribune* and the *New York Daily News*, helped cartoonists create many of America's most popular comic strips.

If the cartoonist draws a political figure often enough he is likely to develop some symbolism for him that goes beyond his physical features. Back in the mid-1950s when Adlai Stevenson and Estes Kefauver were running for president and vice president on the Democratic ticket, the conservative editorial cartoonist for the *Los Angeles Times*, Bruce Russell, never failed to show them with holes in their heads. (L. D. Warren, another conservative who drew for the *Cincinnati Enquirer*, in a cartoon labeled "Mr. Double-Talk," showed Stevenson with two mouths: one labeled "SPEND," the other labeled "TAX CUT.")

People as Animals

Like many editorial cartoonists, especially those who worked at the turn of the century, Homer Davenport delighted in picturing prominent officials as animals. In this cartoon, captioned "June in the Political Swamp," you will probably recognize the frog as Theodore Roosevelt; but you may not recognize the long-stemmed, long-beaked bird as Thomas C. Platt, boss of the Republican Party in New York. Readers of the time could recognize Platt by the eyes and eyebrows and by the strands of hair at the top that formed into a dollar sign. That was a trademark Davenport developed for Platt and often used.

And Davenport was able to make a woodpecker out of William Jennings Bryan. Although Davenport was one of few big-city cartoonists to support Bryan in Bryan's first run for the presidency (in 1896), by the time "The Great Commoner" ran a third time, Davenport had tired of him.

In 1903 after Governor Samuel Pennypacker (the name is a cartoon in itself) made an angry speech to the Pennsylvania legislature demanding that cartoonists be "drawn and quartered," an assemblyman introduced a bill prohibiting "the depicting of men as birds or animals." Newspaper cartoonist Walt McDougall, as he describes it in *This is the Life!* promptly "made a whole page of portraits in which every prominent official from the Governor down was portrayed as a vegetable, some of the portraits being exceedingly felicitous, and the bill died a natural death from ridicule."

Perhaps the cartoonist best known in our time for depicting politicians as animals is not an editorial cartoonist but a comic-strip artist, the late Walt Kelly. In *Pogo,* many public officials, including Senator Joe McCarthy and Vice President Spiro Agnew, appeared in animal form.

The Tyranny of Caricature

For some public figures, like Secretary of State Henry Kissinger, the cartoonist doesn't have to consult a photograph. As a matter of fact, a photograph would throw him off; Kissinger no longer looks like his photograph. He looks like the stereotype the cartoonists have established: a man with an enormous nose, horn-rimmed glasses, kinky hair, a downturned mouth, and a slightly rotund body. Just the briefcase alone is almost enough to say it's Kissinger.

Presumably Kissinger, a man of awesome sophistication—and attractive enough to have been something of a ladies' man before a second marriage—can take all the artistic kidding.

Reports vary as to how the victims of caricature react to seeing themselves in print in so unflattering a form. Nixon was said to be greatly disturbed by the relentless attacks by Herblock of the *Washington Post* from the late 1940s on. Even the unshaven look was an annoyance. Defending his practice of showing Nixon with a "five-o'clock shadow," Herblock in *Special Report* reproduces a photograph showing that this was the way Nixon looked. "But I wouldn't have pictured . . . [the shadow] if it had not seemed to me to fit what I considered to be . . . [his] political thuggery." When Nixon won the presi-

dency in 1968, Herblock drew a cartoon of a barber shop with a sign: "THIS SHOP GIVES TO EVERY NEW PRESIDENT OF THE UNITED STATES A FREE SHAVE.—H. Block, Proprietor."

One of the most maligned of politicians was the headline-hunting mayor of Los Angeles, Sam Yorty. A Paul Conrad cartoon showed Yorty talking on the phone with men in white suits in the background holding a straitjacket. Yorty was saying: "I've got to go now . . . I've been appointed Secretary of Defense and the Secret Service Men are here." Yorty sued Conrad for $2,000,000—and lost. Libel laws are interpreted these days so as to give the cartoonist almost free rein, provided in his attacks he concentrates on the public rather than the private life of his subject.

Other politicians, at least on the surface, enjoy the notoriety, and often write to the cartoonists requesting the originals of the caricatures to frame and hang in their offices. J. R. Cochran in *Inside Comics,* a quarterly, reports that John Ehrlichman and other Nixon administration staff members ridiculed in *Doonesbury* wrote to Garry Trudeau (unsuccessfully) for the original strips.

In their excellent survey of editorial cartooning, *The Ungentlemanly Art,* Stephen Hess and Milton Kaplan suggest that Richard Croker, a turn-of-the-century politician, "must win some kind of award" for gathering cartoons about himself—and publishing them! In his book, *Political Cartoons Gathered by Their Target—Richard Croker* (ca. 1901), Croker wrote: "To my friends whose confidence was unwavering when the shafts were barbed with malice and falsehoods, and when wit or humor fashioned the arrow, mingled their laughter with mine, this collection from leading American Cartoonists is offered."

5

The Magic of Drawing

All art—and especially cartoon art—is illusion. Like the magician on stage, the artist who calls himself a cartoonist titillates his audience with his repertoire of visual effects.

These are some of them.

The Cliché

Clichés abound in the cartoonist's world. He uses them shamelessly: the Zs that indicate sleep; the scrambled letters and punctuation marks that stand for cursing; the lightbulb that says "idea"; the puffs of smoke that follow someone on the move; the sweat marks (or tears) to help show pain, worry, sadness, and even mirth.

See how easy it is, using cartoonists' clichés, to suggest drunkenness or near-drunkenness. Bubbles coming out of the mouth of one man, his necktie undone; eyes crossed on another man (a useful device if used sparingly); eyes half-closed on a third. The fact that one of the men is leaning precariously helps, too.

Sometimes cartoonists make fun of the clichés they depend upon. Charles Addams in a *New Yorker* cartoon shows a monk—a scribe—asleep at his post, pen in hand, his head resting on the manuscript he's been working on. He's obviously asleep. But that is no ordinary Z above his head. The Z is one of those fancy illuminated initial letters we associate with the literature of the Middle Ages. More recently, in a *New Yorker* cartoon, Nurit Karlin, using three panels, shows a day-dreaming character walking along a New York street thinking about an exotic island (there is one of those thought balloons above his head). In the last panel, to his chagrin, the balloon is hung up on one of those arrow street signs, caught and apparently punctured as the character walked by.

Shortcuts to Drawing

The cartoonist uses the simplest possible devices to depict the most complicated of scenes. For instance, to show a large flock of birds flying, all he needs is a series of stretched-out *M*s, preferably made with slightly curved lines.

Cartoonists' shortcuts have come in for some kidding, too. Steve Allen in his *Bigger Than a Breadbox* (Rowland B. Wilson did the drawings) offers a four-panel gag cartoon of a hunter watching a flock of geese (or ducks): the hunter shoots, he makes his hit and runs to retrieve it, and, in the last panel, surprised and disappointed, he holds up for us to see—two slightly limp *M*s.

On the mechanical level, the convertible with its top down has made drawing less of a strain for the cartoonist. Popular enough in its day, the convertible nevertheless did not have the appeal in real life that it had in movies and cartoons. The reason for the preponderance of convertibles in the popular arts was simply that it was easy to show what people inside convertibles were doing.

In this cartoon, for example, the task was to show a man trying to back into a too-small parking space, helped along, but not much, by his wife. Had this been an ordinary car with a top on it, you couldn't have seen much of the man inside the car, at least from this angle. Or, if the car had been drawn from inside, you couldn't have seen very easily what was going on outside.

But the convertible is not the only answer. Another is to show the car from a lower-than-usual "camera angle." That way the roof does not hide so much of the interior. Still another is to show the car in a normal view and then take cartoonists' license and give the car an abnormally high roofline. Ed Sullivan manages to do this very well in a small-space cartoon in his *Stained Glass* series. He shows not one but two car interiors, with a little foliage along the highway as well.

" THAT'S JUST YOUR OPINION··· I THINK
CALIFORNIA'S KIND OF NICE!"

Courtesy Ed Sullivan and
Avant Features, Canfield, Ohio.

Other shortcuts to drawing include the elimination of wrinkles, buttons, and shoelaces and the cutting down of the number of fingers. Figuring a comic stripper draws an average of eight characters a day, that's thirty-two fingers a strip, if all the views are side views. Going the three-finger route, the cartoonist will save himself a total of 2,912 fingers for the year, not counting Sundays. Walt Disney knew what he was doing all right when he laid plans for the hands of Mickey Mouse.

The Fickle Line

A sweeping, wavy line in the hands of a cartoonist (or any artist) suggests grace and movement. A zigzag line suggests dissension and discord. Or lightning or electricity. In his short story, "The Car We Had to Push," James Thurber, acting as his own illustrator, chooses to illustrate the· sentence, "Electricity was leaking all over the house." He shows a woman reading a book, looking up at a light fixture with a bulb missing. Out of the socket heading down toward the nervous woman is a series of short zigzag lines.

A series of short, wavy lines radiating outward from the item being drawn suggests heat or light or even an unpleasant odor.

A series of short, straight lines radiating outward suggests newness or cleanliness.

A series of horizontal parallel lines helps to emphasize width, which is why people on television look better fed than they do in real life. A series of vertical lines helps to emphasize depth.

Parallel lines irregularly spaced, running up and down in a kidney-shaped area, suggest water. Up and down across the surface of a desk, such lines suggest shine. Running diagonally in a rectangular shape, they suggest glass; over the surface of a cube, ice.

By changing only slightly the nature of his pen strokes the cartoonist can alter drastically the nature of a character.

Consider these two faces: alike in every respect except for the handling of the near-beards.

By running some more-or-less even strokes across the chin on the first face, the cartoonist says: "This fellow hurried off to work this morning without stopping to shave. But he's not a bad sort, really." He merely has what the ads used to call a "five-o'clock shadow."

We have a little less sympathy for the second fellow. That stubble, indicated with short, irregular strokes, suggests a man who truly lacks grooming. If he drinks, you can bet it's muscatel.

The Cartoonist's Bag of Tricks

As part of his routine, a magician invites a member of the audience on stage to "help" him with one of his tricks. The cartoonist invites audience participation, too, by leaving out some lines in order that the reader may finish them in his mind. Or the cartoonist subdues the idea so that the reader has to work on it a bit in order to fully appreciate it.

The lead cartoon for one of Andre Francois's books, *The Tattooed Sailor*, shows a sailor with no shirt, his pants rolled up to the knees. Tattooed on the man's chest is the trunk of a woman. On his legs are tattooed the woman's legs. The man's pants hides the rest of her, but the reader sees that it is a whole woman and wonders what the tattooing must look like where the legs join the body.

With a cartoonist in command, people and animals do things they couldn't otherwise do. In Heinrich Kley's world, snails not only grow to enormous proportions; they also engage in racing.

From *The Drawings of Heinrich Kley.*

A simple prop, combined with a stereotype, can be invaluable to the cartoonist. Here are two more faces, essentially the same. By changing a raised brow to a frown, making the eyes squint, hiding the buck teeth, and substituting a pipe for a cigarette, the cartoonist is able to make a thinking man out of a near imbecile.

Like words, drawings can carry double meanings. A favorite trick of the cartoonist is to make a drawing that reads one way at first glance and another when it is given a second inspection. For example, an editorial cartoonist named Murschetz drawing for the *Suddeutsche Zeitung*, Munich, shows a regular line chart, labeled "Consumer Price Index," with the graph line shooting upward. But, looking closer, you can see a character representing German Chancellor Helmut Schmidt climbing the boxes that form the chart as though they were chicken wire, holding on with one hand and pushing the graph line downward, bending it as though it were a wire or hose. Baringou in *France Observateur* some years ago showed what at first glance appeared to be the American flag; but upon closer inspection the bars turned out to be jail bars with blacks imprisoned behind them.

Another trick is for the cartoonist to draw a cartoon within a cartoon. Al Ross does this in *The New Yorker* when he shows a couple in their living room watching a television screen. On the screen is the same couple—watching themselves on a television screen. And on *that* screen is the same couple . . . and so on. Warren Miller in the same magazine shows an ancient of Rome emptying a cornucopia by turning it upside down and shaking it—only to have another cornucopia come out of it, and out of *that* cornucopia still another, etc.

The comic strips have been known to feature strips within strips. Al Capp's "Fearless Fosdick," parodying *Dick Tracy,* is good enough to break away from *Li'l Abner* and become a strip on its own.

Still another trick is to make an item much bigger—or much smaller—than in real life. Jack Ziegler in *The New Yorker* shows a man raking leaves who has stopped to pose for a picture. Like a fisherman holding up his catch for all to admire, the man holds up a leaf as big as he is.

A cartoonist can convert an ordinary human body to a body quite out of the ordinary. Paul Mandel for a Chas. Pfizer

& Co. advertisement shows a man drinking from a bottle. The man is in pure outline. The content of the bottle, in color, is shown running down the man's throat to about neck level; from neck level to the feet, there is solid color. The effect is that of a man as a transparent, empty vessel being filled up by liquid.

Perhaps no one has taken more liberties with the human face and figure than Basil Wolverton. Following are some of Wolverton's "Preposterous Pictures of Peculiar People Who Prowl this Perplexing Planet" as put together by publisher William W. Spicer.

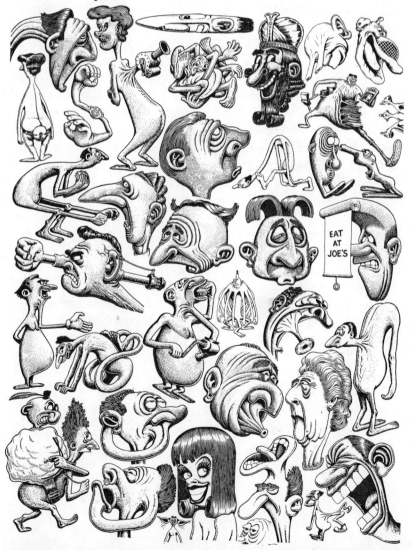

Courtesy of William W. Spicer.

Gustave Verbeek for the *New York Herald* from 1903 to 1905 did comic strips that could be read both right side up and upside down. You can see them in *The Incredible Upside-Downs of Gustave Verbeek,* published in 1969 by The Rajah Press. Another book of combination right-side-up and upside-down cartoons is Peter Newell's *Topsys & Turvys* published in 1974 by Dover Publications. Newell was also a turn-of-the-century cartoonist.

The more inventive the cartoonist, the better.

In one of Vip's cartoons for *True* that goes back to the early 1950s (the idea has been used by other cartoonists since) a man walks down the street carrying an umbrella. The rain is coming down in sheets—from *under* the umbrella, but nowhere else. Two men are watching, and one says to the other: "Nothing goes right for Filstrup."

A different version of this—Al Capp has used it—is to show a gloomy character (without an umbrella) walking around under a cloud. It is raining, but only on him.

For the *New York Times* Victor Juhasz draws a tree that has been "cut down" by a logger standing nearby with his ax; there is a three-foot gap between the bottom of the trunk, where the tree has been cut, and the stump, but the tree is still standing.

Charles Addams in *The New Yorker* shows one of his awful interiors—a bathroom—with a mirrored wall cabinet showing that a man is brushing his teeth. The tube is on the sink and the water is running, and the mirror image is unmistakable. But there is no one standing in front of the sink.

In a *Saturday Review/World* cartoon, Lo Linkert shows a couple of men marooned on an island. The horizon line is a dotted line. And just above it is lettered: "TEAR ALONG THIS LINE." One man says to the other: "I'm game if you are."

Mort Temes in a three-panel gag cartoon for *Maclean's* (Canada) shows a couple of men on a raft in the middle of the ocean, one pointing to a small sailboat on the horizon. They paddle wildly to get to it, and when they do they find it is—a small (toy) sailboat.

To illustrate a September 9, 1974, cover blurb on "Why Nixon Did Himself In: A Behavioral Examination of His Need to Fail," *New York* artist Haruo Miyauchi shows Nixon hanging himself, pulling upward on a rope he has tied around his neck. He is several feet off the ground. A person in real life couldn't possibly lift himself off the ground like that, but such restrictions do not stop the artist or cartoonist.

On the title page of a children's book he edited and illustrated, *A Storybook*, Tomi Ungerer shows a hand holding on to a ladle, stirring a pot of soup. The rest of the body has sunk into the soup. But the hand still is stirring.

Sometimes the cartoonist has his characters admit they are only cartoon characters. John Norment in *Saturday Review/World* shows two birds sitting on a tree branch. One says to the other: "I'm really a bluebird, but this magazine doesn't print its cartoons in color."

All in a Single Drawing

Only in recent decades has the photographer had his wide-angle, telescopic, and fisheye lenses to distort and bring together. The cartoonist has always had this facility.

Nor is time necessarily a deterrent. In the following cartoon you can see that it is possible to show the actual

connection that sent the ball over the fence, the batter rounding second, the pitcher, the infield, and the outfield of the opposing team (such as it is), and even the fans in the stands—all in one panel.

The following combination montage and portrait was drawn by Chris Ragus for a poster advertising *Squanto,* a play written by Jim Magnuson and produced at Princeton in 1973. The play is described by the author as "an epic of the American past replete with pilgrims, Shakespeare, Caliban, Spanish nuns, the ghost of Elizabeth I, and the host of the first Thanksgiving," all of which Ragus captures in one intriguing piece of art.

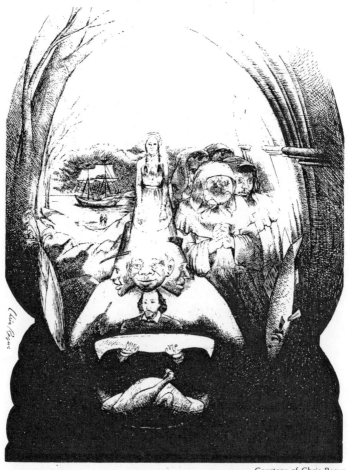

Courtesy of Chris Ragus.

Bil Keane in a Sunday version of *The Family Circus* shows a mother leaving a living room full of guests to get her son to recite for them "the cutest poem" he learned at school. The son is seen by the reader hiding under a bed in his room on a second level. How does Keane depict all this in a single panel? By showing a cutaway of the bedroom that ordinarily would be hidden by the stairway.

The cutaway can be a real challenge to the cartoonist. One of the most impressive ever done was of the Pentagon. It was run as a two-page spread in *Life* a decade or more ago. Most of the departments were shown, and many of the top officials were caricatured. The artist was the late Carl Rose, of "I say it's spinach. . . ." fame.

A recent cutaway that comes close to rivaling the Rose masterpiece is one run on the cover of a company magazine, the *Integon Listener,* on the occasion of the purchase by Integon

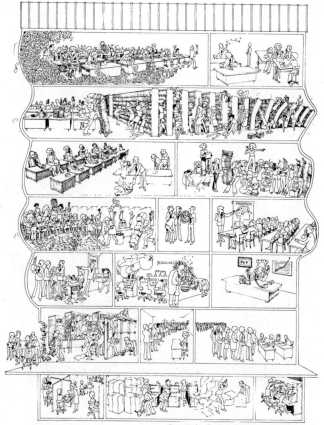

Corporation of part of another insurance company. An article inside the magazine explained that the purchase meant increased activity at corporation headquarters. The cover blurb said: "Integon is Bulging at the Seams . . . and for Good Reason."

Keith Stuart is the artist. He put hundreds of cartoon figures to work inside his cutaway front view of the building. As the blurb says, the building is really bulging. On the second floor you see that part of the wall has even broken away. Letting your eye wander from room to room here you'll notice, eventually, that people in one department, in the upper right part of the building, occupy their time flying paper airplanes. One suspects that Stuart, a freelancer, is kidding some people in the art department of Integon.

Showing the Impossible

Much of what happens in cartoons couldn't possibly happen in real life. In one of his classic cartoons that predates his haunted-house period, Charles Addams showed a skier who has passed a tree, one of his tracks going around the left side, one around the right. Psychiatrists have used the cartoon to test the reasoning power of their patients.

Pat Oliphant, when he was the *Denver Post* editorial cartoonist, resurrected the Addams scene in late 1974 to show that President Ford, at the time on a skiing vacation in Colorado, had dismissed too easily some charges that the CIA had engaged in domestic spying. Ford, whose tracks in the cartoon had encircled a tree marked "CIA" and then come together again, is shown saying to a companion: ". . . So I said to the tree, 'Tree, I won't tolerate anything like this!' And that was that."

Another effect that belongs only to the cartoonist is the one that shows a character doing the impossible until he realizes it *is* the impossible. When he loses confidence or realizes that what he's doing can't really be done—and only then—he becomes a victim.

We most often see this in animated cartoons. Through stupidity or misfortune, a character finds himself out in space, in a state of suspension. When he realizes it isn't possible for him to be out there like that, he falls. It is a temporary demonstration of mind over matter.

In the print media as well as in animation, it takes a series of drawings to bring this off. Johnny Hart in *B.C.* shows a character who trips over a rock at the edge of a cliff and loses his glasses. He just lies there in midair, shaken up a bit but in no immediate danger. He reaches for his glasses, puts them on, looks around, and as soon as he sees where he is and senses the impossibility of it, he falls rapidly and roughly to the ground. It is a fall of immense proportions, but the character, although battered, is able to pick himself up and walk away.

Showing movement in a single drawing is no problem. To make a head turning, the cartoonist simply draws two or three short, curved lines on either side. Or he draws the head several times: a side view, a three-quarters view, a front view, slightly overlapped, with only one of the heads fully defined. Doug Marlette shows how in this *Charlotte Observer* cartoon.

"FOOD CRISIS? WHAT FOOD CRISIS?"

Courtesy of Doug Marlette.

In the next cartoon you have some rather complicated movement in a single panel—the kind of movement you might expect in an animated film. For his book of tongue-in-cheek advice on playing tennis, Jack Roberts shows how a person can avoid using a backhand. ". . . a ball on the other side [the backhand side] is patently unreasonable, and a quick and right-thinking player realizes this immediately. . . . So he simply runs around it and hits the ball with his friendly forehand. The critics of this maneuver say that you'll never learn a backhand that way, and they have a point. Meanwhile, if you've returned the ball to your opponent's backhand, you have a point." Roberts shows this by drawing the player facing a backhand situation, and then drawing him again meeting the ball with a forehand stroke.

Copyright 1974 by Jack Roberts.
Used by permission.

If he is inventive enough, the cartoonist can show action that occurred some time before the moment that is captured in a single panel. Consider the problem of showing a man taking his seat in a theater. How does the cartoonist say that the man is about to sit down rather than that he is about to leave? To help the reader see that the man is half into a chair rather than half out of it, the cartoonist shows: (1) the man with his overcoat on, fully buttoned, (2) his hands holding onto the crease of his pants, and (3) his body slightly off balance, as though he were falling into the seat. The cartoonist also shows footprints leading in from outside.

Footprints are a handy device. John T. McCutcheon used them to advantage in "The Mysterious Stranger," his famous cartoon drawn in 1904 for the *Chicago Tribune* to show an unprecedented switch of Missouri voters to the Republican Party. The footprints dramatized the fact that the state was no longer standing where it had been standing.

This cartoon is remarkable for its clarity and simplicity in a day when political cartoons drawn by lesser artists had to be studied before their messages came across. McCutcheon directs attention to the two principal characters through use of solid blacks. Notice with what economy of drawing

McCutcheon suggests the other states. The cartoon is worth studying, too, for the variety of expressions: the pleased look of the other states, the slightly guilty look of Missouri, the disturbed look of the Solid South.

Here's a problem for the cartoonist: how to show that a father and baby are related. You could see a resemblance in real life, all right, but the resemblance would be too subtle to register in a cartoon. The cartoonist solves this problem by putting the same face on the baby, mustache and cigar and all, that he puts on the father. Only the body and dress are different.

Here's another problem: how do you show printing on a folder when the folder must be seen in context with the people using it? How do you show the folder big enough so the printing can be read? You can exaggerate its size, of course; but that might introduce a complicating factor. It is better to put it well in the foreground as in this drawing of a middle-aged couple planning a vacation. Perspective comes to the rescue by allowing the cartoonist to draw the folder large in relation to the figures in the background.

Showing the Intangible

Drawing's primary use is to show tangible objects and people. But it can also be used to show intangible things.

Take the problem *McCall's* had illustrating an article on "Do-It-Yourself Divorce." The magazine could have used a photograph or drawing of a couple angry with each other. Or a courtroom scene. Hinrichs Design Associates, Inc., handling the design and art job for *McCall's*, chose instead to show a standup paper-doll arrangement of a bride and groom with a dotted line between them. Words printed along the dotted line said: "CUT HERE." A big hand and a pair of scissors were shown cutting the couple apart.

To illustrate an ad promoting a television program about "Hank Aaron: Babe Ruth's Successor," on WMAQ-TV, Alex Murawski drew a candy bar that looked like a Baby Ruth but on closer inspection turned out to be a "Hank Aaron" bar.

The assignment for the following cartoon was to show that Oregon couples were rushing to Washington State to get married because at the time there was less of a wait. That's a little hard to illustrate. You can't very well show the phenomenon literally. You show it by putting your characters on a map, the map drawn in perspective. The characters in this kind of a setting must be oversize, of course, and overwhelming. You make the couple look marriage minded by (1) getting them to hold hands and (2) showing the man holding a ring. Only an idiot would run like that with a ring in its box with the lid open, but once again: this is Cartoonland.

"Everybody Talks about It . . ."

It is not quite correct to say that nobody does anything about the weather. A cartoonist can do plenty. Working for the *Eugene Register-Guard* and facing a dull day for news, I have often turned out a fearless attack on the long, hot spell—or, more likely for Oregon, the long, rainy spell—only to have the weather break, just before the paper goes to press. My influence on the weather comes with a heavy penalty assessed against my credibility. Readers do not understand the time involved between a cartoon's inception and its production; they think the cartoon was drawn a half hour before the paper reached their doorsteps. When they have to pull the blinds to cut down on the brightness outside, the better to take in my cartoon about the rain, they conclude that I am not a very astute observer.

N. Wylie Jones, in his article about Jeff MacNelly, reports that the *Richmond News Leader* cartoonist has similar problems with the stock market. "Jeff seems to have come up with a foolproof way to make the stock market rise," Jones writes. "When the stock market has been falling for days, he draws a cartoon about the fall, then the stock market jumps at least 10 points the next day—sometimes the same day—just for spite."

One of the many reasons for admiring *Mad* magazine is its ingenuity in dealing with life's vicissitudes. In 1960 John F. Kennedy ran against Richard Nixon for president and won. The next day, on newsstands across the country, there appeared the new issue of *Mad* with Kennedy on the cover along with this blurb: "*Mad* congratulates John Kennedy upon his election as President. We were with you all the way, Jack!"

Now an issue of a magazine is printed many days before it hits the newsstand. How could *Mad* take such a chance? It was to be a close election. When the reader turned the magazine around he soon found out: he found another cover that carried the same congratulatory message, but directed to Richard Nixon.

Newspaper editorial cartoonists sometimes take similar

precautions at election time, but without their tongues planted in their cheeks. They do congratulatory cartoons for both candidates and have plates readied. When the election returns are in, the editor picks the appropriate cartoon and plops it into its hole.

But a weather cartoon hardly rates all that planning. The cartoonist takes his chances.

I was lucky with a cartoon one summer commenting on the arrival, however late, of sunny weather in Oregon. The sunny weather remained until after the cartoon appeared.

"Been waiting long?"

How do you show an unreasonable passage of time? I used the time-worn analogy of the always-late wife (this was in pre-Women's Lib days). It's obvious that a lot of time has passed by: (1) the cobwebs, (2) the ticket on the car, (3) the hint of a beard beginning to grow on the distraught man, (4) the multitude of cigarette butts, and (5) the approaching darkness, suggested by the Zipatone and the drawing of the streetlights.

To depict hot weather it is not necessary always to show the sun. For a navy publication in the South Pacific during World War II, I did a cartoon showing how unbearably hot it was by simply showing a sailor's head and neck protruding from a puddle of—butter?

Sometimes shadows alone do the job. The greater the contrast between their blackness and the figures' whiteness, the hotter the day.

To show rain: some uneven parallel lines running diagonally, along with drops and puddles. When the rains result in floods, it is necessary to do more. The preceding cartoon shows the result of floods one Christmas in Oregon. Many families who otherwise would have been together had to celebrate with distances intervening.

To show snow: a few flakes in the air; a concentration on tops of trees, roofs, etc.; and sunken footprints, drawn in three dimensions. Usually, those characters outside would be bundled up, but in this cartoon, I wanted to show that the father had stepped outside only momentarily; and I wanted to create sympathy for the girl by showing her unprepared for the cold. (The "Saturday Market" was a collection of sidewalk stalls set up by local craftsmen to sell their wares.)

Actually, the cartoonist doesn't really need the obvious devices of comic art to depict the weather. There are no swirling lines to indicate wind, no parallel lines to indicate rain in the following drawing. No raindrops. No puddles of water. No clouds.

The effectiveness of the drawing lies in the tension of balance and in the contrast between the straight, stiff lines in back of the figure and the ballooning lines in front. You can feel the high wind even though it does not show.

The drawing also illustrates the possibility of arranging the composition of a figure to conform to the shape of a letter from the alphabet, in this case a "Y."

The Look of Sound

An earlier chapter recorded the contribution of Roy Crane to the language of action. Crane is not alone in coining and using words to depict action. "GLITCH!" goes a man as he steps into dry dirt in a *Mad* cartoon by Al Jaffee. Even a candy maker has gotten in on the act with a bar called

"Skrunch." The wrapper bears the slogan: "World's skrunchiest candy bar." I don't find the word in my dictionary. But maybe in the next edition?

The rules say, at least so far as cartoonists are concerned, that the sound words must be in all-caps, preferably ending in exclamation points. And, to be really effective, they should be in outline letters, with shadows, perhaps, to make the letters stand out. A few stars or other typographic effects nearby don't hurt.

New action words come along with increasing frequency. Henry Martin in *The New Yorker,* commenting on this phenomenon, shows two men fighting. Just above them is lettered "KRONK!" "ZAP!" and "ZUT!" One onlooker says to the other: "What ever happened to 'POW,' 'BIFF,' and 'BAM'?"

Another recent phenomenon in the comic strips is the use of *descriptive* words as *sound* words. Charles Schulz shows Snoopy typing, and near the dog are the words "TYPE, TYPE, TYPE." Brant Parker has a character in *Wizard of Id* reading, helped along by "READ, READ, READ." Johnny Hart in *B.C.* shows a character sneaking up on an ant pile: "SNEAK, SNEAK, SNEAK." You can tell a descriptive word from a sound word by the lack of exclamation marks.

Animals can talk as human beings do in the strips. Or they can talk in "ARF! ARF!"s or "CHIRP! CHIRP!"s. But sometimes the cartoonist invents a new animal language. Charles Schulz chooses to have the little bird-friend of Snoopy's talk in a series of short, vertical lines with little hooks at the ends: sort of like a series of lowercase *l*s.

Creating the Creator

During the "Death of God" debate among theologians in the 1960s, *Time* commissioned a cover by Larry Rivers: a collage making use of a da Vinci version of God, putting Him in a coffin. It turned out that the cover was "too complex." And for the first time in its history, *Time* went with an all-type cover. God proved to be too much for *Time.*

Christ has been drawn and painted often enough, but God as a visual subject proves to be illusive. Not for cartoonists, though.

In the *New York Times* Al Kaufman, in an illustrative cartoon, shows God as a big hand reaching down from the clouds. Noah and crew are building the ark, just starting to hook a sail to a mast. The big hand carries a sign that reads "NO SAILS."

J. B. Handelsman in a *New Yorker* cartoon tries his hand at God by showing him as a large semi-transparent figure in the sky, with flowing long hair and beard, and with lines of brightness radiating outward. In this cartoon God tells a poet in the forest: "Trees are made by gods like me, but only a fool like you can make a poem."

6

The Art of Stereotyping

Digging one day in the library stacks, one of my resourceful graduate students came onto a slim and singular volume called *Analysis of Human Nature, Book Four: Features, Gestures and Emotions* by somebody named Floyd Foster Barnes. Knowing I would be interested in the writings of a fellow three-namer, he passed it along to me. The book bore a 1923 copyright date but no publisher's imprint; it was a book so much in the vanguard, apparently, that it had to be published by the author himself.

I have no way of knowing what the first three books in the series propounded, but Book Four, anticipating later writers with their you-are-what-you-eat and even you-are-what-you-throw-away themes, makes the point: You are what you look like. The shape and placement of your eyes, nose, mouth, chin, and ears tell a great deal about your character and personality.

Take the eyes. These are "the windows of the soul." Or: "the mirrors of the mind." Sensing that their eyes betray them, people turn their eyes down or away when they engage in lies or other subterfuges.

But people can't hide some characteristics associated with the eyes. For instance: Barnes points out that the normal space between the eyes is the width of an eye. If the space is wider than that there is, obviously, more room for brains; hence, the person with such eyes is one of "originality and sound judgment." But if the space is unreasonably great, as on a cow, the individual is likely to have little personality and, frankly, few opinions of his own. Barnes writes: "His eyes let in too much vision for him to concentrate on any abstract opinion."

The same problem occurs with large, wide-open, protruding eyes, regardless of spacing. "It is not necessary for purposes of sight for the eyes to be so wide open and protruding," Barnes writes, somewhat testily.

More handicapped still is the person whose eyes are set close together. Such a person, Barnes suggests, is narrow-minded, even treacherous.

The best kind of eyes to have are small, deep-set, preferably blue, and slanting downward at the outside edges—good news to those of us of Swedish persuasion. Small, deep-set eyes are a sign of a deep-thinker, Barnes declares. With the upper lid drawn partially over the eye, there is a more limited field of vision. "Thus the mind is less disturbed by external impressions, and can occupy itself with the matters it undertakes, without interruption. Small eyes see less, but comprehend more." Furthermore: ". . . most of our geniuses have small eyes and over-hanging brows. And when the eyes appear to be slanting downward, it is a sign of executive ability, keen mentality, and [here's the bad news] a degree of pessimism."

And consider this: "Thick eyelids, especially when they are red, denote the presence of passion and sensuality. Fullness under the eyes is generally accompanied by ability in languages, or the power of oral expression. Most orators and public speakers possess this trait. Do not confuse this, however, with the discolored, puffy condition which indicates kidney ailments and a general lack of eliminative powers."

As for the nose, Barnes sees a relationship between size and energy. The larger the nose, the more energy and strength, because a large nose means large lungs. "All big business men and women have fairly large noses, and the majority are *markedly* large." (Italics mine.) The shape strikes Barnes as significant, too. For instance, if the nose is concave its wearer is subject to inaction. And he's probably obstinate. But to his credit, the concave-nose type has a good memory.

A big mouth suggests to Barnes a good digestive system and accompanying good cheer.

On the subject of excessively thick, protruding lips, Barnes minces no words. These mean an "abnormally developed sexual nature, and many times an indolent, unenterprising disposition." But there is this to consider: "One occasionally sees very full lips which are compressed to such an extent that they do not seem as large as they are. This individual has decided tendencies towards the faults which we have listed above. But he has reasoning power to realize the baseness of these faults, and the necessary self-control to rid himself of them. He has himself in hand and never lets his baser instincts get the better of him. This is one of the many ways in which a man may change the appearance of his features. We often see pictures of men who at twenty had full-protruding, careless, characterless lips, and who at forty have disciplined those lips into a firm and determined line. This type of lips is admirable, for it shows sentiment and generosity, as well as self-control."

A short upper lip belongs to the fellow who values praise highly. He cares what people think of him. "Most actors and public speakers have short upper lips."

On the subject of teeth: those that protrude show a greediness for food. Small, short teeth belong to the narrow-minded.

A strong chin is a dead giveaway for strong will, of course. A dimple on the chin is a sign of enthusiasm. A ball on the chin is a sign of energy.

Ears close to the head say that the individual is conservative. When they are large and protruding the person is generous, he has executive ability, and, understandably, he has musical ability.

Writing much later in the Barnes spirit in an article in *Ladies Home Companion* (not to be confused with *Ladies' Home Journal* or the defunct *Woman's Home Companion*), Virginia Morris sets out to popularize the work of one Professor William H. Shelton of Columbia University. Instructing her women readers in the art of husband picking, Ms. Morris divides the breed into three body types: Ectomorph (thin and nervous), Mesomorph (muscular), and Endomorph (plump and cheerful).

The thin and nervous man, she reveals, wakes up unrefreshed and harried, eats a small breakfast, is ill at ease, likes to work alone, is more concerned with his own than with world problems, doesn't like strenuous exercise, prefers female to male companionship, is amorous, likes the "feeling of security that small rooms give him," prefers chairs with high and shallow seats. ". . . Do buy a hard mattress" for him, Ms. Morris advises.

The muscle man eats plain food and plenty of it, likes spacious rooms, makes decisions easily, likes games of chance, likes hunting, and "as a lover, he is classified as medium."

The plump and cheerful man eats often and pleasurably and "he'll help with the dishes occasionally," is a good salesman, is popular "but seldom strays from the fireside." Ms. Morris advises: "Try to manage at least one upholstered lounging chair for him and a soft mattress. He takes sensuous pleasure in luxurious furniture and thick rugs." But she adds: "His sexual drive is low."

To determine a person's traits through analysis of his physical appearance, you need not encounter him personally.

According to Robert U. Akeret you can do the job simply by studying his photograph. Akeret explains how in *Photoanalysis,* a book Peter H. Wyden, Inc., brought out in 1973.

We even have members of the medical profession getting into the act. Suffering some years back with a digestive disturbance (unfortunately, I don't have one of Barnes's big mouths) I struggled to the office of a nearby physician. He didn't subject me to any tests. He simply sized me up and decided my trouble was not in the stomach as I had suspected. As he explained: "You are small-boned, hairy-armed, with many moles and freckles. That type always has trouble in the lower digestive tract."

Psychologist Samuel V. Dunkell finds that the position you assume in sleep tells a lot about your personality. The *New York Daily News* reports his saying that if you sleep on your side in a semi-fetal position you tend to be "a fairly secure personality." But if you assume a full-fetal position, curling yourself around a pillow, you are insecure. If you sleep on your stomach you "want to control and organize everything" around you. You are a powerful person. People who sleep on their backs are generous. Dr. Dunkell further observes that if a married couple sleeps back-to-back "usually a divorce is not too far away."

In the mid-1960s *Newsweek* reported the observations of a gynecologist making a study of the relationship of breasts to brains. The doctor's conclusion: "The better the brain, the smaller the breasts, and vice versa." Not that his conclusion gained immediate acceptance. "The idea just doesn't stack up with my observations," responded Dr. Charles M. McLane of Cornell University Medical College.

On Half-Believing

There may be those among the social scientists who would question the validity of many of these observations. And on an intellectual level, most of the nation's cartoonists, probably, would regard them largely as fraudulent. Haven't all of us been fooled by those magazine features that ask us to match mug shots of real-life persons with their correct occupations? Invariably, we make bank presidents out of mechanics and radio announcers out of accountants.

And yet: cartoonists—all of us—continue to rely on facial features to tell our readers something about the character of the people we draw. The stereotypes are too firmly entrenched to dislodge. Only the most obnoxious of them—the ones with racial overtones—have withered away. It comes back again to the nature of the cartoon. The message is too hurried, the space too restricted to engage in more precise communication.

And maybe the cartoonist, with so many hours at the drawing board, half-believes in the stereotypes, as the editor at a respected book publishing house that brings out a book on astrology half believes that the stars have a bearing on one's life. One of Malcolm Muggeridge's observations applies, although it may be a bit harsh in this context: "In all deception, whether of governments, or demagogues, or press lords, or media pundits, or advertisers, down to little con-men and columnists and street-corner *exaltes*—the ultimate doom is that the deceiver comes to believe his own deceits."

Cartoonists are on safer ground when they attach significance to the *movement* of facial features rather than their size and shape. There can be little argument, for instance, over the meaning of the winking of an eye, the wrinkling of a brow, the screwing up of a face, or the nodding of a head. In a blockbuster of an ad in *Publishers Weekly* in late 1974, the publisher Frederick Fell announced a new book, *Face Language,* by Robert L. Whiteside, that "shows you how to interpret the positions and movements of the eyes, mouth, lips, eyebrows of persons you are speaking with (or even see on TV) so that you understand what is in their minds as well as what is on their lips." The book obviously was cashing in on the popularity of a 1970 book published by Julian Messner, *Body Language* by Julius Fast.

The Eyes Have It

Whether or not the eyes are true indices of physical or emotional health, so far as the cartoonist is concerned they are the key to facial expression. They need not—they should not—be complicated. Two simple dots often are all that's needed. It's where on the face the cartoonist puts them and how he coordinates them with the eyebrows that's important.

Often the cartoonist draws circles around the dots that represent the eyes. But the most famous cartoon eyes are the ones the late Harold Gray gave Little Orphan Annie: two small ovals, hollowed out. David Levine in an appropriate gesture borrowed the eyes to do his caricature of Svetlana, Stalin's daughter.

Following are six common expressions or conditions indicated by eyes in coordination with brows: bashfulness, gladness, worry, anger, weariness, and hurt.

For use in indicating expression, the nose is of little importance to the cartoonist. True, he delights in exaggerating its size, at least for male characters. On the other hand, he may leave it out altogether, as when he draws a head-on view of a pretty girl.

With Help from the Hands

Sometimes the cartoonist needs to bring in the hands or other parts of the body to round out the expression or condition. Even in real life people use parts of their body other than the face to express themselves. "We rub our noses for puzzlement," writes Julius Fast in *Body Language.* "We clasp our arms to isolate ourselves and protect ourselves. We shrug our shoulders for indifference, . . . tap our fingers for impatience, slap our forehead for forgetfulness."

Consider this poor fellow, just after tax time. The face tells part of the story (the turned-up eyebrows and the turned-down mouth), but the pulled-out pockets and the extended hand, palm out, fingers down, help the man explain: "That's all I've got. I'm wiped out."

Hands play a vital role in the expressions in the following cartoon, helping the judge round up a juror from off the street (all very legal in an emergency, according to the news feature for which this sketch was made) and helping the tapped one respond, "Who, me?"

A Glossary of Expressions

Here, for whatever use the reader chooses to make of it, is a glossary of expressions and conditions that can be suggested by the cartoonist mainly through manipulation of facial features. (It is considered good form for the cartoonist, as he draws, to work his own face into the expression he is trying to depict.)

Anger—Brows slanting inward and downward, close to the eyes, with the mouth turned down. For extreme anger, "redden" the face with tone made of thin, parallel lines and open the downturned mouth to show teeth.

"Please! Think of the children..."

Anger is depicted in the preceding cartoon not only by facial expression but also by clenched fists and a pointed finger. Several other expressions in this cartoon deserve notice. One is worry, as seen on the face of the little boy. Note the eyebrows, the sweat mark, the finger in the mouth. Pleading is shown by outstretched arms, hands pointing downward, palms facing forward. The little girl's concern is shown mostly by the folded hands. The evidence of disarray in the room, barely suggested, helps create the illusion that something is amiss.

Boredom—Eyes sleepy or closed, with hand in front of open mouth to stifle a yawn.

Cleanliness—Thin lines extending outward from the subject. He looks shiny.

Defensiveness—Arms spread, with hands pointing downward, palms exposed. The character is explaining his position. There is a look of worry on his face.

Embarrassment (caught-in-the-act division)—Big, silly smile, with too many teeth showing, accompanied by worried look. Snoopy often shows this expression.

Evil—Mouth turned up, as in a smile, brows turned inward and downward, as in anger. An expression almost impossible in real life but easy enough in a cartoon.

Fear—Eyebrows drawn diagonally and raised at the center, eyes wide open, hair standing on end, mouth open and turned down.

Fingers-scratching-blackboard look—Eyes closed, with frown and with thin-lipped mouth closed in zigzag line.

Goodness—Halo over the head.

Grief—The character holds his head in his hands, shoulders humped, with a worried look on his face and perhaps a tear or two showing. If you want your grief-stricken character to cry, throw his head back, close his eyes, open the mouth, and turn it downward.

Happiness—Mouth turned up, eyes closed (optional). To turn happiness into a laugh, throw the head back, as in the cry, open the mouth, but turn it upwards. Tears are versatile. You can use them here, too.

Impatience—The character drums his fingers and frowns.

Innocence—Eyes looking heavenward. If the innocence is feigned, the character whistles nonchalantly.

Inspiration—A lightbulb is shown over the head, usually

inside a balloon, with bubbles connecting the balloon to the head.

Intelligence—Deep-set eyes are shown squinting, and the forehead is high. There is a pipe in the mouth (male version only).

Love—There is a heart over the subject's head—or two hearts with an arrow going through. The expression on the face can be one either of stupidity or happiness, depending on your point of view.

Misery—The expression on the face combines aspects of both worry and grief.

Old age—Thin lips, with short lines running into them top and bottom (to suggest lack of teeth); wrinkled face; skinny neck; bags under the eyes; very little hair; loose-fitting clothing; stooped. The body often is full enough, but the limbs are like toothpicks.

Pain or injury—Stars drawn at the ends of thin line extending outward from the victim. You may include a crossed patch of adhesive tape, even though the victim has not really had time to dress his wound (cartoonists' license). Use Xs for eyes. Put a heavy circle around one of the Xs.

Puzzlement—The character scratches his head and maybe looks a little worried. You could include a large question mark above his head. I'm not sure why the head scratching works in a cartoon (none of my puzzled friends act that way), but it does.

Self-satisfaction—Eyes closed, brows raised, mouth slightly upturned, head thrown back a bit. In the following strong, graceful, confident pencil sketch of a businessman for an advertisement for Time-Life Multimedia, Charles Saxon, to better show the look of self-satisfaction, utilizes for eyes and nose the space that ordinarily would be reserved for forehead.

Used by permission of Time-Life Multimedia.

Stupidity—If you don't mind the unfairness of the stereotype, you can show your character with eyes half-closed,
chin receding, teeth bucked, mouth partially open, forehead low.

Surprise—Eyebrows raised, mouth open. To show extraor-
dinary surprise, you can show the character tumbling
over backwards, with the soles of his shoes showing, and
the word "PLOP!" nearby.

Timidity—Put the character's finger in his mouth. Or have him staring down at his feet and make him look worried. Maybe you could put a weak smile on his face.

Worry—Eyebrows drawn diagonally, slanting outward; forehead wrinkled; mouth turned down. The subject may have his finger digging into his collar, pulling it away from his neck.

Youthfulness—The face is round, the forehead abundant.

Often the point of a cartoon depends upon the pitting of one expression against the other. To put his gag across in a *Stained Glass* syndicated panel, it was necessary for cartoonist Ed Sullivan to clearly portray anger in one character, feigned innocence in another.

" *...* AND PLEASE LET DAD BE A BIG WINNER IN THE STATE LOTTERY! "

Courtesy of Ed Sullivan and Avant Features.

Symbols and Stereotypes: the Difference

The symbols that editorial cartoonists invent and use are deliberate. They are clearly labeled. The reader recognizes them for what they are: stand-ins for the real thing.

Stereotypes, on the other hand, evolve gradually and result not necessarily from normal thought processes but from unconscious bias and maybe uncritical observation. They become the quick and easy way to communicate.

Nor can we fix the blame—if there is blame in using stereotypes—on any one group of cartoonists. All cartoonists use them. Liberals—who make the most noise against stereotypes—are as guilty as conservatives. To the liberal cartoonist, a conservative is an old lady in tennis shoes; to the conservative cartoonist, the liberal is a shaggy-haired double-domed buttinsky if not a bomb thrower. Al Capp, as a liberal, was as merciless in his use of stereotypes of conservatives as he was later, as a conservative, in his use of stereotypes of liberals. (In Capp's defense, let it be recorded that he told his critics, and they seem to have multiplied since he turned his attacks on the left, that he fights lunacy wherever it may be found.)

The following cartoon shows two cartoonists' stereotypes from the 1960s; the tweedy professor and the hippie student. The unpressed herringbone suit with the leather

patches at the elbows, along with the pipe, probably still serve; but the student dress—and hence the stereotype—changed a bit in the 1970s: wire-rimmed glasses in place of the horn rims, and flair or bell-bottom pants. The silly expressions are eternal.

I have found that in some cases—in editorial cartoons where I don't want to label the figure as "Faculty"—the tweed suit and pipe do not communicate readily enough. In those cases I put a cap and gown on the figure. Not that professors ever really wear those robes (except to commencement exercises), but the robes do more obviously symbolize the academic life.

Some of his best friends

What you see here is a cartoon for any occasion: a cartoon that at first glance seems to come down hard on—

what? The beauty of the cartoon to its creator is that it doesn't commit him to any cause except the disapproval of political extremism—a safe enough stance. The cartoon could be used against the left or the right. The only group likely to take offense would be cigar manufacturers, who would much prefer seeing nice guys using their product. The industry has worked hard to erase an image coming out of movies of the 1930s suggesting that only gangsters smoke cigars.

For the newspaper reporter, the cartoonist shows a trench coat and, stuck in his hatband, a press card. I have never seen a real-live reporter carrying his press card that way, but it's a well-established stereotype, and I have never cartooned a reporter otherwise. You'll notice, though, that in the preceding illustration, drawn for a program for a conference on school-community relations sponsored by an organization of teachers, I did not use the once-popular old-maid stereotype at the desk. A client is a client.

Of course, that may not be enough of a concession to the times. It may be argued that the male-female roles could be reversed in this cartoon. The teacher could be a man; the reporter could be a woman. After all, men teach in elementary and secondary schools, too; and women are becoming better represented in all areas of the communications industry.

The question the cartoonist has to ask himself, though, is: Will the cartoon read just as clearly that way?

Ed Sullivan in the following *Stained Glass* cartoon assigns a woman to a reporter's role, but his reason may be that the reporter is from the women's section of a paper, where women have always been employed, rather than that he is willing to break away from the male-reporter stereotype. At least he is able to convey "reporter" without relying on a press card.

"OUR READERS WILL REALLY LOVE *THAT!* WHAT *ELSE* HAVE YOU LEARNED SINCE YOU LEFT THE PRIESTHOOD?"

Courtesy of Ed Sullivan and Avant Features

The Fully Clothed Nude

While the figure in real life measures seven or eight heads in height, the figure in a cartoon measures three or four. The large head gives the cartoonist room to manipulate the facial features so important to him in establishing expression and mood. Not content with the large head, the cartoonist may go a step further by eliminating the forehead (provided the character is not a child) to achieve even more room for expression.

In drawing kids, the cartoonist further exaggerates head size. The *Peanuts* characters, for instance, are about half head, half body.

Some other characteristics of cartoon kids: they have a tendency to stick out their stomachs, although their backs remain ramrod straight. Their limbs are straight, like stovepipes, thickest, perhaps, at the wrist and ankle. And kids hold their hands differently from adults.

The more the cartoonist learns about anatomy, the more possibilities he discovers for distorting the figure. He can learn about anatomy through books, of course, but, better, he can enroll in a life-drawing class or go out on sketching trips. When I attended the Art Center School (now the Art Center College of Design) in Los Angeles, I used to walk the several blocks west to the Farmer's Market, there to spend the late afternoon at one of the terrace tables sketching the interesting and varied characters who came to shop, eat, or wander past the booths. I felt less self-conscious about what I was doing when I was in the company of other sketching students, but nobody in bustling Los Angeles paid much attention to what the other fellow was doing anyway. My subjects seldom noticed that they were posing. Of course, I had to move quickly with my pencil, but that is good training for a cartoonist.

For both faces and figures the cartoonist avoids easy-to-do side views and offers his readers, where possible, three-quarter views, front views, and back views.

Jim Consor in a sketch of an exercising woman for an ad for The New York Health Club chooses a back view so that he

Courtesy The New York Health Club, Inc.

can show the face—a pleasant one—and, at the same time, a part of the body needing conditioning. He has given the woman's gym suit a texture to tie it to the texture of the hair, thus unifying the drawing.

A major lesson the cartoonist learns from his life classes or sketching trips is that every movement of the body brings on a countermovement. For instance, when the hips are pulled in one direction, the shoulders are pulled in the other, as in the following figure.

In drawing any figure for publication the cartoonist starts out by roughing in the body and then fitting clothes around it. In the inking-in process, drawing the figure is largely a matter of drawing clothes.

A drawing of two thoughtful men displays some of the possibilities. The fellow on the left shows how a thin, loose-

fitting shirt can be made to contrast with tight-fitting pants. The fellow on the right suggests that when the cartoonist wants to indicate a thick, woolen cloth, he does it by drawing in bolder, choppier strokes.

In the following drawing Zella Strickland gets by with just clothes (and shadows) in depicting a sinister character to accompany a review of a crime movie. (The publication is *The Western Critic* of Boise, Idaho. Editor Dwight Wm. Jensen says that Ms. Strickland "for several years was the only Idahoan supporting herself wholly as a freelance artist.")

The cartoonist has two kinds of wrinkles or folds to contend with: loose folds (zigzag lines) occur wherever there

ZELcA

Courtesy of *The Western Critic*.

is a concentration of extra cloth, as at the elbow when an arm is bent. Tight folds (straight lines) occur where the cloth is pulled, as when a leg is stretched in a long stride. In the drawing on page 236, notice the right fold in the pants of the expansive gentleman at the left. Notice the loose folds at the bend in the arm of the wary gentleman standing at the right. At his knees, there is a combination of both folds, caused by the natural sag of trousers and by the fact that he is pulling up the trousers slightly by keeping his hands in his pockets.

Fat characters in cartoons are likely to have tight folds, skinny characters loose folds. Notice the tight little fold at the armpit of the man at the left.

It is a temptation for the cartoonist to get too caught up in wrinkles, as George Wunder did in the strip he took over from Milton Caniff: *Terry and the Pirates.* Gag cartoonists, who simplify their work more than most other cartoonists, often show no wrinkles at all, even when elbows and knees bend. It would be as much of a mistake to draw in every wrinkle as it would be to draw in each button and every shoelace.

Generally, the rules for folds in cloth apply also to wrinkles in the face. The cartoonist avoids wrinkles for fat characters, but when he does use wrinkles, they would be tight, presumably because the skin is being stretched by too much flesh. Skinny characters, especially if they are older, would have some wrinkles. In the preceding cartoon, notice the wrinkles at the chin line, caused by sagging flesh, in the gentleman at the right. The fat character, every bit as old, has a wrinkle-free face.

Len Norris of the *Vancouver* (British Columbia) *Sun* presents a study in fabrics in a cartoon showing a speaker overreacting to a new Public Officials Disclosure act in Canada. Note how Norris uses different kinds of lines to

"...may I ask, sir, have you thoroughly read the new Public Officials Disclosure Act..."

Courtesy of Len Norris.

suggest heavy material in the drapes, lighter-weight material in the table cloth, and still lighter material in the shirting, and then turns to solid black to suggest still another material. And see how it all contrasts with the sagging flesh of a man well past his prime.

Finally, to borrow a title from a Nora Ephron article in *Esquire*, "A Few Words About Breasts." In the cartoonist's world there are no flat-chested women any more than there are any small-nosed men. Every figure needs a protuberance, or the cartoonist feels somehow he has failed to draw a funny picture.

Nor does the fact that the torso is fully covered present any problem. The cartoonist simply inks in the figure as though there were no clothes there and then, at the last moment, just before turning his cartoon in to the editor, saves himself any possible censure by demurely putting some hint of clothing at the top, say a double line to represent a turtleneck. Al Capp since the beginning has specialized in breasts of this genre, displaying them with great abandon, never having to stoop to the obvious device of the low neckline.

But gag cartoonists, especially those submitting to the

men's magazines, have been high on cleavage: either the *I* type, or, in more hysterical moments, the *V* or *Y* types. Cartoonists are able even to make something of small breasts (far right). The low-slung, no-bra look is less in evidence in cartoons than out there in real life.

And, inevitably, a pretty body in Cartoonland accompanies a pretty face. You can see in the following sketch the hopelessness of any attempt to defy this convention.

7

Style and Technique

Those who admire the drawings of the late James Thurber, I notice, do not draw much. I suspect that if they drew pictures, their pictures would look like Thurber's. When they praise Thurber they strike a blow for nonartists everywhere. Or maybe it's another case of praising the idea while not noticing the drawing.

Thurber was as surprised as anyone when his drawings began to appear in *The New Yorker*, where he worked as an editor/writer. For a good part of his later sub-career as a cartoonist, Thurber, nearly blind, had to draw in broad sweeps with a thick crayon pressed against a large sheet pinned to a wall. For all editor-in-chief Harold Ross knew, the staff was putting him on by insisting that he publish the Thurber drawings.

Nor did Thurber have any illusions about his drawing ability. One of his most famous cartoons showed a woman on all fours on top of a bookcase, with a man and his wife nearby talking to a visitor. Says the man: "That's my first wife up there, and this is the *present* Mrs. Harris." Thurber had tried to show the first wife on a staircase, but he had had trouble with the perspective. Ross, ever cautious, asked Thurber if the crouching woman were alive or dead.

Oh, alive, Thurber assured Ross, because "my doctor says a dead woman couldn't support herself on all fours, and my taxidermist says you can't stuff a woman."

Despite the sorry draftsmanship in the Thurber drawings there was a quality in them that made them unique. Call it style. Nobody was able to duplicate the Thurber look, although there were plenty of cartoonists around who drew badly enough to try.

Harold Gray (*Little Orphan Annie*) was another cartoonist not likely to win any prizes for his drawing ability, but there was a strength of style there, too, that gave his work charm and made it instantly recognizable. When he died, his syndicate tried desperately to find someone to keep Orphan Annie alive. Several artists tried. All failed. "Horrible things have been happening to Little Orphan Annie," wrote Paul Richard in the *Washington Post*. "Leapin' Lizards, she looks awful!" Finally the syndicate had to begin reissuing the early strips to satisfy Annie's dedicated, super-Republican fans.

Another comic-strip artist whose drawing might be called into question but whose style made him a giant in the field is Chester Gould (*Dick Tracy*).

Then there are the cartoonists whose styles are not necessarily distinguished but whose drawing is impeccable, even inspirational: people like Alex Raymond (*Flash Gordon* and *Rip Kirby*), John Prentice (*Rip Kirby*), Hal Foster (*Tarzan* and *Prince Valiant*), John Cullen Murphy (*Big Ben Bolt*), and Burne Hogarth (*Tarzan*).

Some comic strips managed to hold on to large audiences with little to distinguish them in either style or drawing: *Boots and Her Buddies, Smilin' Jack, Mickey Finn, Archie.* The most that could be said for these strips from an art standpoint is that the lines were clean and reproduced well. The most conspicuous example of non-art in the comic strips would have to be that short-lived watery imitation of *Dick Tracy: Dan Dunn.* But don't underestimate its influence. *Dan Dunn* may have caused any number of cartoonists in the 1930s to think about launching their own strips. If *Dan Dunn* could make it, anything could.

One of the current marvels of the cartoon world is a one-column panel called *Love Is . . .* , which appears to have taken its cue from a Determined Productions book by Charles Schulz: *Happiness Is. . . .* Despite a glaring deficiency in drawing, in style, and in idea content, this "warm and tender" feature enjoys "tremendous reader acceptance," according to the Los Angeles Times Syndicate.

But, fortunately, popularity does not embrace only such amateurish efforts. Milton Caniff among the adventure-strip artists has enjoyed widespread adulation for both drawing and style, first in *Terry and the Pirates* and later in *Steve Canyon.* The masterful Caniff touch is not easily duplicated.

Already you have seen evidence of the combination of high style and superb drawing in Roy Crane's work. In the following 1941 example, Crane handles figures, props, fire, and smoke convincingly but still manages to retain an element of the comic in the figure stretched out on the deck in the concluding panel. (To explain one of the props: Easy had earlier been chained to a bed.)

Reproduced by special permission of
Newspaper Enterprise Association (NEA).

Among the purely *comic*-strip artists, a surprising number managed to combine good drawing with a unique style.

George McManus (*Bringing Up Father*), with his sophisticated sense of design and his beautifully controlled line, was one of these. So was Cliff Sterrett (*Polly and Her Pals*).

In the preceding example—from 1935—you can admire Sterrett's beautifully composed panels and uniquely drawn characters, including one of comicdom's best cats. Those buildings seen through the window are typically Sterrett. So is the tile floor, drawn in faithful perspective. Although the strip was named after Polly, it was her father, Sam Perkins, who most often took center stage. Like only a few others, this strip died when its creator retired in 1958. No one else could possibly have taken over.

Among gag cartoonists, the most admired today probably is George Price, a long-time *New Yorker* regular who delights in depicting unusual and unpleasant older characters, poor-taste furniture with every detail intact, and the backs of television sets with all those wires and plugs. Price combines one of the most unusual styles in the business with some of the best and most precise draftsmanship.

Some who admire his style may make the mistake of thinking that Price's genius lies in the outline that seems to separate into two lines at times and then merge back into one. Looking at a Price drawing you get the impression that the ink runs dry as he pulls a flexible pen across the sheet. The two parts of the pen point seem to separate and then come back together again. It is probable that Price encourages this look by actually going back to his solid lines and, using opaque white, painting a white strip down the center of some of them. But the double-line effect is only a surface characteristic. It is not what gives a Price drawing its unique quality.

What really marks George Price as an artist is the design he builds into every part of his drawing. Take any part of a Price drawing and analyze it: you find in it an exquisite set of proportions, one shape beautifully contrasting with another. Price does not just draw a wrinkle at the elbow in a bending sleeve; he constructs it to make it relate to other lines and shapes around it.

And there is solidity there. Just with outlines and Ben Day tints (he seldom uses washes and never solid blacks) Price makes each of his works look as though it were carefully chiseled out of stone.

Price is one cartoonist who seems to improve with age. His cartoons of the late 1930s and early 1940s, in style, showed little of the promise of what was to come, although from the start his gags were of a superior quality. I remember a vintage Price-ism: a cartoon showing a woman trying out a hat and making a face, sticking out her tongue, wiggling her hands with her thumbs stuck in her ears. The old Bronx cheer. A long-suffering salesman was standing behind her saying: "A simple 'Yes' or 'No' will be sufficient. . . ."

Another of the greats among gag cartoonists was Peter Arno. Arno, a man who felt a sense of destiny, considered himself first an artist, then a cartoonist. A cartoonist, he said, "should be capable of producing a minor masterpiece in any medium."

He added: "Hundreds of young people have come to me for advice and appraisal of their work. For years I've been depressed by the low level of their aspirations. Their ignorance is colossal. Hardly one of them has even known the name (let alone studied the work) of a great painter or draftsman—of this or past centuries. All they know are the newspaper strips and tenth-rate magazine hacks. Their idols are dyed-in-the-wool mediocrities."

Arno said his effects were achieved only through "pain and toil, concentration, . . . revision, nervous expenditure, great aspiration, and continuous elimination of tasteless detail. . . ."

Going back further—to the beginning of the century—we rediscover the work of another cartoonist who was also first an artist. As a matter of fact, he emerged from out of the ranks of painters to dazzle readers with his pen-and-ink masterpieces. He is the enigmatic Heinrich Kley.

Dover Publications, in the introduction to *The Drawings of Heinrich Kley* (1962), calls Kley "one of the greatest cartoonists of modern time." Certainly in his day, as a contributor to humor magazines in Germany, he was immensely popular, with several collections of his works issued between 1909 and 1923. The Germany that emerged from World War I largely forgot him, and little is known of his later years. It is not certain when he died; like Ambrose Bierce, he seems simply to have disappeared.

It is difficult, too, to categorize him. The drawings he produced were certainly not conventional; they were cartoon fantasies, satirical, erotic, sometimes shocking, as when he showed an African woman nursing two baby elephants or a monster roasting tiny human beings on a stick over an open fire, sprinkling them with salt.

From *The Drawings of Heinrich Kley.*

In the preceding sketch, a study in balance and tension, you see his admirable draftsmanship and his fine-pen technique.

Another cartoonist who was as much artist as cartoonist was Boardman Robinson. After working as an illustrator/cartoonist for the *New York Morning Telegraph*, the *New York Herald*, *The Masses*, *The Liberator*, *Harper's Weekly*, and the *London Outlook*,

The

Boardman began his teaching career at the Art Students League in 1924.

To adequately display this powerful editorial cartoon of Robinson's, *The Masses,* militantly anti-war, gave it a full two-page spread (each page was 10½″ × 13¼″). The year was 1916.

Editorial cartooning at about this time tended to divide into two main schools so far as technique was concerned: pen-

ter

and-ink drawings, which were more touching than argumentative; and grease-crayon sketches on rough-textured paper, combined with bold brush strokes, that championed social and often radical causes. "Saber-toothed cartoons," Max Eastman called them. Cartoons of the former school flourished in the Midwest; of the latter, in New York.

R. A. Lewis, whose editorial cartoons for many years appeared on the front page of the *Milwaukee Journal*, was among those cartoonists and artists who went to Boardman Robinson to learn the grease-crayon technique. Robinson, in turn, had been greatly influenced by eighteenth- and nineteenth-century satirists in Europe who made lithographic prints. Because many of the cartoons of this latter period showed garbage (or ash) cans to symbolize slum areas, the style became known as the Ash Can School.

Lewis himself was liberal but never doctrinaire; his attack, if telling, was usually gentle, despite his bold style.

Among his admirers was Herblock of the *Washington Post*. (Herblock as a newspaper cartoonist goes back to 1929.) "His drawing combines sureness and a simplicity with a delicate craftsmanship which make his work particularly appreciated by professional colleagues who understand the subtleties of his skill," Herblock observed.

Opposite is an excellent example of the Lewis touch: a cartoon drawn the day after the December 7, 1941, attack on Pearl Harbor.

Perhaps the best-known exponent of the Ash Can style among American newspaper cartoonists was Daniel Fitzpatrick, who spent nearly five decades with the *St. Louis Post-Dispatch*. His successor, Bill Mauldin, who moved on to the *Chicago Sun-Times*, bears some of the marks of the Ash Can style, but his work has always been more playful and more detailed than the work of the artists who came up in *The Masses* tradition.

Counterfeit Styles

The Mother Earth News in its first issue said that ". . . you will find that the best cartoon instruction in the world is only

If There's Another Job to Do, We'll Do It

as far away as the nearest printed cartoon." As this magazine saw it, the beginning cartoonist can simply lift a little something from three or four cartoonists he admires, and presto! He has a style of his own. Which is precisely what many second- and third-rate cartoonists have done.

Even more reprehensible has been the practice of some beginning cartoonists to study the work of a single cartoonist, duplicate it verbatim, and then set out to cash in on it. What satisfaction can there be, aside from the monetary, in devoting one's career to the production of counterfeits?

Almost never does the imitation capture the flavor of the original. A rival panel to *Grin and Bear It* didn't come close to duplicating the relaxed artistry of George Lichty. The several advertising illustrators who try to duplicate the sweeping brush or pencil strokes of *New Yorker* contributor Charles Saxon (you find their work in ads in the medical journals) don't fool the connoisseur.

Sometimes the imitators become so numerous that the style itself, even in the hands of the originator, grows tiresome. Pat Oliphant, the *Washington Star* editorial cartoonist, and Jack Davis and Mort Drucker, the *Mad* cartoonists, to some extent suffer from overexposure brought on by their countless imitators.

Not that the beginning cartoonist does not derive some benefit from imitation. "We all begin by imitation," says Milton Glaser, the designer/illustrator and a founder of Push Pin Studios, New York. "The penalty for consistent imitation, unfortunately, is the erosion of personal vision and artistic sensibility."

The secret is for the cartoonist to do his imitating at the early stages of his development and for only a short period of time. He should move out on his own as soon as possible, determined to infuse his work with his own personality, with the thought of eventually developing a style different enough from any other to be instantly recognizable.

The temptation is great to draw in the style that for the

moment seems to prevail in the field where the cartoonist chooses to operate. It was difficult in the mid-1970s, for instance, for the new editorial cartoonists on newspapers to avoid the horizontal format and single- and double-tone chemically produced shading that had only recently grown so popular and that represented a' breakaway from the Grease-Crayon School.

Dugald Stermer, commenting on the fine-line caricatures of David Levine, which represented a very different style for the time, cited "David's desire not to fall into the political artist trap, in the way that the quasi-socialist realists of the thirties did; the Heroic Worker, Bloated Capitalist School of painting."

Not only does the professionally motivated cartoonist try to lay claim to an exclusive drawing style; he also stakes out a subject area for himself, if he can. And it isn't just the comic-strip artist who does this. Before the fatal accident in his Jaguar, *The New Yorker's* Sam Cobean ("His drawings were beautiful—he drew more easily than anyone I ever knew," Charles Addams said of him) had the daydream—a balloon above a man's head, usually with a nude involved—pretty much to himself because of repeated use. And before Cobean, Addams fenced in the haunted house and the macabre. In more recent times, *Playboy's* Gahan Wilson cornered the market on weirdos and sick humor. (Example from his syndicated Sunday feature: a man is shaking hands with another man with three heads, and he's saying: "Of course I remember you.")

The newly aware may not appreciate these priorities. My young son came running to me one day with a Charles Addams collection from my library. "Look, Dad!" he shouted, the mark of discovery on his face. "Someone copied the Addams family from TV!"

Changing Styles

A comparison of Charles Schulz's first strips in the early 1950s with his latest strips shows a pronounced change in style. Most other comic-strip artists have changed their styles, too, and always gradually enough so that their readers have not been aware of the changes. The cartoonist often makes his changes unconsciously, partly as a result of his maturing and partly as a result of his awareness of changing tastes among his readers.

Garry Trudeau with his *Doonesbury* started out with a style that can best be described as "Yellow-Pages Modern." For one thing, it was too weak to stand the reduction the strip had to take to appear in the newspapers. After a few years Trudeau has been able to polish and strengthen his drawing, although it still cannot compare to the work of Charles Schulz, Mort Walker, Johnny Hart, Russ Myers, Dik Browne, Al Capp, Art Sansom, Brant Parker, the late Walt Kelly, or others of the humorous-strip artists.

Some comic-strip artists manage to keep their features alive without adapting their styles to the times. Their followers are loyal enough to hang on, seemingly endlessly; in fact, they would object strenuously to any change in their artists' approaches.

Once a cartoonist develops a style that suits him it is easy for him to fall into the rut of reproducing the same figures and props in cartoon after cartoon. Some of the nation's most successful cartoonists—and I would have to include the great Herblock among them—work in styles so predictable that their cartoons, from a drawing standpoint, are no longer fun to anticipate. These cartoonists might just as well have rubber stamps made of the characters and props; creating their cartoons, then, could be simply a matter of stamping out the characters in the various arrangements necessary.

A gag cartoonist who has changed styles completely in recent years is *The New Yorker*'s William Steig. It used to be difficult to tell a Steig cartoon from a Syd Hoff. Today Steig is among the most experimental of cartoonists, in some respects rivaling Saul Steinberg. There is a playful, flossy, unreal quality to Steig's work now. What he creates lies somewhere between spot illustration and gag cartooning. Not long ago he showed what could have been an idyllic setting from the past. A man with a loaf of bread, a jug of wine, and thou. But thou was loudly and angrily nagging at him. He looked glum indeed.

Reamer Keller, another gag cartoonist, has operated quite differently. "My big problem is [that] my style has remained consistent over the years," he says. "Sure wish it would improve!" But in Keller's case, why should it? There is a quality there—a style—that sets him well apart from the general run. Vip has the quality, too.

In cartoon illustration—especially in the field of advertising—the look of today, whatever that might be, is more important than in other areas of cartooning. The advertising fraternity, whatever its immunity to criticism, cannot tolerate the criticism that it is not "with it." The hot cartoonist of the 1950s is not likely to appeal to the advertising agency art director of the 1970s, unless there has come about a general revival of the cartoonist's style.

Of course, advertising agencies direct their clients' campaigns to specific audiences, and if an audience is of an age group that appreciates an earlier style, a cartoonist from that era might well do a better job for the client than an upstart.

Given a choice, an agency would rather hire a name cartoonist—one with an established comic strip or a string of published gag cartoons in general-circulation magazines—than an unknown cartoonist, regardless of style.

In 1967 Volkswagen of America hired many of the best-known gag cartoonists to do gags about The Bug and published the results in *Think Small,* a small hardbound book distributed by its dealers. Vip was there. So was George Price.

On page 254 is one of two George Price cartoons done for the *Think Small* book.

If you look closely you can see the "split line" technique in several spots in the drawing: down the right edge of the pole supporting the parking meter, for instance; and where the left

"He's the one luxury we allow ourselves."

leg of the passerby joins the bottom edge of his suit coat. That old lady sitting in the right front seat is a familiar character in Price's cartoons.

The cartoonist looking for advertising commissions can, if the times move away from him, wait until they swing back around again, but that may not be in his lifetime. If he can manage it, he adjusts his style to fit the art directors' fickle tastes.

Revivals

Styles do have a way of returning to favor. What's "in" for a few years goes out again, and then a new wave of cartoonists sets the standards. Often the new standards look remarkably like the standards of a previous generation.

It is true that the underground cartoonists, with their crowded compositions, multiplicity of lines, and deliberate crudeness of style, greatly influenced the straight cartoonists of the 1970s. But study the work of Robert Crumb, the most admired and imitated of the underground cartoonists (he did the art that inspired the "Keep on Truckin' " bumper stickers), and you can see the influence of turn-of-the century cartoonists F. Opper and Zim and later cartoonists George Herriman and Basil Wolverton.

Versatility

Not only does a cartoonist face the problem of changing with the times, but he also faces the problem, if he is into advertising and editorial illustration, of working in several styles simultaneously.

Don Thompson shows his versatility in ink styles in *Aramco World Magazine,* a company publication of the Arabian

American Oil Company, Beirut, Lebanon.[1] His three different
line illustrations were done for three different articles in a
single issue. The biggest is one of several done for an article
entitled "Diary of a Dig." It has a pleasant sketchy look,
probably accomplished with pen and ink or possibly a Pentel
or Rapidograph. It is a sort of sophisticated version of the
childlike sketches of Hendrik Willem van Loon.

The tightly drawn, highly stylized second illustration
showing three gunmen is one of several for "The Bey from
Virginia." This drawing has an Aubrey Beardsley look to it—
dated and decorative.

The third Thompson example is one of several done for
"Aesop of the Arabs." It is done in heavy strokes, not unlike
what one might achieve with a linoleum block or woodblock,
but without the crudeness. (Of course some woodcuts are
anything but crude.) The art also has a calligraphic look about
it, the flow of the lines carefully controlled. Note the
simplicity in Thompson's handling of the feet.

Of course, for a single article requiring more than one
illustration, the cartoonist would use the same style throughout. Furthermore, he would create his drawings so that they
would take the same reduction. If one were to be played up
more than the others, the cartoonist would draw it bigger.
Otherwise, the drawings within the article would vary in line
strengths. Unity would suffer.

The following illustrations are evidence of the growth
and versatility of Irwin Caplan, starting with a gag cartoon he
did for *The Saturday Evening Post* at the end of the 1950s (Caplan
began freelancing in New York right after World War II). The
other pieces include a line drawing of a landmark house in
Seattle, one of a series he did for Cone-Heiden, a printing
company; "The Common Loon," another line drawing, but
more stylized, used as a cover for a Pacific Northwest Bell
publication (McCann-Erickson, agency); a very contemporary
cartoon with old-fashioned crosshatching, used to illustrate
the headline "Gaco Sticks With You All the Way" in an ad for

---

1. Part of the material in this and the "Techniques Unlimited" section
appeared in a different form in "The Look of the Book," a column I write
for *IABC News,* monthly publication of the International Association of
Business Communicators.

Courtesy of Irwin Caplan.

...or. Stop beginning every sentence with 'confidentially'."

THE SATURDAY EVENING POST

THE COMMON LOON

With so many homes to choose from and Washington Mutual dying to lend you the money at new low interest rates, why aren't you out looking for a home?

WASHINGTON MUTUAL SAVINGS BANK

Gaco Western, Inc. (Kraft, Smith & Lowe, agency); and finally
a whole ad put together and drawn by Caplan in an Art Deco
style. Even the typeface—Windsor Bold—seems to fit the
mood. (Kraft, Smith & Lowe again was the agency.)

"Past experience in gag cartooning and writing, for me,
has been of enormous help in conceptual thinking when
applied to general graphic design problems," says Caplan, a
half-time lecturer in the Graphic Design Department of the
School of Art, University of Washington.

Two Basic Styles

It is possible to reduce the various styles to two: tight and
loose.

A tight style is marked by careful planning and controlled outlining and texturing. The cartoon looks as though it
took hours to draw. And it probably did. Hugh Haynie among
the editorial cartoonists draws in a tight style. Haynie also has
a mannerism (not to be confused with style) which sets his
work apart: a too small border out of which juts the major
figure or prop in each cartoon.

A loose style is marked by sweeping, carefree strokes.
You get the feeling the cartoonist thoroughly enjoyed himself
while he produced the drawing and that he didn't spend much
time on it. Maybe he did; maybe he didn't. Robert Osborn,
whose work appeared for so many years in *The New Republic,*
George Lichty, and Charles Saxon all draw in a loose style.

"If your drawing is simple, or doodle-like," says Jules
Feiffer, "it's not because you don't know how to draw, but
rather, because after considerable experience, you've arrived
at a shorthand style stating exactly what you want to state—
without any extras at all. This takes a hell-of-a-lot of time—it
can take forever. I'm still trying to figure out my style."

Often the loosely drawn cartoon you see in print resulted
from several tries. And perhaps chunks of several drawings
were pieced together to achieve the fresh, unlabored look.

The preceding drawing *was* done in a hurry, with just a few unconnected brush strokes pulled across rough-textured paper. The reader sees almost no detail. (If he is literal minded, he had better not count the fingers on the sailor's hand.) And yet this rough sketch says enough: that a sailor is being remembered at mail call. His elation is suggested by that tiny line emanating from the back of his head.

For many years the loose style has been on the ascendancy. The "roughs" that gag cartoonists submitted to magazines were bought "as is" and sent directly to the engraver. As Lord Peter Wimsey is made to say in a Dorothy L. Sayers novel, *Unnatural Death:* "The rough sketch is frequently so much more convincing than the worked-up canvas."

Paul Peter Porges (he signs his work "Porges") as a gag cartoonist (he's also a masterful oil painter) changed from a tight, heavy-line style—"The Grand Rapids School," he calls it—to one much freer. "One has to be extremely flexible in this field," he says. "You can't be smug and say, 'I've got a good, cute style and I'm going to exploit it and drain it to the end.' You have to be with it, see what's going on, and be aware of the handwriting on the wall. Always try to be one step ahead, as far as market potentialities are concerned. There's no such thing as a secure style."

But the 1970s saw a renaissance of the tight style,

especially in editorial cartoons, illustrative cartoons, and cartoon creations. Just as fashion relaxed its grip and made room for almost any dress style, so did the mass media find room for tightly drawn cartoons as well as loosely drawn ones.

One of the most beautiful tight styles today belongs to Bud Blake, a former advertising agency art director who does a cute-kids strip for King Features: *Tiger*, less cerebral than *Peanuts* and not nearly as funny, but still worth studying for the art alone. Blake's line is sure and clean, with each panel thoughtfully arranged. His solid black accents are masterfully placed.

We have a tendency to associate detail and decoration with a tight style. But tight drawings, like loose drawings, can be simplified. When a tight drawing is simplified, it is called a stylized drawing. Following are two examples.

The one on the left is a carefully executed drawing (artist unknown) where detail is sacrificed to both simplicity and boldness. In fact, the car and its passengers are reduced to an abstraction. Despite the lack of detail, you read the drawing immediately as a car, and you see right away that it carries several passengers. The drawing was used in a company magazine published by the Exxon Company and in similar magazines during the 1974 energy crisis as a heading for columns promoting car pools.

The other example—from *Chemical Chronicle,* a publication of the Chemical Bank, New York—is an anonymous drawing used to illustrate an article on financial counseling for employees. Notice that the outline is bold and uniform. The eyes are simple dots. Not only has detail been eliminated (no eyebrows, no folds in the ears), but only parts of the faces are shown. Yet the point comes across immediately: one person talking to another. Some observers call this kind of art "posterized art." It is especially useful for any printing meant to be seen from a distance.

Line and Halftone Processes

Unlike paintings, cartoons are created specifically to be reproduced. The originals are likely to show scars where the cartoonist has scraped away unwanted lines with a razor blade. Or there may be patches of paper or white paint over which the cartoonist has redrawn a face or corrected some lettering. No matter. The camera used in the reproduction process does not notice.

That is, it doesn't notice unless the cartoon is to be reproduced by the *halftone process.* In that case, scratches and patches *will* show. Cartoons that require the halftone reproduction process include wash drawings; paintings in either transparent or opaque mediums; some pencil drawings; and photographs of three-dimensional art.

Cartoons that can take *line reproduction* include pen or brush and ink drawings, with or without Craftint, Grafix, Ben Day, or Zipatone shading; grease-crayon drawings; scratchboard drawings; and prints from woodblocks or linoleum blocks.

A word about Craftint and its present equivalent: Grafix. These are drawing papers or boards into which is built a pattern of fine, perfectly parallel (single-tone) or cross-hatched (double-tone) lines that give the cartoon the illusion of grays. The pattern doesn't show until the cartoonist brings it out by brushing on a chemical solution. Crane made the most of the technique in the early years. Today, it is a technique used by many if not most of the editorial cartoonists who work in a horizontal format, among them Pat Oliphant, Jeff MacNelly, Paul Szep, Doug Marlette, Bill Schorr, and Don Wright.

Ben Day is a pattern applied by the printer, either on the negative or on the plate. The cartoonist indicates where he wants the Ben Day to go with light blue shading. The light blue does not reproduce in the line process.

When the cartoonist wants to stay in command of where the shading is to go in a cartoon destined for line reproduction, he uses Zipatone or any of several other brands of shading sheets. These transparent sheets come with any number of patterns: dots, parallel lines, crosshatched lines, herringbones, etc. The reverse sides of these sheets are lightly waxed to make them sticky enough to attach themselves to the drawing. The cartoonist cuts away unwanted parts of the shading with a single-edged razor blade or knife.

Grease-crayon drawings start out as pen or brush and ink drawings on rough-textured paper. The shading is applied with a grease crayon that deposits pigment on the unrecessed parts of the paper.

Scratchboard drawings start out as layers of solid black paint spread out on hard-surface paper. The drawing is done by scratching away parts of the ink with a blade or knife.

The advantage of line reproduction to the cartoonist is that he knows ahead of time exactly what the cartoon will look like when it is reproduced, even if the work is reduced or enlarged. Black is black; what's black will show up as black. With a halftone, the cartoonist is never sure. The printed cartoon always carries some surprises. The screen used in the halftone process to break up gray areas into a pattern of dots may interpret tones as darker or lighter than the cartoonist intended. And, of course, any smudges, scratches, patches, or folds will show up in the final print, possibly as dark blurs.

The advantage of the halftone is that it gives a

photographic quality to the work and allows for subtle tones of gray. There are two kinds of halftones: (1) square or rectangular halftones, where a faint tint of gray extends across the whole of the cartoon; and (2) highlight or dropout halftones, where the white of the paper comes through occasionally to provide greater contrast. The latter is preferable to the former.

Comic strips and editorial cartoons are almost always reproduced by the line process. Some gag cartoons are reproduced in line, some (wash drawings) in halftone.

It makes no difference how the publication is printed— whether by letterpress or offset lithography; the cartoon ends up either as a halftone or a line reproduction. An advantage of offset—a printing process that has overtaken letterpress in publications work—is that the screen used in the halftone process can be fine, for greater detail, even though the paper is newsprint-like in quality. Furthermore, it is cheaper to reproduce art—line or halftone—by offset than by letterpress because photoengravings are not involved.

Peter Arno and Charles Addams, more than any other gag cartoonists perhaps, made wash drawings popular. Letterpress reproduction on high-quality paper in *The New Yorker* gave their cartoons sparkle.

A wash drawing is a sort of watercolor painting, but it is done in various shades of gray rather than in colors. The gray comes from watered-down india ink or from a tube of lampblack. The usual procedure is to make several puddles of wash, each a little lighter than its neighbor. After first outlining the drawing in regular india ink and allowing the outlines to dry, the cartoonist begins painting in the tones, starting with the lightest. (He can always go back and darken the tones. He can't go back and lighten them.)

In doing a wash drawing, the cartoonist must work fast— and on heavy paper or illustration board with a semi-rough surface—or "tooth"—that will accept the wash and not wrinkle. To escape a muddy look, the cartoonist avoids painting over any area that is still wet. Before painting in any washes, of course, but after the inked outlines are thoroughly dry, the cartoonist erases any pencil lines made in the preliminary sketching stage.

Following are two of my own wash drawings done for newspaper reproduction. For reasons too complicated to go into here, it was necessary for me to use a fluorographic solvent in place of water, but the drawing and painting process was essentially the same as described above.

"TAKE A FEW STEPS BACKWARD, WHY DON'T YOU...."

The first was an editorial cartoon commenting on a bill being considered by the Oregon legislature some years back that would have closed down Sunday businesses. The second was used to illustrate a nostalgic newspaper feature on America's one-time fascination with radio drama. The article made the point that in some ways radio was more absorbing (consider the "Men from Mars" broadcast in the late 1930s) than television ever became. To do this cartoon I had to go to my files to find examples of 1930s furniture and dress—and, of course, an example of a 1930s radio. The washes here help emphasize the light coming from the two lamps. They also emphasize the light on the radio dial.

You may notice a couple of vertical lines just to the right of center and at the top. They illustrate the sensitivity of the halftone process. The cartoon had been stored under another cartoon that had a piece of Scotch tape attached to it; the tape bled slightly and left yellow marks on this cartoon. I couldn't paint the marks out without disrupting the gray tone, and the camera couldn't ignore the flaw. Had the cartoon been done for line reproduction. . . .

In the latter part of the nineteenth century, Georges Seurat, Paul Signac, and other impressionist painters in France developed a technique of putting small dots of pure colors on canvases and letting viewers "mix" the paints optically. They called their technique "Pointillism." The half-tone reproduction process, which came later, made use of the same principle. Dots of varying sizes, printed in black ink on white paper, could be read as shades of gray.

In the following illustration for a present-day ad with the headline, "In Business, You Have to Know Almost as Much as You Pretend to," Sean Harrison made use of Pointillism to draw his own halftone. You can see the change of tone as the dots merge into black areas. Even the signature is in "halftone." I put halftone in quotes because this work, as presented to the printer, is already "screened" and ready for line reproduction. It really is a line drawing.

S. Harrison

Courtesy of Information for Business, New York.

Techniques Unlimited

I attended a high school large enough to support a weekly eight-column printed newspaper. Although offset had taken over a sizable portion of the yearbook market in those days, it had not yet made inroads into the newspaper business. We could not afford photoengravings, so for art in the paper, a staffer had to take the bus downtown and beg plates from the two metropolitan newspapers. If we wanted to run a student cartoon, we had to get the cartoonist to make his own plate. This meant he had to sketch out his ideas on a piece of linoleum and then carve out those parts he didn't want to show.

As editor/artist I did my share of these cartoons, and I still have scars on my hands to prove it. The Speedball cutting tool I used would often slip across the slick, hard surface of the linoleum and plant itself into my left hand, which held the block down.

Eventually I developed a routine of warming the linoleum in an oven, making it soft and easy to carve. And I developed the art to a point—this was important to me—that made the cut indistinguishable from a regular line engraving. Thin lines with few solid blacks.

It wasn't until much later, as a professional, that I developed an appreciation for linoleum block printing as an art of its own. I did not realize, in my salad days, that every medium has its strengths. Just as brush strokes added to the enjoyment of a fine painting, I discovered, so did boldness and crudeness add to the enjoyment of art used commercially. Linoleum block printing was, after all, similar to woodcut art, an example of which you see in the following work by a nineteenth-century English writer and illustrator, Joseph Crawhall.

I have in recent years tried to duplicate the crude linoleum-block look with scratchboard and with matchsticks rather than pens and brushes—anything to maximize and capitalize on the imperfection of lines. I have even worked small and asked my editor to enlarge my drawing rather than reduce it.

A cartoonist should force himself to change mediums once in a while and, sticking to one medium, use the tool in different ways. If he is a pen-and-ink man, he should try unfamiliar pen points. If he has always drawn in pen and ink he should switch to a brush; and he should try the more painterly mediums, like washes (black water colors) and opaques (oils, temperas, and acrylics). In his morgue he should have a file of examples of various art mediums and styles to turn to to stimulate his imagination.

Among comic-strip artists, Roy Crane was the great experimenter. Early in his career he used pen and ink, pretty much in the manner of all the early cartoonists. Occasionally, when he wanted the effect of disaster or tragedy, he would slip his readers a strip that used grease-crayon shading, in the manner of Robert Minor, Boardman Robinson, and other somber editorial cartoonists associated with *The Masses.* In the mid-1930s he began using Craftint. Craftint gave Crane's work a more polished appearance, in one way improving it, in another detracting from its spontaneity.

Tony Auth, the editorial cartoonist for the *Philadelphia Inquirer,* says, "I don't think . . . that . . . cartoonists have to use the same kind of paper every day, or . . . a particular pen or brush. The way you do a drawing ought to be determined by the problem that a certain drawing presents."

Any drawing tool will work, provided it makes a mark clear enough and black enough to be picked up by the camera.

One cartoonist, Jim Berry (*Berry's World*), does his final sketch with an ordinary dark-lead pencil, scrubbing his lines on the paper to give them thickness and strength.

Comic-strip artists work mostly in pen and india ink; editorial cartoonists in brush and ink and, for shading, grease crayon or Grafix; gag cartoonists in pen or brush and ink and, for some publications, washes.

But other tools are used, too. The nylon-tip marker has lately proved popular with many cartoonists. Unfortunately, the point wears down quickly, and the line becomes thick and slightly fuzzy; but sometimes the cruder look of a line made with an old Pentel or Flair is to be preferred to the fine-line look it offers when new. An interesting effect can be had with the nylon-tip marker by chopping off the tip and making a chisel-point instrument out of it.

Should the cartoonist want to draw in a decorative style using a uniformly fine line, he should try a Rapidograph technical fountain pen. As with a Pentel, he can make his drawing without ever lifting the instrument from the paper. The haughty and fashionable (for the mid-1970s) young lady in the preceding drawing was drawn with a Rapidograph. The pen comes in a variety of point strengths, from micro thin to macro thick. This drawing was done with an "extra fine" pen (No. 0), which is still four pens removed from the Rapidograph with the finest point. If the cartoonist plans to have his drawing reproduced, it doesn't pay to go to too fine a point; the printer will have trouble reproducing the drawing.

Compare the woman at the left with the man at the right, who is drawn in brush (No. 1 red sable) and ink. Notice that some of the drawing is in shadow—in solid black. Working this way, it is necessary for the cartoonist to establish a light source. Here it comes from in back of the man. So brilliant is the light it obliterates much of the outline of the back of the man's suit.

I offer these two drawings together to show basic applications of the Rapidograph and the brush, but ordinarily, a cartoonist would not combine two different techniques in a single cartoon. An exception can be seen in a Saul Steinberg cover for *The New Yorker* (November 23, 1968). It was a family portrait, each member drawn differently: a middle-aged salesman-type in bold Speedball lines, an old father in crosshatching, a fragile daughter in weak pencil strokes, a flighty mother in scribbled lines, a child in the stick-figure style we associate with children's drawings. He did a similar *New Yorker* cover (January 6, 1975) when he showed a drawing of various drawing instruments: the pen and the ink bottle were drawn in pen and ink; the color pencil was drawn with a color pencil; the ordinary lead pencil was drawn with an ordinary pencil; and the brush was drawn in watercolor, with a brush.

Alfredo Alcala, a top comic-book artist (*Marvel Comics*) who lives in the Philippines, invented his own drawing tool: a "fountain brush." He got tired of constantly dipping a brush into a bottle of india ink, so he got a Chinese brush, ripped off the bristles, got an old fountain pen, unscrewed the tip, and worked the bristles into the end. Apparently there are some commercial versions available—made in Japan and Germany.

There is also the possibility of pasting pieces of paper together to make cartoon collages.

Of course, an ordinary ballpoint pen, with black ink, can be used for drawing cartoons, too. Art-supply stores make available a ballpoint with india ink cartridges. But most cartoonists find a ballpoint, with its lack of flexibility, a less than satisfying drawing instrument compared to others that are available. And anyone who takes pride in his handwriting or who dabbles in calligraphy and is used to a regular fountain pen or an Osmiroid would become apoplectic at the suggestion that he use a ballpoint. His reaction would be a little like that of that highly cultured gentleman in a classic Peter Arno cartoon being helped out of a classy restaurant, badly shaken after overhearing a young couple at the table next to him ordering Scotch and 7-Up.

Another tool useful to the cartoonist is the camera. Adventure-strip artists and some editorial cartoonists use a camera to take pictures of relatives, friends, and even paid models, which they can refer to while drawing. A Polaroid Land Camera is especially useful because with it the cartoonist can have his printed reference material within seconds.

If the cartoonist does his work as sculpture, he needs to photograph it finally, of course, so that his publisher will have the necessary art from which to make a halftone.

The combination photograph-and-cartoon technique—especially when it involves a photograph head and a cartoon body—has been overused, but it is a technique still useful in the hands of an artist with talent. On page 272 is an excellent example, dreamed up by NEA graphics director Rudy Hoglund, who made the photographs, and drawn by Art Sansom, whose strip is the subject of the advertising. NEA ran this ad in *Editor & Publisher* to promote *The Born Loser*, one of its most popular offerings. Take time to observe all the mishaps that occur to Art Sansom in the panels.

There has developed in photography a movement that John Peter, the magazine designer, calls "concept photography": gimmick photography used as if it were an editorial cartoon, often on the cover of a magazine. For the January

The Born Loser

"Hi! I'm Art Sansom. I do The Born Loser comic strip for NEA."

"In it I try to portray the universal human experience of falling flat on one's face."

"I've observed that many people suffer one pratfall after another."

"I watch everybody. I take notes. I've become a student of the human condition."

"Still, I can't explain why some people seem destined to be losers."

"But thank heaven for the losers. They give me an endless source of inspiration for my strip."

"I hope you're considering The Born Loser for your newspaper. Hundreds of newspapers use it and, I'm proud to report, my strip is Number One in many recent surveys."

"There's nothing like a winner. Or a Born Loser."

NEA Newspaper Enterprise Association

The Born Loser is just one of the many fine newspaper features available as part of the NEA Daily and Sunday Services. For information and rates, contact Dick Johnson or Ron Hawkins, 1200 W. 3rd St., Cleveland, Ohio 44113. Phone: 216-621-7300.

Courtesy of Newspaper Enterprise Association (NEA).

1974 cover of *Harper's*, for instance, Sheila Berger, art director, and photographer Jimmy Saratochiello, to illustrate the blurb "The Arabian Fantasy," bought a gas pump nozzle and hose and rented a carpet; put the carpet on a platform in a studio with plastic foam underneath to make it look wavy; put a stiff wire in the gas pump nozzle and hose to make it stand up; silhouetted the studio shot and then superimposed it on a photograph of sky. Result: a flying carpet with a symbol of oil.

Another tool used by some cartoonists is the airbrush, which sprays gray water color in various and gradual degrees of intensity, giving the drawing roundness and a kind of super-realism. Robert Grossman used the airbrush technique to unite a series of cartoons for full-page ads sponsored by New York Life in the 1970s. The headline for the following illustration, which ran in *Ebony*, reads: "The Woman Who Works. New York Life Believes She Needs Protection as Much as a Man."

Courtesy New York Life Insurance Company.

Even wire can be used. As part of its permanent collection, the Museum of Modern Art, New York, has a wire-construction figure by Alexander Calder (he's the artist who did the flashy paint jobs for Braniff International planes) called "The Hostess," a snobbish-looking lady carrying her eyeglasses on a stick, walking stiffly along, apparently on her way to greet some guests. Paul J. Sachs in his *Modern Prints & Drawings* calls it "witty, waggish, and sophisticated. The characterization is based on keen observation and endless practice; an ingenious invention by a shrewd Yankee tinker."

But to start with, the cartoonist will probably want to try the time-tested and still popular drawing pen: a metal point that the cartoonist sets into a wooden holder. An art supply store offers the cartoonist a bewildering assortment of points, some stiff, some flexible. Fortunately, the price per point is still a matter of pennies; the cartoonist can pick up several and try them to discover which one most suits his style. Basil Wolverton, to display his spaghetti-and-meatball style, uses a Gillott extra fine 1068 and a Gillott 303. Reamer Keller, the gag cartoonist, reports: "Sometimes I use a penpoint that will splay out nicely (Esterbrook #788), or a brush—and on the pages of cartoons I do for the *N.Y. Sunday News:* [a] Speedball #4." *The New Yorker's* Barney Tobey, whose style can best be described as juicy and satisfying, after trying all kinds of tools, settled for an old fountain pen, which he dips into india ink.

The Drawing Process

The born cartoonist draws constantly, not necessarily to produce pieces he can use or save but to register in his mind the quirks of body structure, movement, and expression. He learns to draw rapidly. When the time comes to produce a cartoon for publication, he may, in his haste, ignore what he has learned through observation, putting too many or too few fingers on a hand, for instance; but nobody minds much. What he does try to avoid is making a basic mistake in construction, such as putting the thumb on the wrong side of the hand, easier to do than you might imagine.

Getting it wrong is not peculiar to cartoonists. The writer Louis Nizer is quoted in *Grit:* "When a man points a finger at someone else he should remember that four of his fingers are pointing at himself." A nice thought, but not probable unless the man is someone drawn by Charles Addams or Vip.

Another writer—for a religious magazine—used a three-legged stool as a figure of speech. Shorten one leg, he said, and the stool will wobble. Not so, wrote in an alert reader. A *four*-legged stool with one leg shortened will wobble, but not a three-legged stool.

Some years ago a major newspaper, to reach media buyers in advertising agencies, ran an ad with art like the following drawing. Each gear was supposed to represent some good quality of the paper. The three qualities worked together to make the paper a good medium to advertise in. So the text said. But could gears placed like that work at all? Some readers thought not, and the newspaper made a necessary adjustment in the art by disengaging the two bottom gears from each other.

For most cartoonists, the idea phase—even for an illustrative cartoon—takes more time than the drawing phase. Once the cartoonist has his message worked out and his composition visualized, he can, depending upon his work practices and drawing style, dash off his drawing in a matter of minutes. For some cartoonists—and for some cartoons— the drawing may take much longer. Rube Goldberg is said to have worked as long as thirty hours on some of those cartoon inventions of his.

Russell Myers, who does *Broom Hilda*, draws rapidly—as if

the room were on fire, as he puts it—with an ordinary fountain pen. "I get it done as spontaneously as I'm able to. I make a lot of mistakes, use a lot of white paint, and if the retouch paint industry went out of business, I'd have to go into the aluminum-door game tomorrow." He draws in a size three times larger than it will appear in print. The reduction minimizes the imperfections.

Typically, the cartoonist sketches out the cartoon in light pencil lines first, erasing and redrawing; then, when he's satisfied with the arrangement, he inks in the lines. He works from top left to bottom right to keep his hand off lines that may be slow in drying. But Glenn Bernhardt says, "I've never finished a drawing without smearing a pen line."

Inking for some cartoonists is merely a matter of careful tracing. For others, it involves additional drawing, because as they ink they change their minds about, say, the size of a nose or the length of an arm. My own tendency is to trace lines that are only suggestive, so that my finished product looks considerably different from the rough pencil sketch. I have a kind of I-can't-wait-to-see-how-it-will-turn-out feeling as I ink in. Using a brush rather than a pen I can expect some happy accidents, because a brush more than a pen has a tendency to surprise you by its sudden turns and swellings.

In an unfinished drawing (p. 277) from the Peacock Collection at the University of Oregon, you can see how cartoonist Homer Davenport sketched in his cartoon with rough pencil strokes and then went over them carefully in ink. Davenport worked large, in almost a poster size. His drawings were greatly reduced to minimize any imperfection in the lines.

We do not know why Davenport did not finish this cartoon. Possibly he was not satisfied with the likeness he had achieved for Theodore Roosevelt. Nor do we know the occasion for the cartoon. It may have been a first try at the famous "He's Good Enough for me!" cartoon. If it was, Davenport changed the final version considerably.

David Seavey, staff artist for *The National Observer,* unlike

other illustrators and cartoonists, does not sketch in rough outlines with a pencil. From the start, he works in ink.

First he does a preliminary sketch. Then he slips it under a sheet of frosted acetate or tracing paper and redraws it, again in ink, making whatever adjustments are necessary. He repeats the process any number of times—until, as he puts it, "the necessary refinement is achieved."

All in Line

There are lines. And there are lines. They range from the confident, carefully turned calligraphic lines of Hank Ketcham and the late Walt Kelly to the squiggly lines of Edward Koren of *The New Yorker* and the nervous lines of R. O. Blechman.

**WOULD A SMALL TOWN HAVE THE
COUNTRY'S MOST MODERN TRANSIT SYSTEM?**

Blechman's nervous-line technique can be seen in a cartoon used by the *Oakland Tribune* as an illustration for an ad designed to reach media buyers in agencies with the message that the *Tribune* is "The biggest paper in Northern California's biggest market." (The agency that prepared the ad is Botsford Ketchum Inc.) Blechman is perhaps best remembered for his animated art for the talking stomach commercial sponsored by Alka-Seltzer.

The original nervous outline—that of Chon Day—came about accidentally. As Day tells it, he got a bad batch of drawing paper during the shortages of World War II. The paper was rough or "sticky" enough to cause his pen to stumble as he drew. He rather liked the effect, and thereafter sought out the paper. "I never was much for using a rule for getting straight lines anyway," he says. Day's simple, innocent style allowed him to get away with an occasional nude in family magazines in the days when nudes in print were a novelty. An editor at *This Week* told Day there was no objection at the magazine because his nudes were "as sexy as vegetables."

A different kind of outline can be had through a process known as contour drawing. In this process, the cartoonist never lifts his drawing tool off the paper. The tool has to be a

Rapidograph, Pentel, or similar instrument that doesn't have to be dipped periodically into an ink bottle. A more extreme version is blind contour drawing, a process where the cartoonist doesn't look at what he's drawing until it's finished.

WHAT'S WRONG WITH THIS PICTURE?

Courtesy of *Topics* magazine.

Mark S. Fisher for a back cover illustration for *Topics,* a publication of New England Telephone, Boston, used an unusual technique in which his lines swell at points where they run into other lines. The answer to the headline, by the way, was "Everything." The copy under the drawing went on to explain that "we're in the middle of a serious and continuing energy shortage. . . . So if you don't really need it, don't plug it in, drive it or turn it on."

Cartoonist Frank Farah's problem in a newspaper adver-

Does City Hall Need Electric Headache No. 54?

Vote **NO** on Portland City Measure **54**

tisement was to get across to Portland voters the idea that City Hall had enough problems without taking over a major electric power company. He uses an "antiqued" decorative style for his nearly full-page cartoon to show what City Hall might look like if the measure passed. It didn't. (McCann-Erickson was the agency.)

For side views, a cartoonist has the option of drawing in silhouette form, as Dorothy Bond has done here for a decorative item that goes on all her business stationery. The beauty of a drawing like this is that it can be reduced substantially from its original size with no danger that detail will be lost.

'WHAT'S GOOD FOR GM IS GOOD FOR THE COUNTRY...(GASP)... WHAT'S GOOD FOR GM IS GOOD FOR THE (WHEEZE) COUNTRY...(GASP)...WHAT'S GOOD FOR (PUFF) GM...IS...(PUFF)... '

Courtesy of Pete Wagner.

Pete Wagner, as editorial cartoonist for the University of Minnesota's *Minnesota Daily,* makes use of the silhouette technique to show Uncle Sam giving a push to the auto industry in harrowing 1975. Wagner includes just enough detail inside the silhouette to make his figure read well. And he adds some texture to the foreground to keep it from being monotonous. (As a student at Minnesota, Wagner saw his work reproduced in several metropolitan dailies and *The Progressive* magazine. College Press Service syndicated his cartoons.)

Shadows
It is possible for the cartoonist to draw without resorting to outlines. He uses shadows. To do this, the cartoonist first decides where the light is to come from. Then, using solid black or texture, he fills in those areas not likely to be

illuminated. He uses some hard-edged shadows and some soft-edged shadows. Hard-edged shadows occur when an object protrudes in front of the subject, blocking off the light. Soft-edged shadows occur where light leaks around a curve. The cartoonist tries to organize his shadows into large masses. Too many small shadows can result in a busy, cluttered look.

"I saw in the paper that every drink you take shortens your life four hours."

"Nonsense, if that were so I would have been dead long before I was born."

A cartoonist named Petersen in *Klods Hans*, Copenhagen, Denmark, for a pre-World War I illustrated joke shows how one can draw almost wholly in shadow.

The great David Low in a cartoon for the *London Telegraph*

made dramatic use of light and shadow to illuminate Benito Mussolini's lifting of the lid of hell in 1935, the year the imperialistic dictator invaded Ethiopia. This cartoon is worth studying for what it teaches about shadow placement when the light source comes from below. The strength of the cartoon comes from Low's use of grease crayon on rough-textured paper.

THE MAN WHO TOOK THE LID OFF.

Among comic-strip artists, Milton Caniff has probably made the most dramatic and consistent use of shadows. In the first two panels of a three-panel *Steve Canyon* strip from 1969 (shown close to actual size) you see Caniff at his spectacular

best in dealing with a light source. In Panel 1, using a bird's-eye view, he actually shows the source of light as well as the shadows cast by the source. Like spokes on a wheel, the shadows move outward from the source. Caniff also beautifully contrasts a tone of pen strokes with solid areas of black.

In Panel 2 he changes to a worm's-eye view and moves in close. Notice how he organizes his shadows into masses to keep his compositions from taking on a too-busy pattern. Caniff does not draw every wrinkle.

NO TROUBLE WITH THE GIRL AND THE OLD ONES—THEY WUZ SO BUSY WATCHIN' THE ICE SHOW THEY FORGOT TO LOOK FOR MEANIES!

On page 286 the complete strip is shown in a size closer to its printed size. Although each panel shows a different scene, when viewed together the panels form one well-composed piece of horizontal art. Note how the figures of one panel lead the eye into the figures of the next.

The all-shadow look can be achieved by the photographer, too, when he asks that his photograph, with its range of tones, be handled by the printer as though it were line art. Photographing it as line art, the printer allows all the middle to light tones to drop out and all the middle to dark tones to

add themselves to the solid black tones. The high contrast print, then, looks like a line drawing done in shadows.

Courtesy of David Seavey.

David Seavey, staff artist for *The National Observer*, eschews outlines in a sketch of Dwight Chapin, President Nixon's appointments secretary, in favor of shape and texture. He treats areas of the face as units almost unto themselves. Viewed in their entirety by the reader, the units add up to a well-drawn face, with all the details necessary to distinguish it from other faces. A great advantage of this kind of drawing is that the reader becomes involved. He uses his own imagination to furnish the missing outlines.

Even though he works shadows into figures and props, the cartoonist may leave them out of the faces, especially if the faces are small. Shadows can get too complicated on a small face. You can see, in the preceding cartoon, how shadowless faces coexist with a shadowed prop. Notice that the black shading on the car's left side is not brought all the way forward. It stops rather suddenly. And you see only a suggestion of black shading on the hood and on the right fender. Nor does the black extend all the way down in back on the left side. This adds to the roundness of the body. It also suggests a shine to the car's finish.

The lesson here is that it is not necessary to spread the

black all the way to the edges as you use it. Using black in a drawing is not like using color in a coloring book. Neatness does not necessarily count.

I leave it to your imagination what this couple is trying to escape from. But the black shadow under the car, removed as it is from the wheels, clearly establishes the fact that the car is moving right along.

Even without shadows, the cartoonist can help the reader feel a source of light. Where there would be shadow, the outline grows heavier. Notice how heavy the outline grows below the man's left arm.

A drawing of John F. Kennedy's "Eternal Flame" provides another example of roundness achieved through blackness that does not spread all the way to the outer edges of the items being drawn—in this case a disk and a cone. The medium is brush and ink and grease crayon on a rough-surface paper. The pattern created by the crayon, typical of what you find in editorial cartoons of the Mauldin-Herblock school, is strong enough to allow the cartoon to go as a line rather than a halftone reproduction.

Note how Ed Sullivan in the woman-reporter cartoon in Chapter 6 uses floating chunks of Zipatone that don't necessarily conform to the shape of areas where they are placed. This is called "off register" shading.

Texture

The cartoonist has a choice of two kinds of texture: mechanical or hand-drawn. Mechanical textures include sheets of thin plastic on which a pattern has been printed, like Zipatone; drawing paper with a built-in pattern; and the Ben Day process. Hand-drawn texture is anything the cartoonist wants to make it, just so it's clear enough to reproduce. For instance, it can be drops splattered from a toothbrush whose bristles, after an application of ink, are rubbed with a knife blade. Most commonly, hand-drawn texture is made with parallel or crosshatched pen strokes.

Sometimes the cartoonist tries for a more intricate texture, as when he puts a pattern onto a suit. In doing a suit pattern, he can either follow the contours, or he can lay his pattern flatly, as though he were using a sheet of Zipatone. Using the latter approach, the cartoonist comes up with a more stylized drawing.

A stipple-pattern Zipatone was applied to the sand area shown in the following cartoon. Because that pattern is so different from the others, it helps unite the sand castle to the shoreline and explain to the reader that the waters have moved in to destroy the boy's work.

Three distinct textures work together to give strength and solidity to the drawing. The sky employs some rather ordinary pen scratchings: sweeping lines, made with a flexible drawing pen. These lines are made with a swinging motion, keeping the wrist stiff, using the elbow as a pivot. The cartoonist can only get three or four lines down before he has to dip his pen in the ink again. Should he do a large mass of

this kind of texture, he'd probably want to use a Rapidograph.

The ocean area is drawn with a brush. Blacks are contrasted with whites; wavy lines are contrasted with zigzag lines.

The preceding Jim Seavey illustration for a *National Observer* article on prison systems is a beautiful study in pattern and texture, all hand drawn. It is also a study in contrasts. Notice especially the contrast between the wrinkles in the clothing and the harshness of the brick wall; and between the crosshatch shading in the center of the drawing and the parallel-line shading at the far right. Notice also that the figure in the foreground is detailed; the figure up in the tower is in silhouette. The units of the drawing hold together into an interesting, irregular shape, and this shape is contrasted with a line (with character of its own) that boxes the drawing off into a rectangle.

Marvin Mattelson uses very different kinds of hand-drawn textures for part of an Amtrak ad run in college news-

Courtesy of Amtrak.

papers with the headline: "There's a New Rule of Thumb for Weekends and Holidays. Amtrak." The primitive roundness is reminiscent of some of the art found in underground comics, which probably helps make the art appropriate to its audience. (The advertising agency is Ted Bates, New York.)

ABOUT TIME TO START SOMETHING

A contrast of textures—fine-line shading, crosshatching, polka-dot pattern, solid blacks, and shimmering blacks—gives the preceding cartoon from the *Montgomery* (Alabama) *Advertiser* an appeal it would not otherwise have. Note with what economy the cartoonist—a man named Spangler— suggests industrial activity at the shoreline. The year is 1912. Spangler uses a scene that anticipates one from Theodore Dreiser's *An American Tragedy* (1925) to show that Prohibition, which was yet to come in this country, might hurt the economy of Birmingham, the state's industrial center. It is difficult to figure out exactly where the cartoonist stands on this issue, for neither of the two characters in the boat looks very admirable.

Texture, made with sweeping and sometimes over- lapping pen lines, helps establish the fact in the following cartoon that a job is only just begun. The black in the boy's shirt and the black just in back of the housewife who hired

"IT'S TIME FOR ME TO GO HOME NOW,...."

him to do her lawn help make the figures stand out. And because the caption refers to time, a little black is employed to make the boy's watch show up.

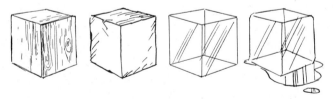

These cubes show some ways in which texture can better define what the cartoonist draws. Short, parallel strokes with an occasional swirl suggest wood; short, choppier strokes with a more ragged outline suggest cement; mechanically straight lines suggest glass or plastic; straight lines with some roundness at the cube's corners (and a puddle of water) suggest ice.

Color

When she was a student at the University of Oregon, Kay Fraser, who writes books on tole painting for Sterling Publishing Company and Crown Publishers, New York, came down with something diagnosed at the infirmary as "black, furry tongue." As she tells the story, a doctor gave her a handful of orange sticks, and, at his direction, she dutifully scraped her tongue twice a day. But a week later her mirror told her that the condition persisted. Only after a cold she had been fighting died out and she quit taking those Smith Bros. licorice cough drops did her tongue return to its normal color.

Let an unfamiliar color take the place of a familiar one, and we become uneasy. Color greatly influences our lives.

When we are depressed, we "feel blue." When angry, we "see red." If our political inclinations move too far to the left, we're "red" or at least a little on the "pink" side. But if our health is good, we're "in the pink." Afraid of a fight, we're "yellow." New on the job, we're "green." If we overwrite, we deal in "purple prose." Taking on a task and putting our best into it, we "do it up brown." Before becoming sensitive to the racial implications of "black" and "white" we said the outlook was "black" when hope was gone (although, on the positive side, we operated "in the black" when we made money in our business). It was mighty "white" of us to lend a hand to our neighbor when he needed help.

Just as your looks can give your character away, so can your color preferences, if we can believe what some psychologists tell us.

One Swiss psychologist has even gone so far as to suggest that how we adjust our color television sets shows what we're really like. As reported in *Behavior Today* (September 16, 1974), Dr. Max Lüscher, "after testing thousands of viewers," concludes that if we tune in for the reds we are oversexed and aggressive; if yellow, we are optimistic and trusting; if bright blue, we are lazy—but easy to live with; if dark blue, we are weak, shy, and dangerous when crossed; if purple, we are "possibly" homosexual, or maybe handicapped or pregnant.

All of which interests the cartoonist. The act of distorting and exaggerating color can achieve effects for the cartoonist every bit as funny or satirical as his other acts of distortion. The trouble is, he doesn't often get a chance to use color. It is too expensive to reproduce.

From the printer's standpoint, there are two kinds of color: spot and process. Spot color is color prepared apart from the original art, usually on an overlay of frosted acetate. The cartoonist makes a separate drawing not only for black but also for each primary color needed. If, for instance, his cartoon is to carry some red inside a Santa Claus suit, he would make a separate drawing of the red, which would be photographed by the printer for a second plate. For the Sunday comics, staff artists at the syndicates, using the cartoonist's original drawing as a base, make three more drawings: one for the yellow plate, one for the red, and one for the blue. The four plates used together (black plus the three primary colors) create the illusion of full color. The color is spot color.

The second kind of color, process color, much more expensive to produce, *starts out* as full color, all in one piece. Perhaps the cartoonist has applied various hues of watercolor to his drawing. Perhaps he has done his work in opaque paints. Or he has used chalks or crayons. Only cartoonists who do cover cartoons for *The New Yorker* and a few who submit cartoons to *Playboy* and similar magazines enjoy this luxury.

Usually, the cartoonist works in black and white. But there is such a thing as "black and white color." It goes back to texture and pattern.

The idea is to use pattern, texture, or tone for areas where you'd like real color to be. Such a drawing, of course, is cheaper to reproduce than a drawing with real color.

The "color" in the following cartoon is provided by solid

ROY PAUL FOR THE EUGENE REGISTER-GUARD

"REMEMBER, DEAR—HE'S JUST LEARNING"

areas of black and by areas that have been covered with Zipatone. You see four different Zipatone patterns: on the lawn,
the man's pants, the woman's hair, and the woman's dress.
(An explanation of the cartoon: Tongue Point, at Astoria,
Oregon was a Job Corps center that came under attack from
critics when an unpleasant racial incident occurred. The
woman is trying to convince her husband that he should be
tolerant.)

The following cartoon is another example of black and
white color. The "color" is applied (a brush and black india
ink) in swashes that make no attempt to extend themselves all
the way out to the edges of their areas. As a result, the
cartoon has a roundness it would not otherwise have. It has a
sort of painterly quality. There are little hints of dry-brush
technique (ink allowed to run out and take on the texture of
the rough-surface paper). A few parallel lines of shading and
some wrinkles add to the effect.

ROY PAUL

The drawing has a juicy look, making it more interesting than it would be if it were rendered in a continuous outline and solid blacks. (The problem here, by the way, was to illustrate a story about the trials of a judge at a children's pet parade. You can see that the poor judge is getting more static from the parents than from the kids themselves, which was the point of the story.)

The Cartoonist as Student

There are always exceptions. Len Norris, the widely admired editorial cartoonist for the *Vancouver* (British Columbia) *Sun* (described by Walt Kelly as "the greatest in the business") is a self-trained artist. He took some art courses at night school during the depression, but, he says, they didn't do him much good. George Price attended no art schools. He got his training making drawings for underwear and hosiery ads. But the biographical information on today's cartoonists indicates that most underwent some training in professional art schools or college art departments. A few have backgrounds in the fine arts as painters. A few others, like former advertising agency art director Ted Shearer (*Quincy*), moved over from the broader field of commercial art. Milton Caniff and underground cartoonist Denis Kitchen are journalism school graduates.

Staff artist Jack Barrett of the *St. Petersburg* (Florida) *Times* not only studied art at the Pittsburgh Art Institute and Carnegie Tech, but he also has taught life drawing and illustration courses at the Ivy School of Art. Irwin Caplan earned a fine arts degree from the University of Washington. Bill Crawford, editorial cartoonist with NEA, earned one from Ohio State. Eldon Dedini studied at Chouinard Art Institute, Bill Mauldin at the Chicago Academy of Fine Arts, Brant Parker at Otis Art Institute, John Prentice at the Art Institute of Pittsburgh, Mort Temes and J. B. Handelsman at the Art Students League. Gluyas Williams studied art in Paris.

It seems reasonable to assume that formal training in the arts helps the cartoonist. Of course, there is some danger that academic regimentation could stifle individuality, but a firmer grip on the principles of design and a more thorough knowledge of basic drawing anatomy is worth the gamble. An art school can greatly broaden the cartoonist's vision.

"If I had it to do over again," says Mort Drucker, who does those beautifully tight caricatures for *Mad*, "the only change I'd make would be attending art school or a university with a good art department. Being self-taught means being limited by your innate talent, personal experiences, and influences. You try to learn through imitation, and while some growth is possible in this manner, it depends upon the expertise of the artist you emulate.

"Art teachers, professional instructors, and most of your fellow students make you more aware of the *thinking* end of art, which is a lot more difficult to learn by yourself."

At one time correspondence courses probably played a more important role than art schools in the lives of cartoonists. What these courses lacked in solid training they made up for in inspiration.

By all odds the most influential correspondence course—partly because it came along at the right time, when careers in cartooning were as glamorous as, later, careers in the movies appeared to be, and partly because its instigator was an impressive if not widely published cartoonist (he was a syndicate executive)—was The Landon Course of Cartooning out of Cleveland. Many of the early comic-strip artists, including Roy Crane, studied with the Landon school.

The lessons came in a typewriter typeface, the sheets sandwiched between dark brown or gray wrappers and held together by staples at the top. Each lesson ended with the note: "Dictated by C. N. Landon." The illustrations— "plates"—were printed on loose sheets of glossy paper. Following is one of them, from a lesson on perspective.

Figure 1 shows that there can be more than one V.P. (vanishing point) on the horizon line (notice that the barn door has its own V.P.), and a V.P. need not be within the drawing.

Figure 2 shows that if you want to depict a crowd, it is a good idea to plan your horizon line high in the picture (giving the reader a bird's-eye view). Note that the fence, house, and telephone lines, because they are parallel to each other, share the same V.P.

Figure 3 shows how to handle wheels in perspective (the front wheels are supposed to be different in size from the back wheels on this wagon), and Figure 4 shows exaggerated perspective (sometimes called foreshortening). "In drawing a sketch of this kind where objects or a part of the figures are in the extreme foreground, be careful to see that the figure tapers off in proportion," Landon dictates. "This is an excellent idea for both the cartoonist and comic artist to bear in mind, although exaggerated perspective should not be used too much."

Other correspondence courses came along. Several still operate today, including the Famous Artists Cartoon Course, Westport, Connecticut (which Jessica Mitford almost killed off in a devastating attack in *The Atlantic*), and Art Instruction Schools, Minneapolis, the school Charles Schulz studied with and later worked for. And several less expensive and less comprehensive courses advertise themselves in *Writer's Digest* and the *Popular Mechanics*-type magazines. But no course of today could possibly stimulate the dreams of greatness that the Landon course did.

8

Not by Art Alone

The cartoonist may come up with an intriguing idea, turn out a flawless drawing in a unique style, and still fall short of producing an effective cartoon. The cartoon may not be well designed.

Design involves a decision about which figures and props should go into a cartoon and which ones should be omitted. It also involves decisions about exact placement of these items within the cartoon frame.

The Principles of Design

Bing, in *Simplicissimus,* Munich, Germany, in a pre-World War I cartoon, shows that the design of the panel can be more important than the actual drawing (p. 302).

The principles of good design are universal. They apply to a cartoon as they apply to a fine painting, a piece of sculpture, a building, even a floral arrangement. They boil down to these: that the items used create some kind of a visual balance, either symmetric or asymmetric; that they be seen in

"THAT WAITER REFUSES TO LEND ME A DOLLAR NOW, YET I HAVE FOUNDED NO LESS THAN FOUR RELIGIONS RIGHT HERE IN THIS CAFE."

logical sequence; that their placement create pleasing proportions; that they be unified; and that, despite the unity, one item stands out in contrast against the others.

Robert Minor's powerful graphic commentary on labor strife in Pittsburgh, drawn for *The Masses* in August 1916, makes good use of these design principles.

Drawn by Robert Minor.

PITTSBURGH

The balance here involves a tension between the diagonal thrust of the soldier pressed against (or through) the collapsing arc of the worker. The sequence is clearly left-to-right. The viewer first sees the soldier and his weapon and follows the thrust to the victim. Had the cartoon been flopped, with the worker on the left, the readability of the cartoon would have been impaired.

The beauty of the proportions in this drawing is a little harder to identify. Essentially, the proportions work because they are unequal. There is, in the space allotted, more drawing than there is non-drawing. You don't get the feeling here of half art, half white space. And the white space you do see looks as if it were planned and not just left over. Each chunk of white space is of a different size and shape. From the standpoint of horizontal space allotment, the figure on the left is wider than the figure on the right. From the standpoint of vertical space allotment, the weapon is placed above the center so that the drawing does not divide vertically into equal halves. Good proportion, with few exceptions, is proportion that involves units and spaces of unequal dimensions. The unity in this cartoon is achieved through consistently strong crayon strokes and through triangular composition. No question about it: the drawing holds together.

Finally, Minor succeeds in introducing an element of contrast into the cartoon by matching the force of the one figure against the receptivity of the other. In other cartoons, contrast is often more pronounced: for instance, one figure is made much larger than another. But such handling here would have made this drawing more a caricature than a savage commentary.

Among modern-day cartoonists worth studying for their keen sense of design is Charles Saxon, *The New Yorker* cover artist and gag cartoonist, already cited in this book for his superb draftsmanship. Following is one of his advertising cartoons.

Saxon arranges his elements to give this cartoon a *U*

"Could you spare $12.00 for a fifth of Chivas Regal?"
Courtesy General Wine and Spirits Company.

rather than a square or rectangular shape. To simplify the composition, he arranges his elements into units of three: buildings, figures, car. And the figures themselves number three. Through "camera angle" Saxon hides other figures and cars one would expect to see on a busy New York street. He hides them because they are unnecessary to the cartoon's message. He draws just enough of the car to establish what kind it is, necessary to the point of the cartoon.

To tie everything together, he lets the figures overlap each other, and, stepping back, he allows the *group* of figures to overlap the buildings and car. To provide a further tie of figures to car, Saxon arranges the top of the open car door so that it lines up with the rich man's shoulders, creating an optical axis. A similar axis occurs between the bottom of the car window and the chauffeur's waist.

Mixing his mediums—ink, wash, and pencil—Saxon uses scrub strokes to make the wily panhandler stand out from the black-suited rich man. Such strokes make the panhandler's clothes look old and wrinkled.

The silhouette of a cartoon is important to its design. If the figures and props combine to make an irregular rather than a rectangular silhouette, the cartoon becomes more interesting to contemplate and, more important, easier to read.

An unknown cartoonist (we have only his initials: R.K.) for *Die Muskete* in Vienna, Austria, back in 1912, relies on silhouetting and overlapping to bring unity to this cartoon ridiculing the suffragettes. (The cartoon carries both a title, "The Olympic Games," and a caption, "Miss Suffragist wins first prize for 30 window panes and 2 minister heads in one minute.") Pretend for a moment that all the figures are completely blacked in; the overall shape of the cartoon, then, would be dramatically irregular and therefore interesting. The overlapping of the figures holds the crowd together. No one figure is isolated. R.K.'s cartoon can be admired for its simplicity of execution in a day when the typical cartoon was all aclutter.

One way to show contrast is to use parallel structure. Parallel structure is as important in drawing as it is in writing. In the following drawing, used in a heading for a federal-government-funded newsletter on education, my job was to show that both young and old were playing student roles. So I drew essentially the same desk, over and over, in a straight line; then I put one set of figures on one side, one on the other. The reader gets the feeling that the oldsters are, well, just a little out of place, which is the feeling I wanted to portray.

In drawing groups like this, it is necessary to worry about equal representation, especially these days with liberation all around us. Both sexes, all nationalities, and all races must share in the glory. With only ten openings here, I had to give this problem some thought. That I ended up with six females and four males was not necessarily influenced by the fact that my boss for this job was a feminist. As in one of the other cartoons in this book, I stepped into one of the roles myself. And at no expense to the reader I included a caricature of my feminist friend. That is one of the luxuries permitted the cartoonist: to slip caricatures or names of friends into published drawings. The late Walt Kelly used to amuse his friends by lettering their names onto the sides of those skiffs he showed floating in the swamp.

The Value of Nothing

How the cartoonist *doesn't* use his space is almost as important as how he *does* use it. The shape and placement of white space is vital to the design of a cartoon. Ideally, the white space should be concentrated in one or two areas, not scattered throughout the cartoon.

"HAVE WE FORGOTTEN ANYTHING?"

In the preceding cartoon, the white space helps give full display to the fire, which, when the cartoon ran in the Eugene *Register-Guard,* was printed with some solid red. The elements in this cartoon are arranged in a sort of circle so that the reader follows around clockwise and stops at six-o'clock: the fire.

"HAVE I TRIMMED DOWN ENOUGH FOR YOU, DOCTOR?"

The doctor's office cartoon, like some other cartoons in this chapter, shows how overlapping of elements helps unite them. In addition, this cartoon illustrates the importance of silhouetting. As in the angry-women cartoon, the various elements here, filled in with black, would form a strong silhouette. Looking at the top of the cartoon, you see that the patient's head is higher than either the diploma or the medicine chest. If these lined up across the top, the composition would be less alive. Even the signature has been located to help form the basic silhouette.

For the Sake of Variety

The cartoonist whose work appears frequently in any one publication should try to vary his style and technique. His politics, if he is an editorial cartoonist, may make his stands predictable, but at least he can offer the reader some surprises in the nature of the idea and the way it is presented.

What makes Paul Szep so satisfying a cartoonist is his willingness to vary his technique and materials. Each day that a *Boston Globe* reader turns to the editorial page he may be in for some kind of visual surprise.

A cartoonist ought not to be saddled with a given vertical or rectangle to fill each day. Ideally, he should let the subject matter dictate the format. This becomes difficult for the cartoonist who is syndicated to newspapers that must plan their space ahead of time.

An interesting exercise for the cartoonist is to see if he can convert a normally horizontal scene, say of a parade, to vertical. Or vice versa. Can he, for instance, show a man leaning out of a high window, but in a horizontal rather than a vertical composition?

Giving It Substance

Although the cartoonist usually draws in terms of out-lines, he thinks in terms of solids. He may find it useful to imagine that what he is drawing is right there on the paper and that he is tracing around it. Or he may try to imagine that, even though he is using a pen, he is sculpting his figure, chiseling it out as though it were of solid material. At any rate, he tries to give his drawing substance. While he draws, the cartoonist gives consideration to the foundation on which the figure rests.

The sketch of a father and son talking shows two ways of handling weight. Before I was able to show weight for the

father, I had to construct the chair and then determine where the man's rear would settle into it. I chose to do an over-stuffed chair. This made the problem of seating the man different from what it would have been had I put him on a hard chair.

In the case of the boy sitting on the floor, I decided to divide the concentration of weight by letting the boy partially support himself with his left arm. Keeping his arm and back stiff and bending him slightly forward, I was able to build a triangle. I gave the triangle a solid base by allowing the boy's rear to flare slightly at floor level. There is no better way to create the illusion of weight than through triangular construction.

Even walking figures have a base, a feeling of solidarity. The reader should sense the weight. Notice that each of the persons in the preceding sketch has the ball of one foot planted firmly on the ground as the other foot stretches forward. You can see how the action works both from a three-quarters and from a side view.

It is a good idea for the cartoonist to set the stage—to rough in the room and the furniture or the outside scene—before he brings on his characters. Then he can establish his bases for them.

Setting the Stage

The cartoonist doesn't need much to set his stage. Just a hint of a wall, an edge of a piece of furniture; if the figure is out of doors, a bit of grass and maybe a tree trunk, a hill, a rooftop. Charles Schulz has taught us not to let the background become busy enough to interfere with an easy reading of the figures. J. B. Handelsman's three-in-a-bed cartoon in Chapter 2 suffers slightly from a too-detailed painting above the bed, a painting that has nothing to do with the cartoon's point.

It doesn't take much to change the character of a cartoon prop. A few strokes here, a bit of tone there—and any picture can change dramatically. The sketch at the left represents a house badly in need of attention. The roof sags, the chimney crumbles, windows break, the front door hangs precariously, the grass gets out of hand, filth and garbage pollute the walk in front. Now, to create an entirely different illusion: straighten the roofline, draw an even pattern on the roof, do some landscaping (no trouble at all with a brush and india ink and a bit of Zipatone), plant a tree, leave the walks clear—and you have an entirely different setting.

In this cartoon, the reader gets the idea right away that the characters are in a store. The scene obviously is indoors, but the people are wearing outdoors garments. That in itself is almost enough to say "store." To further establish locale, there stands a merchandise counter, but only part of one; and you see a support column, common to big department stores. "PRICES AS MARKED" pretty much wraps it up. That one of the packages being carried is gift wrapped suggests Christmastime, which was when this cartoon was run: to illustrate a story on how shoppers that year were being more careful about considering prices than they had been in the past. The glasses on the man suggest watchfulness.

The trend in cartoons is to simplify. The less detail the better. But some cartoonists like to give their readers extra rewards for studying the cartoons closely. A number of editorial cartoonists—Pat Oliphant among them—put little characters in lower corners who carry on their own conversations. Bill Holman, the comic-strip artist who did *Smokey Stover*, filled his panels with sideline puns in pictures and signs and promoted nonsense words like "Foo" and "Notary Sojac" that had nothing to do with the story line.

"I need a car that will last me ten to fifteen years...while they complete their discussions on public transit routes."

Courtesy of Len Norris.

Len Norris of the *Vancouver* (British Columbia) *Sun* likes to give his readers their money's worth. In one of his typically saturated cartoons, you see the wife of a car buyer kicking a tire, as new-car buyers are supposed to do. The action has no bearing on the point of the cartoon, which is to ridicule the inordinate amount of time public officials are taking to work out public transit routes. Nor does that impossible posture of the car buyer have anything to do with the idea. Or the fact that his shoelaces are untied. But these effects add to our enjoyment of Norris's work.

The Vantage Point

The point from which the cartoonist does his drawing—whether from near or far, whether from high above the subject or from the level of the ground—makes a big difference in what he can show. He chooses his "camera angle" as a chess player chooses his next move.

The preceding sketch illustrates how a bird's-eye view and a worm's-eye view can affect a figure and a prop. In the bird's-eye view the head, much bigger than the feet because of foreshortening, appears to be sunk into the shoulders. In the worm's-eye view, the head is pin-sized compared to the legs and feet. And in a semi-side view like this, one shoulder partially hides the head.

The beginner trying these views will probably find it harder to do the figures than the props. A briefcase or table is easy enough because it starts out as a box. The cartoonist may find that by conceiving his figures at first as boxes, he has an easier time of it. After figuring out the perspective for the boxes, he puts the figures inside and then erases the boxes.

When school busing caused such a furor in Boston in 1974, Doug Marlette of the *Charlotte Observer*, drawing his analogy from history, which was appropriate for Boston, made the following comment.

"THE COLOREDS ARE COMING! THE COLOREDS ARE COMING!"

Courtesy of Doug Marlette.

Note the low horizon line, which gives him a worm's-eye view and permits him to focus attention on the horse and rider. Marlette is able to get a celestial body, a church, a bus, a cobblestone street, a street lamp, and some store fronts into the picture in addition to his horse and rider, and still keep his composition simple.

Courtesy of Jeff MacNelly.

Setting up the vantage point at ground level gives cartoonist Jeff MacNelly of the *Richmond News Leader* a chance to allow the back of the truck to loom large, leaving plenty of space for the signs so necessary to make his point on the occasion of Nixon's stepping down from the presidency to be succeeded by Ford. There were many Ford-car allusions early in the Ford presidency; this was one of the most imaginative of them.

The drawing of the truck is masterful. What gives it its character is the toe-in of the wheels and the roundness of the cab and fenders. MacNelly achieves his roundness through skillful use of doubletone Grafix paper.

Courtesy Reader's Digest Association Inc. © 1974.

To illustrate a *Reader's Digest* anecdote involving a printed message on the bottom of a pair of skis, Roy Doty decided to avoid showing the message itself. That would have given away the punch line. Besides, in a smaller-than-life-size drawing there wouldn't have been room. So he chose this camera angle, shooting from the other side, using the fallen skier to frame the onlooker.

Like all Roy Doty illustrations (and Roy Doty seems to be everywhere in the magazines), this one is remarkable for its clean, tight lines and well-conceived composition. The slant of the trunk of the upright skier nicely parallels the slant of the diagonal ski at the left. To further organize this picture, Doty draws each pole to point to a foot of the downed skier. Doty confines his blacks to the skier in the foreground to help place the upright skier in the distance.

The Cartoonist as Writer

Among artists, the cartoonist today may be the true renaissance man. His drawing ability and design sense may be only part of the picture. He may also find it necessary to develop an ability to express himself as a writer.

Reviewing Edwin Newman's *Strictly Speaking: Will America*

Be the Death of English? for *The New York Review of Books*, David Levine, the caricaturist, said, "This delightful book points up all my [writing] weaknesses. It is precisely why I draw pictures." But Levine was protesting too much. He was as much at home in his review as he is each week in *TNYRB* illustrating reviews written by others.

As Chapter 1 points out, many of our best cartoonists either wrote professionally before turning to cartooning (there are a lot of ex-reporters in the ranks) or they write articles and books, including novels, between stints at the drawing board. The typical review of the latest Herblock collection of cartoons and comment, admittedly with some extravagance, inevitably concludes that "he writes as well as he draws." A reading of the autobiographies of Walt Mc-Dougall, John T. McCutcheon, Art Young, and David Low should convince anyone that card-carrying writers have no monopoly on communicating clearly with words.

And much of cartooning *is* writing. An adventure strip is a novel. A comic-strip or gag cartoon is—or can be—humor of a verbal as much as a visual nature. Both the gag cartoon and the editorial cartoon need captions worded with painful precision.

Among the cartoonists, the editorial cartoonist acts always as his own writer, although, if he is weak in this area, he may get a lot of editing from the editorial-page editor. The comic-strip artist and the gag cartoonist often get outside writing help. Of course, some of the writing is of a lower order.

Perhaps the two most important words or phrases in the early days of the strips were "WHAT TH—?" and "PLOP!" Everyone knew the character was really saying "What the hell?" but "hell" was too rough for most publications, and especially for newspapers, which were meant to be read by all the family.

"PLOP!" lettered outside any balloons, was a sound-effects word, meant to accompany the straight man in the last panel as he fell over backward in a faint in response to some outrageous remark made by his partner. Bud Fisher with his *Mutt and Jeff* did as much as any cartoonist to establish this routine.

The writer/collaborator in a comic strip gets credit inside the cartoon or in a line at the top, but the writer for a gag cartoon remains content with his 25 percent of the take. Yet, a whole army of gag writers exists, methodically sending their 3 × 5 cards describing their gags to cartoonists they want to work with. They share this in common with the unbylined writers for the confession magazines: nobody ever hears of them.

With its penchant for accuracy, *The New Yorker* in its masthead listing cartoonists for an issue (a recent service to readers) precedes the list with "Drawings" not "Cartoons" presumably because so many of the gags come from writers and are assigned to the favored cartoonists by the editors.

Should we admire the work of Robert Day, Barney Tobey, George Price and the others any the less for this? Probably not, any more than we would discount an important speech coming from a Franklin Roosevelt or John Kennedy because a ghost writer was involved.

But the cartoonist or politician who leans entirely on others for writing help may one day regret his neglect of this facet of his work. The story is told of a senator who began to take his speech writer for granted. Picking up a speech just before he was to go up on the platform, he did not even bother to read it over before delivering it. So he began: "Tonight I am going to give you the solution to the problems of inflation and unemployment." Turning to the next page, he saw only one line: "You're on your own now, you old windbag."

The difference between a politician and a big-name gag cartoonist is that at least at one time in his career and probably sporadically throughout it the cartoonist writes his own stuff. I don't know whether it was Robert Day himself who wrote the gag for that unforgettable cartoon showing the empty football stadium with the radio announcer in the booth saying, "Well, folks, here it is starting time! . . . One moment while we take a look at that little old schedule" (it goes back to 1940), but he deserves the thanks of cartoon lovers everywhere for whatever role he did play.

What's in a Name?

In a humorous piece from *The New Yorker,* writer Calvin Trillin calls a youth camp "The Eleanor Roosevelt Camp for Social Awareness and Weight Loss." In one of his novels, Peter DeVries has a practical joker whose last name is Sandwich talk his wife into naming their son Hamilton. It isn't until some time later that the wife discovers that the boy, naturally, will be called "Ham."

Into the public domain has gone that favorite name for a law firm: Dewey, Cheatham & Howe.

I have long held out the hope of founding a newspaper at Newport News, Virginia: the *Newport News News.* If my first name were Pierre, I'd open a clothing store and call it Robes Pierre. There's a song I'd like to write: "A Pretty Girl Is Like A Malady." There's a book I want to do on the fringe groups in religion: *Everything You Always Wanted to Know About Sects.* I also have a story in mind about a fellow who flits from woman to woman leaving his mark—his name would be Hickey Freeman.

Among the comic-strip artists Chester Gould (*Dick Tracy*) probably deserves the prize for introducing the most improbable lineup of characters—mostly villains—over the years. No small part of his contribution is the names he gives them: "Pruneface," "Gargles," "Nothing Yonson," "B.O. Plenty," and "Gravel Gertie."

Picking a name for a strip is serious business. Sometimes, as with *Wash Tubbs,* the major attention gradually shifts to another character, and the strip has to be renamed. Charles Schulz has never been happy with "Peanuts"; he wanted "Charlie Brown" in the title.

Alliteration often plays a role: *Beetle Bailey, Big Ben Bolt, Brick Bradford, Bugs Bunny, Dan Dunn, Donald Duck, Mickey Mouse, Hagar the Horrible, Half Hitch, Krazy Kat, Mandrake the Magician, Moon Mullins, Moose Miller, Polly and Her Pals, Priscilla's Pop, The Katzenjammer Kids, Thimble Theater, Tim Tyler's Luck, Toonerville Trolley, Winnie Winkle.*

A little rhythm helps: *There Oughta Be a Law* and *They'll Do It Every Time.* Or a rhyme: *Dennis the Menace.* Sometimes the name is a pun: *Rick O'Shay, Wash Tubbs.*

The word *little* is—and was—popular: *Li'l Abner, Little Eve, Little Farmer, Little Iodine, Little Joe, Little Lulu, Little Mary Mixup, Little Nemo in Slumberland, Little Orphan Annie, Little Annie Rooney, Little Pedro, Little Sport, The Little King, The Little Woman.*

If you think there are too many "Ace" and "Ajax" companies mentioned in the strips or in gag lines, please understand that it is to protect cartoonists from lawsuits. More realistic names might involve real and identifiable firms, even accidentally, and result in costly litigation if the cartoon mention is injurious to reputation.

Captions

Captions—lines of type above or below the cartoon—are not a consideration in comic strips—the comic strip is a self-contained unit of panels—but they are important to gag cartoons, illustrative cartoons, and editorial cartoons.

The cartoonist letters his caption safely outside the cartoon so that it will not be picked up by the photoengraver or offset cameraman. It is usually set in type and combined with the cartoon itself during the production phase.

Sometimes simple punctuation marks can make or break a caption—and hence a cartoon. In one George Price cartoon in *The New Yorker*, the gag idea rested on punctuation that emphasized an unnatural conversational tone. Price showed a cranky old husband being addressed by his quiet-spoken wife. "Do you suppose you could accept a criticism, which, though not exactly constructive, nevertheless is right on?"

A caption has to be just right to work. Charles Addams in

The New Yorker shows an unpleasant, evil-looking man at a phone booth in a police court. An officer is saying to him, "When I said you were allowed one phone call, I did not mean *another* obscene one." The careful reader might well question the placement of the italics in this one. Try reading the gag line with that emphasis. It doesn't say what the gag writer or cartoonist intended to say. If there has to be emphasis in that gag line, it more logically belongs on the word *obscene.*

There has been a trend in magazine and book photography lately to omit captions. Photographers, when they express a mood with their camera, frequently think that words accompanying the printed photograph are redundant. Let the photograph speak for itself, they argue. Sometimes photographers are right.

Cartoonists also find that at times words only slow down the reader. Some of the best gag cartoons—like Charles Addams's cartoon of the skier whose tracks encircle a tree— don't need captions. A cartoonist for *TV Guide,* illustrating an article on the use of the spitball in baseball, shows a batter watching an erratic ball go by for a third strike with the catcher catching the ball not with the expected catcher's mitt but with a spittoon.

Nor do editorial cartoons always need captions. A cartoon in the *Manchester* (New Hampshire) *Union Leader* showed worms labeled "Revolutions," "Communists," and "Anarchists" eating holes in the map of the United States. The caption read "Worms." But the drawing had already said that. The caption was redundant (as is the last sentence in this paragraph, come to think of it).

Balloons

The use of balloons to carry conversation in drawing goes back hundreds of years. In the mid-1800s, some cartoonists used transparent balloons, allowing some of the background to show through where there was no lettering. And the first balloons were drawn so that the line pointing downward to the talker extended all the way into his mouth. Ralph Steadman uses that style today.

The typical balloon today carries only a hint of a stem pointing to the originator of the conversation. Jules Feiffer and Garry Trudeau don't bother even drawing in the balloon. They are stem-only balloonists.

To indicate that the conversation is coming from a radio or telephone, the stem is shaped like a flash of lightning.

To show that the cartoon character is thinking rather than saying the words, the cartoonist makes his balloon fluffier and constructs the stem with bubbles.

The best tool to use for the lettering in balloons is a nonflexible pen. Some cartoonists use an ordinary drawing pen; others use a Speedball. A chisel-point pen, like those used by calligraphers, also makes a good lettering tool.

The cartoonist uses all caps in his balloons for two reasons: (1) He can letter all caps faster than caps-and-lower-case. All caps require two guide lines while caps-and-lowercase require three. Among comic-strip artists, only Frank King and his successors on *Gasoline Alley* use caps-and-lowercase. And (2) the cartoonist doesn't have to worry about which words are capitalized and which words aren't when he uses all caps.

To give urgency to the conversation, the cartoonist letters it in italics. To step up the volume, he uses bolder or bigger letters than normal.

Walt Kelly achieved extra impact in the conversation of his characters by varying the style of lettering in the balloons. One character talked in a nineteenth-century circus-like typeface. A religiously inclined character talked in Old English.

There are hundreds of typefaces a cartoonist can refer to in doing his lettering. He can buy his own type specimen book to refer to. Sometimes the cartoonist may want to set his letters rather than draw them. He can get alphabets of press-on or dry-transfer letters from any art-supply store. The various mood types put into the balloons that follow come from one New York typehouse: Photolettering, Inc., which boasts about 7,000 different alphabet styles available to its clients.

But for some jobs there is no substitute for hand lettering. The following balloon is inspired by a Mort Walker technique.

The cartoonists who do adventure strips often combine balloons with boxes. The boxes carry the cartoonist's comments. Using this technique, the cartoonist acts as a sort of announcer, helping the narrative. In the early days of *Wash Tubbs*, Roy Crane used a headline style of writing (present tense; no *and*s or *the*s) for his boxes, especially when the action picked up.

Adventure strips like *Prince Valiant* ran *only* cartoonist's narrative; there were no balloons to spoil the composition of the panels.

In today's strips it is necessary that cartoonists be less verbose than before. At Newspaper Enterprise Association (NEA), the Cleveland feature syndicate, a cartoonist is asked to limit his words in balloons to sixty-five per strip.

Gag cartoonists, who ordinarily don't use balloons, occasionally make fun of them. Jack Ziegler in *Saturday Review/World* shows a bunch of people sort of floating along. Above each head is a cartoonist's balloon with the word "HOOPLA" inside. A puzzled bystander says to another: "What's all the hoopla about?" In one of his gag cartoons, Jack Markow shows a man selling balloons in a park. A father and son nearby look surprised, because the balloons are balloons from comic strips with lettering in them. S. Harris makes use of thought balloons in a *Writer's Digest* gag cartoon when he shows a man looking at his wife, and he's wondering: "DO YOU BELIEVE IN E.S.P.?" She's reading the paper, not looking at him, but in the balloon above her head is lettered: "NO."

Even the editorial cartoonists get into the act. Jeff MacNelly of the *Richmond News Leader,* to show that President Ford was "open-minded on all fuel-policy options," drew a thought balloon above the president's head—with nothing in it.

The cartoonist's balloon has been picked up and used by editors and art directors as well. The balloons on page 326 appeared as a full-page, full-color introduction to an article in *Medical Economics,* a magazine published for doctors. The article's title is set, appropriately, in all caps. The balloons, for the sake of variety, take various shapes; and the typefaces inside vary, too.

Rand McNally uses the balloon device (the version

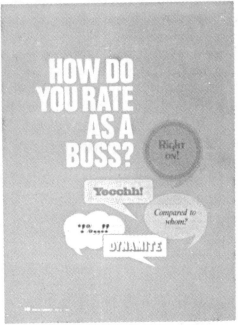

without the outline) in the logotype (signature) for its advertising. You see the name and then the little globe with the compass inside, and off to one side, connected by a thin line, are the words: "and you thought we just made maps," as though the globe is saying the words.

Inside Comics, a quarterly for persons interested in comic books and fanzines, appropriately puts its nameplate on the cover inside a balloon.

Labels

While the comic-strip artist relies on balloons, the editorial cartoonist relies on labels. But he tries to get by with as few as possible.

Logic in labeling is important. For a January 27, 1975, *Newsweek* cover, cartoonist Robert V. Engle drew President

Ford as a knight doing battle with a three-headed dragon. One neck and head represent "INFLATION," one "RECESSION," and one "ENERGY." The trouble with such labeling is that it suggests all three are evil. But is "ENERGY" parallel to "INFLATION" and "RECESSION" and therefore to be slain? Or does the cartoonist really need "ENERGY SHORTAGE" or something similar for his third label?

The cartoonist finds that labels are more necessary on the local than on the national level, because readers do not recognize local political figures as readily as national ones. Local figures often haven't had the media exposure. Nor are local issues so clearly defined.

The beginning editorial cartoonist, suffering from a lack of confidence, tends to use more labels than his established counterpart. The beginner may not even be sure his readers will be able to make out the props he puts into the drawing.

The editorial cartoonist tries hard to produce caricatures that are recognizable enough that he doesn't have to identify them with names. At least he tries to get by with only a set of initials, say on the subject's briefcase. When the cartoonist finds it impossible to draw a likeness (maybe he doesn't have access to a mug shot of the subject) he may show him full figure, from the back, in which case, of course, a full label is necessary.

Back when he was doing editorial cartoons for *Frontier*, a West Coast opinion magazine no longer published, Dennis Renault had occasion to show Ronald Reagan in a track suit, bent down at the starter's line, ready to run for office. Renault, who now does editorial cartoons for the *Sacramento Bee* and gag cartoons for *Playboy,* could have drawn a likeness, all right, but he chose to hide Reagan's face and placed the label right on the seat of the pants of the then aspiring candidate for governor. You got the impression Renault was not much impressed by Reagan's credentials.

Where the label goes is important. If in a light area, the label goes on in black; if in a black area, the cartoonist uses white opaque for his lettering. If there is too little room, he puts the name on a floating label that looks a little like a price tag.

Signs

Mort Temes's *Saturday Evening Post* cartoon showing a sick man in a store looking at greeting cards (he's in need of a shave and wearing a bathrobe) needs no caption, only the sign above the greeting-card display: "GET-WELL CARDS."

Sam Gross in *The New Yorker* shows an anxious man sitting alone in a chair in a bare room. At one end of the room is a door marked "DO NOT ENTER." At the other, a door marked "DO NOT EXIT." In another cartoon, Gross shows a worried man looking at a sign that reads: "DO NOT READ THIS SIGN."

Ed Fisher in *The New Yorker* shows a militant crowd

carrying signs: "DOWN WITH THE ESTABLISHMENT!" "WRECK THE SYSTEM," "NO! NO! POWER STRUCTURE," etc. They are marching down a street along a narrow path in the snow that is being cleared for them by a snow-remover with the inscription on the door: "CITY OF NEW YORK DEPARTMENT OF SANITATION." And a cartoonist named Noonan in *The Nation* shows a middle-aged, middle-class man carrying a sign: "I HAVE NOTHING TO PROTEST AT THIS TIME."

Back in World War II, Private Arv Miller for one of the Armed Services magazines showed an army recruit being examined by a doctor. The recruit has his face pressed against an eye chart, studying an E that is bigger than his head. The examiner says, "That's fine. Now read the second line."

On the home front, in *Collier's,* J. S. MacDonald showed a restaurant scene with a dog seated at the table. A waiter is showing the dog a sign: "NO DOGS ALLOWED." The dog, shaken by the sign, is saying, "Who's smoking?"

Signs, which play a part not only in gag cartoons but also in all the other cartoon forms, require more effort on the part of the cartoonist than balloons do because often the lettering has to be built up and maybe even shown in perspective. Single-stroke letters may not be enough. The sign should look as though a sign painter had done it.

In a *Citizen Smith* panel His Honor, Mayor Dave Gerard (how does he find time to run a city and do a daily syndicated cartoon?), puts some lettering, necessary for the cartoon to make its point, into perspective. Because the horizon line is located near the center, the type arcs upward at the top, downward at the bottom, and runs pretty much straight across in the center of the poster. Gerard has taken some cartoonists' license here with the placing of the poster on the pole. He has made the poster more visible to the reader than to the two male characters who are discussing it.

In choosing the name "Blazx," Gerard is reasonably sure he is not libeling some real-life would-be congressman who

CITIZEN SMITH   By Dave Gerard

"You got to give him credit! He lets you know who's
putting up the campaign money!"

happens to be backed by the Milk Trust, Pork Products, the
Zinc Lobby, and the Peanut Assoc.

If the cartoonist can show the sign or poster in a head-on
rather than a three-quarter view and if he can avoid wrapping
it around a pole, he can use press-on type or dry transfer
letters for his lettering. These letters, which come in
alphabets printed on thin sheets of plastic, can be applied to
the art much as Zipatone is applied.

The way the sign is lettered can be vital to the point of
the gag. Jack Markow once did a four-panel gag cartoon of a
window-sign painter. In the first three panels you saw the
man at work painting signs on various stores. Because he was
working on the inside of the windows, he was always painting
the sign backwards so that it could be read left-to-right from
outside. The last panel showed the sign painter's gravestone.
The lettering on it was—backwards.

As a subtle extra touch, Markow signed his name backwards—which can be dangerous. The printer, in the middle of the photoengraving process, might think the cartoon has mistakenly been flopped and take it upon himself to unflop it. And the cartoon would be bereft of its idea.

The Signature

Early in his career the cartoonist gives a lot of thought to what his signature will look like. What part of the name should be included, he asks himself. And should a little symbolic art—a sort of trademark—go along with it?

For a small drawing the cartoonist may want to use initials only—or no signature at all. A full signature under a portrait for a column, for instance, might be read as the name of the columnist.

Where the signature goes in the cartoon can be important to its composition. It may affect the balance of the cartoon. Often the signature goes next to some prop in the cartoon so that, instead of standing out, it integrates itself into the cartoon.

The cartoonist can have some fun with his signature. Seymour Chwast, the Push Pin Studios man with the flat, primitive, highly designed style, on a *New York Times Magazine* cover drawing made two syllables out of his one-syllable last name:

CHW
AST

Some cartoonists use a script for their signature, as Frank Willard did (*Moon Mullins*); some print them, but with a flourish not used in the other printing within the cartoon, as Edgar Martin did (*Boots*). Fontaine Fox (*Toonerville Trolley*), when he moved from editorial cartooning to comic stripping, followed the practice of running a half a dozen parallel lines above his signature.

Often the signature is a shortened version of the last

name, as "Zim" in Eugene Zimmerman, or an acronym, as "Vip" in Virgil Partch.

A few cartoonists include a prop with their signatures. Elzie Segar (*Popeye*) showed a cigar butt. Reg Manning, as editorial cartoonist of the *Arizona Republic,* drew a small cactus after his name. Marvin Myers (*Zody*) uses the Y in his last name as a martini glass. There is always an olive with a toothpick floating in the top of the Y.

Roland Michaud, who signs just his last name to his gag cartoons, includes a *D* in a circle—a carryover from his early days in the profession when he collaborated with a gag writer, Joe Dibuono, who now is in television production. Michaud explains that he never got around to taking it out.

To keep the signature safely apart from other lettering in the cartoon, some cartoonists, like Milton Caniff, seal it up in a box.

Many cartoonists who use both their names in their signatures abbreviate the first name. Hence: Thos. Nast, Chas. Addams, Geo. Price, Robt. Day, B. Tobey.

Perhaps the most common practice is to sign just the last name. But Claud Smith, *The New Yorker* cartoonist, signs just his first name. A European cartoonist with the first name Harry takes that name and turns it around. His readers know him as Yrrah. (One of Yrrah's cartoons, as shown in *Atlas,* shows a monastery with monks making religious artifacts: miniature crosses with Christs affixed. The monks are busy nailing the Christs to the crosses.)

My use of my first two names on cartoons evolved from my early days when I began selling to comic magazines and trade journals. I had the handicap of the same name (Roy Nelson) as that of a successful *Esquire* and Hearst newspapers caricaturist and cartoonist. So I began signing all three of my names to my cartoons, and that of course took up too much space. Eventually I just dropped the last name.

Lettering

To move into creative areas adjacent to cartooning the

cartoonist needs to make a study of letterform and typography. Letterform involves the design of individual letters. Typography has to do with the way these letters are put together for a particular design job.

Whether the cartoonist does his own lettering or has his letters set in type, he needs to understand what moods his letters can create and how they can be presented for maximum readability.

Typefaces fall generally into two categories: *romans*, with their thick and thin strokes and their serifs (short cross strokes) at stroke terminals; and *sans serifs*, with their single-thickness strokes and lack of serifs. The romans (this book is set in a roman face called Palatino) tend to suggest tradition and dignity; the sans serifs have a more businesslike, modern appearance. They also seem more urgent. There are some serifless types with thick and thin strokes and some even-stroked types with serifs, but, like scripts and other novelty faces, their use is limited.

The cartoonist gets more use out of the sans serifs than the romans. For instance: he letters his balloons in sans serifs. When he uses sans serifs for headings for his Sunday strips or comic-book features, he tends to add novelty to the letters by giving them a third dimension and putting them in perspective.

Trog (Wally Fawkes) plays with sans serifs in a *Punch* cartoon (p. 334). He emphasizes the solid nature of the letters by using three tones: white for the tops, light gray for the fronts, and dark gray for the sides, and then provides contrast for them with solid blacks on the ground and in the clothing of the Charles Addams-like figure with the detonator. The shape of the ground points to the figure, and a spotlight effect calls attention to the dynamite. The high horizon line gives the reader a perfect view of everything that's going on.

The signature seems to be built out of Tinker Toys.

Some of the newer faces coming out of the photo-lettering houses look as though they were designed by cartoonists, as indeed some of the faces have been. Get your-

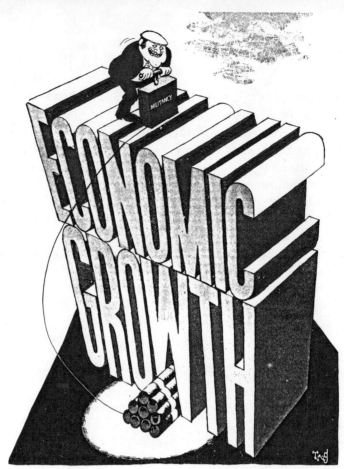

self a type-specimen book from a photolettering house and look up examples of Glaser Babyfat or Chwast Blimp or Push Pin Myopic Open.

It was an underground cartoonist—Rick Griffin—who designed the nameplate for *Rolling Stone* magazine. The light-hearted look and the three dimensions of the letters show the cartoonist's influence. For that matter, it was a cartoonist, Rea Irwin, who designed *The New Yorker* nameplate and the unique display type the magazine uses for titles inside.

In the setting of type, the trend is toward tight spacing, with the thought that the reader should be able to take in wnole words and phrases, not just individual letters. And so the cartoonist drawing his own letters, if he wants them to look contemporary, puts them closer together these days than he might have done a decade ago.

Typesetting houses with photolettering equipment can perform many of the tricks with type that cartoonists perform with lettering. But sometimes hand lettering is the only way to go. A cartoonist who signs his work "Nick," in an illustration for a travel article in the *New York Times*, shows a highway painter who has just painted the words "STEEP HILL" on an incline. It is indeed steep, for the paint at the bottom of the letters has run. The cartoonist's painting of the type in white opaque in the black of the highway was the only way to make the point.

Courtesy of Frank Farah.

Although the basic letterform in the preceding cartoon is available in photolettering, it had to be hand drawn by the cartoonist for this cartoon in order to make it fit perfectly the contours of the airship. Both the lettering and the whimsical art is by Frank Farah, the Portland, Oregon, cartoonist and graphic designer. The small-space ad appeared in Portland newspapers.

In a playful spirit, the cartoonist has been known to build letters of the alphabet out of figures and props, as, for instance, when he designs initial letters for magazine story or book chapter openings. In the mid-1970s *U & lc.*, the publication of International Typeface Corporation, announced the forthcoming publication of a collection of letters of the alphabet, each designed by a different artist using the human form for main strokes of the letters. Among illustrators to be represented were Stan Mack, Robert Grossman, Marvin Mattelson, and Milton Glaser, artists whose works are found in this book. "Ask 26 famous illustrators each to design one letter of the . . . alphabet and what have you got?" asked *U & lc.* "A new alphabet called 'Schizophrenic Obtuse.' "

Letters themselves can provide the central idea for the cartoon. David Weitala in *Saturday Review/World* shows a servant carrying a big, three-dimensional *T* on a tray to his master. The servant: "Your *T*, sir."

When Ralston Purina in the mid-1970s introduced Meow Mix ("Meow Mix" is a registered trademark of the Ralston Purina Company, used on cat food), it featured on the package lettering built with engaging cats falling into position to spell out the name. Milton Glaser was the artist. (The agency: Della Femina, Travisano & Partners Inc.)

Courtesy of Ralston Purina Company.

To show that nothing substantive was coming out of the World Conference on Hunger in 1974, Paul Szep of the *Boston Globe* drew an overfed politician pouring scrambled letters out of a bag into a starving man's empty bowl. If you look closely, you'll find "Words" and "Rhetoric" emerging from the scramble. To make his point, Szep used real letters for the scramble rather than hand lettering. And he used letters from various fonts. But of course the lettering on the bag is Szep's own.

"FOOD FOR THOUGHT."

Courtesy of Paul Szep.

Editorial cartoonists seemed pretty much agreed that the conference didn't solve many problems. Don Wright of the Miami *News* produced a cartoon involving a four-part sequence. A well-fed man wearing a "WORLD FOOD CONF." button is lecturing a hungry child carrying a bowl. Above the man's head is a cartoonist's balloon carrying the word "RHETORIC." In the second part, the man reaches up for the balloon. In the third, he stuffs it into the child's bowl. In the fourth, the child looks out at the audience, *Doonesbury* style.

Tony Auth of the *Philadelphia Inquirer* had the same feeling about what was accomplished at the conference, but his idea involved a different setting. The "customers" starved while the "cooks" argued. The posted menu with nothing written down was a necessary touch.

Copyright 1974 by the *Philadelphia Inquirer.*
Reprinted by permission of Tony Auth.

On another subject, the *Kansas City Star*'s Bill Schorr had fun with blocks in an editorial cartoon making the comment that Leon Jaworski, the special prosecutor in the Watergate case, and President Ford had different ideas as to what to do about Nixon.

Max Bandel in *Wordplay* takes words and draws them in appropriate typefaces, combining letters with art, to produce a clever one-column, drop-in panel for newspapers. "Visual tricks with words," his syndicate calls it. Like Jimmy Hatlo (*They'll Do It Every Time*) and other panel cartoonists ahead of him, Bandel accepts contributions from readers and gives the contributors credit lines.

Jack Wohl also performs tricks with letters in *Pixies*.

Graphic Design

With a good design sense and with a knowledge of letter-form and typography, some cartoonists are getting into a field called graphic design. Graphic design involves the visual planning and laying out of advertising and of pages and spreads in newspapers, magazines, and books. It involves choosing art work and type and coordinating these elements into a pleasing and readable unit. When the designer takes on an administrative role, as when he calls in an illustrator and instructs him on what is needed, the designer assumes the title of art director.[1]

One of the most successful of the graphic designers or art directors to come up from cartoonists' ranks is Irwin Caplan of Seattle. Caplan does it all: he draws, and in a variety of styles; he designates types; he designs; he assembles.

A Caplan-prepared ad (McCann-Erickson is the agency) illustrates some happy solutions to typical design problems (p. 340). First, it shows that good proportion in design often involves unequal allocation of space. Note that the cartoon art by Caplan occupies *more than* half the width of the ad. An equal division between body-copy width and art width would have cut the ad in half—right down the middle.

Note, too, that Caplan has placed the art close enough to the headline type to make of the type and art *one unit*. The fewer the units, the easier it is for the reader to take everything in.

And note that the headline type matches the type in the

---

1. My *Publication Design* (1972) and *The Design of Advertising* (second edition, 1973), both published by Wm. C. Brown Company, Dubuque, go into these matters in detail.

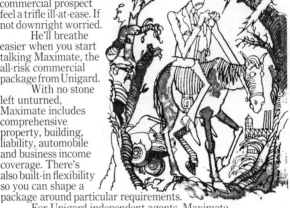
final line of the ad. This helps to tie everything together. Unity is, you remember, a vital design principle.

Finally, note that designer/artist Caplan does not bother to justify the right-hand margin of the body copy. It is set "ragged right." The advantage of ragged-right setting, necessary especially where copy width is narrow, is that the typesetter does not have to put extra space between some words to space out the lines. As a result the body copy has a more even texture. And, more important, it is not necessary for the typesetter to hyphenate any of the words at the ends of lines to carry them over to the next lines. This makes the copy more readable. Right there is the secret of good graphic design: readability. Not prettiness. Not trickery. Readability.

New bestseller!

MARATHON MAN

"A furious crescendo

of action...may well be one of the most unusual thrillers to come by this year."
—Publishers Weekly

"Dazzling
...Try not to let anyone tell you how it ends."—Irwin Shaw

A Book-of-the-Month Alternate • To be a major film, produced for Paramount by Robert Evans & Sidney Beckerman $7.95

A novel by William Goldman
delacorte press
DELL PUBLISHING CO. INC.

Courtesy of Irwin Caplan.

Another good example of coordination of type with art can be seen in a non-outline drawing by Phillip Cimo, an art director with Franklin Spier, a New York advertising agency. Notice how "MARATHON MAN" picks up the black, angular look of the running figure. It was necessary to handletter "MARATHON MAN" in order to make the letters overlap each other and look unaligned. A photolettering house can come close to achieving the same effect, but of course the lettering artist then loses full control. "New bestseller!" to contrast with "MARATHON MAN," was set in photo-lettering.

This ad is a good example of graphic design for a small space, managing as it does to present concisely all the basic information about the book (a novel by William Goldman) plus a couple of review excerpts and information about book-club and movie ties. Notice how the designer uses one hand (the left) of the running figure to point to the book's title and the other to point to the first two words (in boldface) of one of the review excerpts. And one of the toes points to the understated price.

An overriding consideration of the cartoonist contemplating a move into the graphic-design field should be: does he appreciate good letterform and typography? Does he, looking at the following headline for a series of ads sponsored by Benton & Bowles, the advertising agency, see beauty and fit in the roman letters, or is he inclined only to argue against the questionable concept and possible lapse in grammar?

It's not creative unless it sells.

Cartooning as a Career

The professional cartoonist can go about his work in two ways: (1) as a staff artist or cartoonist, working a regular schedule and getting a regular salary, or (2) as a freelancer.

The staff artist or cartoonist enjoys security and fringe benefits, but he often finds himself called upon to do additional work for which he has little aptitude, like map-making, lettering, graphic design, and pasteup.

The freelancer, on the other hand, works when and where he wants to and accepts only those jobs that appeal to him. Or he initiates his assignments. But his income is sporadic. Often it has to be negotiated. The freelancer may find his success rests more on his ability as a salesman than as an artist.

The beginning cartoonist should realize that local media offer him the best chance for publication. With almost all weekly newspapers (there are close to 10,000 of them in the United States) utilizing offset lithography for their printing and now with more than half of the 1,770 dailies gone offset and with most of the others, including the big-city dailies, making plans to switch, editors no longer need avoid local cartoons because "they're too expensive to reproduce." Photo-engraving for most papers no longer is required.

The fact remains, however, that an editor has to pay local cartoonists more than big-name syndicated cartoonists. For a few dollars a week an editor can pick up a daily cartoon from, say, Bill Mauldin, because, under the syndicate system, scores of other papers are chipping in to pay the cartoonist. If the local cartoonist is to profit at all from his work, he is going to have to charge more for a single drawing than the syndicate charges for the week's collection of Mauldins. (The smaller the paper, the less it has to pay the syndicate; rates are based on circulation.)

Even so, considering the amount of space filled and its potential impact, the local cartoon is a bargain. How much is the editor paying in salary and fringe benefits for editorial copy to fill the same amount of space? And how much is he paying for the typesetting?

The big selling point for the local cartoonist is the fact that he can comment on local issues the syndicated cartoonist has to ignore. On the editorial page he can help the editor take a local politician to task. On the news pages he can help the city editor illustrate news or feature stories that don't lend themselves to photographic coverage.

Newspapers aren't the only local market for cartoonists. Most cities have advertising agencies, and most advertising agencies buy art, including cartoons, from freelancers. The advertising departments of the advertisers themselves are also a possible market.

And often the printing establishments in town find it necessary to help their smaller clients with design and art problems. Enter the freelancer or staff artist. Some printers have set up their own art departments.

The agencies, advertisers, printers, and advertising departments of newspapers have access to cheap stock art and free public-domain art (art previously published but for which the copyright has expired), but there is always the problem of finding the piece that exactly illustrates the ad's message or that creates the appropriate mood. Then locally produced art is the answer.

When he has his market correctly assessed, the cartoonist puts together a portfolio of his work and makes his appointments with editors or art directors.

Still, the cartoonist may never be satisfied until he appears in national media. His best chances there probably lie in his submission of gag-cartoon roughs to the few slicks and the hundreds of specialized magazines still buying them. With each contribution of roughs goes a stamped, self-addressed envelope, folded once so that it will fit into the first envelope, to bring the material back. But one recalls the observation Ring Lardner made to another group of freelancers: "A good many young writers make the mistake of enclosing a stamped, self-addressed envelope, big enough for the manuscript to come back in. This is too much of a temptation to the editor."

Rates for gag cartoons, not negotiable, range from a few dollars to several hundred per cartoon, but the competition is staggering. *Medical Economics* in late 1973 reported that it looks at 12,000 cartoon roughs and gag lines a year. It uses one or two percent. The *Rotarian* in 1975 said it looks at 100,000 cartoons each year; "perhaps 50 are published."

One who has made it is Jack Corbett, a university graduate in social science. Corbett worked as a department manager at J. C. Penney for six years before quitting in 1972 to devote himself full-time to freelancing for the magazines. (It took him fifty or sixty submissions before he sold his first cartoon—for $20—in 1970 to the local magazine of the *San Jose Mercury*.) Now keeping 120 batches of ten cartoons each in the mail at all times, Corbett finds he and his family can enjoy "a modest living standard." A highly disciplined man, he consistently turns out at least fifteen cartoons a week for potential sales. One lucky day in 1975 his mail brought him acceptances for nineteen cartoons.

Corbett averages about $35 a cartoon, getting as much as $200 a cartoon from *Playgirl* and as little as $4 from a regional fishing magazine. He tries the best-paying markets first; cartoons that are rejected there go on to progressively lower-paying markets. "Some cartoonists shy away from the small magazines," he says, "but I figure getting $4 for a cartoon is better than throwing it away."

Almost all of his cartoons are purchased "as is" in rough form, but Corbett's roughs, typical of most cartoonists' roughs these days, are polished and always done in ink. Occasionally he will get an okayed rough back from an editor with instructions to finish it in color or supply a color overlay.

The hardest part of the job for Corbett—but the most interesting part—is coming up with the idea. Most of his ideas come through association: looking at other cartoons "until something clicks." A single cartoon or a combination of them will somehow suggest an entirely different subject to him. (This is not the same as taking a cartoon and making a switch, a process used by some cartoonists. A switch is the same basic idea redepicted in a new setting with different characters.)

Corbett buys some of his gags for the "girlie" cartoons he does, but most of the ideas are his own. Not counting the time spent working up the idea, a cartoon usually takes him about an hour to produce. He first makes a thumbnail sketch, and then a fairly finished full-size drawing; this he covers with a sheet of good-quality typing paper and, using a light table, makes a tracing in ink.

Following is one of several cartoons Corbett has sold to *Private Practice*, "the journal of socioeconomic medicine." Note how Corbett's solid yet formless figures contrast to the foamy look of the bed covering. Note, too, the compactness of the composition and the economy of the props suggesting a hospital room.

"*There seems to be some discussion as
to your diagnosis and treatment.*"

In another of his cartoons, this one for *NY Planning News,*
Corbett deals with the topic of increased population.

*"WE DON'T BELIEVE A POPULATION DENSITY PROBLEM EXISTS.
IT'S MERELY A MATTER OF UTILIZING AVAILABLE SPACE."*

Reproduced by permission of
NY Planning News, March-April 1975.

To be successful as a freelancer, especially in the gag-cartoon field, the cartoonist must be uncommonly well organized. He sets up an elaborate bookkeeping system to keep track of cartoons as they go out in various combinations to a wide variety of magazines. He wouldn't want to insult an editor by rerouting a cartoon to him after it has once been rejected. But if the magazine hires a new cartoon editor, the rejected cartoon might well go back to the magazine for another try.

Some cartoonists develop their own business stationery. Paul Szep, the *Boston Globe* editorial cartoonist, designed a letterhead that has his name and affiliation in small type at the top, like the caption for an editorial cartoon, with a box below inside of which he types his letters. At the bottom inside the box is a white embossed signature of the kind he puts on his cartoons.

A cartoonist employed full time by a newspaper or magazine or who has a syndicate affiliation doesn't necessarily remove himself from the freelance market. For instance, Jack Tippit (*Amy*) continues to sell gag cartoons regularly to a wide variety of magazines.

Sometimes a newspaper or magazine objects to a staff member's moonlighting. The reasoning: the cartoonist may be tempted to save his best work for outside sale. At the least, the newspaper expects to be advised of any freelancing by a staff member. The *Milwaukee Journal* once suspended editorial cartoonist Bill Sanders for two weeks without pay for moonlighting without permission. Presumably, Sanders now has things worked out with his editors. The first issue of *Comix Book* (1974), a magazine that tried to bridge the gap between straight comic books and underground comic books, carried an "Alice in Watergateland" feature by Sanders.

Although the syndicates seem grossly overextended in the number of features they make available to the newspapers, it is just possible for an ambitious young cartoonist to come up with an idea to intrigue editors enough to force them, despite newsprint shortages, to find room for it. Garry Trudeau while at Yale made it with *Doonesbury*, hardly worth all the adoration it has been getting but beautifully timed (newspapers were finally ready for some anti-establishment stuff). By 1975 the feature was being run in nearly 500 newspapers, putting it up with the leaders, and it had won a Pulitzer Prize—for *editorial cartooning!*

It helps to be aggressive. Ham Fisher was turned down when he tried to sell his *Joe Palooka* comic strip to the McNaught Syndicate. His drawing was poor. But his sales pitch was so effective that the syndicate hired him to sell J. P. McEvoy's *Dixie Dugan*. He sold it to sixteen papers on his first road trip. But he sold his own feature to forty-two papers, and McNaught had to take it on.

Cartoonists must develop a versatility to survive in the mass media. There is considerable moving in and out of the categories mentioned in Chapter 1. Many of the comic-strip artists started out as gag cartoonists. Many gag cartoonists and comic-strip artists do extra duty as illustrators for articles, books, or advertisements. One of the most versatile was Rube Goldberg, who moved from cartoon panelist (remember those ridiculous inventions?) to comic-strip artist to editorial cartoonist to, when he was past eighty, sculptor (four major exhibitions, 600 sales). So widely recognized were Goldberg's cartoon inventions that at least one dictionary—the *Random House Dictionary of the American Language* (1966)—carried "Rube Goldberg" (listed in the Rs) as a term for any complicated or impractical gadget or scheme. According to Peter C. Marzio in *Rube Goldberg: His Life and Works,* Goldberg became "the only American to have his name become a dictionary word while he was alive."

Where many cartoonists, artists, and graphic designers have moved into photography, only one photographer that I know of has moved into cartooning: the widely reprinted Don Wright, editorial cartoonist of the *Miami News.*

Many cartoonists—Mort Walker, Johnny Hart, and Hank

Ketcham among them—are not content to turn out a single syndicated feature. They have their hand in one or two others. Wayne Stayskal, the editorial cartoonist, also does a syndicated sports panel called *Trim's Arena.* He signs this feature "Trim" (his mother's maiden name) because, he says, he doesn't want his readers to think he is as frivolous with politics as he is with sports.

A surprising number of cartoonists double as authors. Rube Goldberg wrote many books during his long career. Jules Feiffer has written books and plays and movie scripts. Mell Lazarus, who does *Miss Peach* and *Momma,* has written a novel and at least two plays. Shel Silverstein writes hit country-and-western songs. James Stevenson, the *New Yorker* cartoonist, also writes stories for that magazine.

And many cartoonists have gone into painting. One of the most accomplished—he does portraits—is Gib Crockett, retired editorial cartoonist for the *Washington Star.*

Still, only a relatively few cartoonists make a living through their art. They are able to market their work only sporadically. They must rely on other jobs—as graphic designers or pasteup artists, reporters, advertising men, teachers, craftsmen, clerks, or whatever—for regular income. Others may never see their work published. They use their cartooning skills to dress up their letters, entertain their kids, impress their teachers, or, if they lecture, make their work at the blackboard a little more interesting—objectives worthy enough in themselves to merit a study of the art.

Are Editors People?

Looking at the problem realistically, it isn't the reader so much as the editor whom the cartoonist must please if he is to be published. Unfortunately, most editors are word-oriented. They do not think in visual terms. This makes the cartoonist's role as a salesman all the more demanding.

Editors can catalogue any number of shortcomings of cartoonists: their inability to make deadlines, their lack of understanding about what reproduces well and what doesn't; the mistakes cartoonists make not only in spelling but also in the way they depict machinery; a sameness in style; the ideology cartoonists work into cartoons meant only to entertain; the lack of logic in some of their ideas; their failure to include return postage for the return of unsolicited cartoons.

But cartoonists have legitimate gripes, too. Here are some of them:

1. Editors give originals the same rough handling they give a piece of typed copy. A cartoon should not be bent. Nor can it take smudges. Too often a freelancer, getting a batch of rejected gag cartoons back from a magazine editor, has to redraw them before he can resubmit them.

2. The pay schedule for cartoons is often based on prices established ten or twenty years ago or more. An editor has no inkling of the amount of time that goes into a cartoon. The actual drawing is only part of it, as Chapter 2 points out.

3. Editors run all art, including cartoons, too small. The beauty of the cartoonist's line is lost. (Of course, sometimes too-small showings can't be helped, as in a book like this where a great variety of work is necessary.)

4. Because a cartoon doesn't happen to fit a hole on the page, an editor will crop it to fit, not bothered, apparently, by the fact that he may be doing violence to the cartoon's composition. The cartoonist may design the cartoon as a horizontal unit; the editor makes a vertical out of it by eliminating a section.

A lesser offense, but related, is for the editor to misread the angle at which the cartoon is set and tip it into place. As a result, figures may appear to be listing to one side or the other, as though drunk. The cartoonist can eliminate this hazard by enclosing his cartoon in a box, by furnishing crop marks, or by putting dots in each of the four corners and calling the editor's attention to them.

5. Some editors apparently think nothing of changing an editorial cartoonist's caption. But editing cartoonists' captions

is not like editing a story or article. Change one word in a ten-word caption, for instance, and you change 10 percent of the copy. That is too much of a change for an outsider to make. The caption is no longer the work of the cartoonist.

The cartoonist does not like to see a change in his caption because, ideally, he has tailored his drawing to exactly fit the caption.

I have had editors completely reverse my caption so that it would make the point positively rather than negatively. This without giving me a chance to change the expressions on the faces in the drawing to make them fit the new caption. At times I have had to resort to putting my conversational captions in balloons inside the drawing. That at least makes changes more difficult for the editor.

The Test of a Good Cartoon

It is important for the aspiring cartoonist to realize that many considerations beyond mere drawing go into the production of a cartoon. I've tried to make the point that, simple as a cartoon appears to the casual observer, much planning is called for, many decisions must be made. Often all of this goes on before the cartoonist actually picks up his pencil or pen to begin the actual drawing. The drawing, after all this, may take only a few minutes.

And when it is all over, how does the cartoonist know if he has succeeded in doing what he set out to do? In an introduction to a collection of Abner Dean cartoons in the 1940s, Philip Wylie, in an appreciative mood, suggested that readers of Dean's works should be called "beholders." How does the cartoonist know when his work is worth beholding rather than just reading or viewing?

David Low in his autobiography offers a test he applied to his own work: "Are the details nicely composed so that the eye slides easily to the full meaning? Has the drawing the appropriate blend of fantasy and realism to insinuate the satire? Does the wit of its caricature suggest sound judgment of essentials? Do the portraits of the people depicted suggest insight into character? Does the performance fit the intention—not too laboured to defeat the spontaneity, not so facile as to be insignificant? Is it, in short, a good cartoon, or just another plate of hash?"

Bibliography

While this bibliography includes a few books long out of print, it concentrates on those published during the past two decades. It does not attempt to list the countless mass paperback collections of gag cartoons and comic strips and panels.

Abel, Bob, ed. *The American Cartoon Album.* New York: Dodd, Mead & Co., 1974. (Nearly half of the cartoons were not previously published.)

Addams, Charles. *Addams and Evil.* New York: Simon & Schuster, 1947.

———. *Monster Rally.* New York: Simon & Schuster, 1950.

———. *Homebodies.* New York: Simon & Schuster, 1954.

———. *My Crowd.* New York: Simon & Schuster, 1970.

Anderson, Carl T. *Henry.* New York: Greenberg Publishers, 1935.

———. *How to Draw Cartoons Successfully.* New York: Greenberg Publishers, 1935.

Anderson, Doug. *How to Draw with the Light Touch.* New York: Sterling Publishing Co., 1954.

Arno, Peter. *Peter Arno's Cartoon Revue.* New York: Simon & Schuster, 1941.

———. *Man in the Shower.* New York: Simon & Schuster, 1944.

——. *Sizzling Platter*. New York: Simon & Schuster, 1949.

——. *Peter Arno's Ladies & Gentlemen*. New York: Simon & Schuster, 1951.

——. *Hell of a Way to Run a Railroad*. New York: Simon and Schuster, 1956.

Auerbach-Levy, William. *Is That Me? A Book About Caricature*. New York: Watson-Guptill Publications, 1947.

Bacon, Peggy. *Off with Their Heads!* New York: McBride, 1934.

Bailey, John, ed. *Great Cartoons of the World*. New York: Crown Publishers. (A series.)

Baker, George. *Sad Sack*. New York: Simon & Schuster, 1944.

Barlow, Ron, and Stewart, Bhob. eds. *Horror Comics of the 1950s*. New York: Nostalgia Press, 1971.

Batchelor, Clarence D. *Truman Scrapbook*. Deep River, Conn.: Kelsey Hill Publishing, 1951.

Bateman, Michael. *Funny Way to Earn a Living*. London: Leslie Frewin, 1966.

Becker, Stephen D. *Comic Art in America*. New York: Simon & Schuster, 1959.

Bee, Noah. *In Spite of Everything: A History of the State of Israel in Political Cartoons*. New York: Block Publishing Co., 1973.

Berger, Arthur Asa. *Li'l Abner: A Study in American Satire*. New York: Twayne Publishers, 1970.

——. *The Comic-Stripped American*. New York: Walker and Co., 1973.

Berger, Oscar. *My Victims: How to Caricature*. New York: Harper & Brothers, 1952.

Bernstein, Burton. *Thurber*. New York: Dodd, Mead & Co., 1975.

Berry, Jim. *Berry's World*. New York: Four Winds Press, 1967.

Birchman, Willis. *Faces & Facts by and About 26 Contemporary Artists*. Privately printed in an edition of 526 copies, 1937. (Includes biographical information on Peter Arno, Peggy Bacon, David Low, Russell Patterson, Otto Soglow, James Thurber, Gluyas Williams and Art Young.)

Bird, Kenneth (Fougasse). *The Good-Tempered Pencil*. Chester Springs, Pa.: Dufour Editions, 1964.

Blackbeard, Bill, and Williams, Martin, eds. *The Smithsonian Collection of Classic Comic Strips*. Washington, D.C.: Smithsonian Institution, 1976.

Blackbeard, Bill. *The Literature of the Comic Strip*. New York: Oxford University Press, 1976. (A critical history.)

Block, Herbert. *The Herblock Book*. Boston: Beacon Press, 1952.

——. *Herblock's Here and Now*. New York: Simon & Schuster, 1955.

——. *Herblock's Special for Today*. New York: Simon &˙ Schuster, 1958.

——. *Straight Herblock*. New York: Simon & Schuster, 1964.

——. *The Herblock Gallery*. New York: Simon & Schuster, 1968.

——. *Herblock's State of the Union*. New York: Simon & Schuster, 1972.

——. *Special Report*. New York: W. W. Norton & Co., 1974. (Cartoons about Nixon.)

Bradshaw, Percy V. *They Make Us Smile*. London: Chapman & Hall, 1942.

Breger, Dave. *How to Draw and Sell Cartoons*. New York: G. P. Putnam's Sons, 1966.

Brehl, John. *Macpherson*. Toronto, Canada: Toronto Star Limited, 1966. (Cartoons of Duncan Macpherson.)

Briggs, Clare A. *How to Draw Cartoons*. New York: Harper & Brothers, 1926.

——. *The Selected Drawings of Clare Briggs*. 6 vols. New York: Wm. H. Wise & Co., 1930.

Brooks, Charles, ed. *Best Editorial Cartoons of 1972*. Gretna, La.: Pelican Publishing Company, 1973. (First of a projected series.)

Brown, Jerome C. *Classroom Cartoons for All Occasions*. Belmont, Calif.: Fearon Publications, 1969.

Byrnes, Eugene. *Complete Guide to Cartooning*. New York: Grosset & Dunlap, 1953.

Campbell, Mary, and Campbell, Gordon, eds. *The Pen, Not the Sword: A Collection of Great Political Cartoons from 1879 to 1898*. Nashville, Tenn.: Aurora Publishers, 1970.

Caniff, Milton. *Terry and the Pirates*. New York: Nostalgia Press, 1970.

Capp, Al. *From Dogpatch to Slobbovia*. Boston: Beacon Press, 1964.

——. *Who's Who in American Lunacy*. New York: The Macmillan Co., 1969.

——. *The Hardhat's Bedtime Story Book*. New York: Harper & Row, 1971.

Caruso, Enrico. *The New Book of Caricature by Enrico Caruso*. New York: La Follia di New York, 1965.

Cassandra. *Cassandra at His Finest and Funniest*. London: Paul Hamlyn, 1967.

Chase, John Churchill. *Today's Cartoon.* New Orleans: The Hauser Press, 1962. (The work of 140 editorial cartoonists.)

Christ-Janer, Albert. *Boardman Robinson.* Chicago: University of Chicago Press, 1946.

Cleave, Alan. *Cartoon Animation for Everyone.* New York: International Publications Service, 1973.

Cobb, Ron. *Raw Sewage.* Los Angeles: Price/Stern/Sloan, 1970.

——. *My Fellow Americans.* Los Angeles: Price/Stern/Sloan, 1970.

Cole, William, and Robinson, Florett, eds. *Women Are Wonderful! A History in Cartoons of a Hundred Years with America's Most Controversial Figure.* Boston: Houghton Mifflin Co., 1956.

Cole, William, and Thaler, Mike, eds. *The Classic Cartoons: A Definitive Gallery of the Cartoon as Art and Humor.* Cleveland: The World Publishing Co., 1966.

Cole, William, ed. *The Punch Line.* New York: Simon & Schuster, 1969. (Cartoons from *Punch.*)

The Comic Book Price Guide: The Official Blue Book of Comic Values. Robert M. Overstreet, 2905 Vista Drive, N.W., Cleveland, Tenn., 37311. (Annually.)

Conrad, Paul. *The King & Us.* Los Angeles: Clymer Publications, 1974. (Cartoons on Watergate.)

Considine, Bob. *Ripley: The Modern Marco Polo.* New York: Doubleday and Co., 1961.

Cory, J. Campbell. *The Cartoonist's Art.* Chicago: The Tumbo Co., 1912.

Couperie, Pierre, and Horn, Maurice C. *A History of the Comic Strip.* New York: Crown Publishers, 1968.

Craven, Thomas. *Cartoon Cavalcade.* New York: Simon and Schuster, 1943.

Crawford, Charles W., ed. *Cal Alley.* Memphis, Tenn.: Memphis State University Press, 1974.

Crosby, Percy L. *Skippy.* New York: Greenberg Publishers, 1925.

Cruchon, Steve, et al. *Pins and Needlers.* New York: A. S. Barnes & Co., 1967.

Daniels, Les. *Comix: A History of Comic Books in America.* New York: Outerbridge & Dienstfrey, 1971.

Darcy, Tom. *The Good Life.* New York: Avon Books, 1970.

Darling, Jay N. (Ding). *As Ding Saw Hoover.* Ames Iowa: Iowa State College Press, 1954.

Darrow, Whitney, Jr. *Give Up.* New York: Simon & Schuster, 1966.

Darvas, Lou. *You Can Draw Cartoons*. New York: Doubleday & Co., 1960.

Davenport, Homer Calvin. *Cartoons by Homer Davenport*. New York: The DeWitt Publishing House, 1898. (Available as a Finch Press reprint.)

———. *The Country Boy: The Story of His Own Early Life*. New York: G. W. Dillingham Co., 1910.

Dean, Abner. *It's a Long Way to Heaven*. New York: Farrar and Rinehart, 1945.

———. *Cave Drawings for the Future*. New York: Dial Press, 1954.

Dedini, Eldon. *The Dedini Gallery*. New York: Holt, Rinehart & Winston, 1961.

Dille, Robert C., ed. *The Collected Works of Buck Rogers in the 25th Century*. New York: Chelsea House Publishers, 1969.

Dirks, Rudolph. *The Katzenjammer Kids*. New York: Dover Publications, 1974.

Donahue, Don, and Goodrick, Susan, eds. *The Apex Treasury of Underground Comics: R. Crumb and Friends*. New York: Quick Fox, 1974.

Downey, Fairfax. *Portrait of an Era as Drawn by C. D. Gibson*. New York: Charles Scribner's Sons, 1936.

Dunn, Alan. *Who's Paying for This Cab?* New York: Simon and Schuster, 1945.

Durant, John. *Predictions: Pictorial Predictions from the Past*. New York: A. S. Barnes and Co., 1956. (Cartoons from *Life, Judge, Puck*, etc.)

Eller, Vernard. *The Mad Morality: Or the Ten Commandments Revisited*. Nashville: Abingdon Press, 1970.

Esquire Cartoon Album. New York: Esquire, Inc., 1957.

Estren, Mark James. *A History of Underground Comics*. San Francisco: Straight Arrow Books, 1974.

Falk, Lee, and Moore, Ray. *The Phantom*. New York: Nostalgia Press, 1969.

Falk, Lee, and Davis, Phil. *Mandrake the Magician*. New York: Nostalgia Press, 1970.

Feiffer, Jules. *Feiffer's Album*. New York: Random House, 1963.

———. *The Great Comic Book Heroes*. New York: Dial Press, 1965.

———. *Feiffer on Nixon*. New York: Random House, 1974.

Feild, R. D. *The Art of Walt Disney*. New York: The Macmillan Co., 1942.

Finch, Christopher. *The Art of Walt Disney: From Mickey Mouse to the Magic Kingdoms*. New York: Harry N. Abrams, 1973.

Fisher, Ed. *Ed Fisher's First Folio.* New York: The Macmillan Co., 1959.

Fisher, Lois. *Cartooning for Fun and Profit.* Chicago: Wilcox & Follett Co., 1945.

Fitzgerald, Richard. *Art and Politics: Cartoonists of the Masses and Liberator.* Westport, Conn.: Greenwood Press, 1973. (Covers Art Young, Robert Minor, John Sloan, K. R. Chamberlain, Maurice Becker.)

Fitzpatrick, D. R. *As I Saw It.* New York: Simon and Schuster, 1953.

Ffolkes, Michael. *Drawing Cartoons.* New York: Watson-Guptill Publications, 1963.

Foreign Policy Association. *A Cartoon History of United States Foreign Policy Since World War I.* New York: Random House, 1968.

Foster, Walter. *Fun-Sketching—a Pastime that Pays.* New York: The Macmillan Co., 1930.

Francois, André. *The Tattooed Sailor.* New York: Alfred A. Knopf, 1953.

———. *The Half-Naked Knight,* New York: Alfred A. Knopf, 1958.

Fraydas, Stan. *Complete Course in Professional Cartooning.* Huntington, N.Y.: Robert E. Krieger Publishing Co., 1972.

Fredericks, Pierce G., ed. *The People's Choice.* New York: Dodd, Mead & Co., 1956. (Cartoons dealing with the 1956 campaign.)

Frueh, Alfred J. *Frueh on the Theater.* New York: New York Public Library, 1972. (Caricatures.)

Fultz, Barbara, ed. *The Naked Emperor: An Anthology of International Political Satire.* New York: Pegasus, 1970.

Galewitz, Herb, and Winslow, Don, compilers. *Fontaine Fox's Toonerville Trolley.* New York: Charles Scribner's Sons, 1972.

Galewitz, Herb, ed. *Great Comics.* New York: Crown Publishers, 1973. (Reproduction of strips syndicated by Chicago Tribune-New York Daily News Syndicate.)

Galloway, John T., Jr. *The Gospel According to Superman.* Philadelphia: A. J. Holman Co., 1973.

Geipel, John. *The Cartoon: A Short History of Graphic Comedy and Satire.* New York: A. S. Barnes and Co., 1972.

George, M. Dorothy. *English Political Caricature to 1792.* Oxford, England: Clarenden Press, 1959.

———. *Hogarth to Cruikshank: Social Change in Graphic Satire.* New York: Walker & Co., 1967.

Gifford, Denis. *Stop Me! The British Newspaper Strip.* Aylesbury, Bucks, England: Shire Publications Ltd., 1971.

———. *Discovering Comics.* Tring, Herts, England: Shire Publications, 1971.

Gillon, Edmund Vincent, Jr. *The Gibson Girl and Her America.* New York: Dover Publications, 1969.

Gilmore, Donald H. *Sex in Comics: A History of the Eight Pagers.* San Diego: Greenleaf Classics, 1971. (Four volumes.)

Goldberg, Rube. *Is There a Doctor in the House?* New York: The John Day Company, 1919. (Reprint of two magazine articles.)

——. *The Rube Goldberg Plan for the Post-War World.* New York: Franklin Watts, 1944.

——. *How to Remove the Cotton from a Bottle of Aspirin . . . ,* New York: Doubleday & Co., 1959.

Goldberg, Rube, and Boal, Sam. *Rube Goldberg's Guide to Europe.* New York: Vanguard Press, 1954.

Goldwater, John L. *Americana in Four Colors: A Decade of Self-Regulation by the Comics Magazine Industry.* New York: Comics Magazine Association of America, 1964.

Gorey, Edward. *Amphigorey.* New York: G. P. Putnam's Sons, 1972. (Satire in words and pictures.)

Goulart, Ron. *The Adventurous Decade.* New Rochelle, New York: Arlington House, 1974. (Comic strips during the 1930s.)

Gould, Chester. *The Celebrated Cases of Dick Tracy.* New York: Chelsea House Publishers, 1970.

Gray, Harold. *Arf! The Life and Hard Times of Little Orphan Annie, 1935–45.* New Rochelle, N.Y.: Arlington House, 1970.

Greene, Frank F. *How to Create Cartoons.* New York: Harper & Brothers, 1941.

Halas, John, and Privett, Bob. *How to Cartoon.* New York: Amphoto, 1958.

Halas, John, and Manvell, Roger. *The Technique of Film Animation.* 2d ed. New York: Hastings House, 1968.

Hamilton, Wm. *Anti-Social Register.* San Francisco: Chronicle Books, 1974.

Handelsman, J. B. *You're Not Serious, I Hope.* Chicago: Playboy Press, 1971.

Haynie, Hugh. A series published by the *Louisville Courier-Journal.*

Heath, Bob. *Animation in Twelve Hard Lessons.* West Islip, N.Y.: Robert P. Heath Productions, Inc., 1975.

Hecht, George J. *The War in Cartoons.* New York: E. P. Dutton & Co., 1919.

Hefner, Hugh M., ed. *The Twentieth Anniversary Playboy Cartoon Album.* Chicago: Playboy Press, 1974.

Heimer, Mel. *Famous Artists and Writers of King Features Syndicate*. New York: King Features, 1946.

Henderson, Marge. *Little Lulu*. Chicago: Rand McNally & Co., 1945.

Henry, John M., ed. *Ding's Half Century*. New York: Duell, Sloan and Pearce, 1962.

Herdan, Innes, and Herdan, Gustav, eds. *The World of Hogarth: The Lichtenberg Commentaries*. New York: Houghton Mifflin Co., 1966.

Herdeg, Walter, and Pascal, David. *The Art of the Comic Strip*. Zurich: Graphis Press, 1972.

Hergé, *The Adventures of Tintin*, Boston: Little Brown and Co., 1974, 1975. (Series of books reprinting European comic strip.)

Herriman, George. *Krazy Kat*. Edited by Woody Gelman, Joseph Greene, and Rex Chessman. New York: Grosset & Dunlap, 1969.

Hess, Stephen, and Kaplan, Milton. *The Ungentlemanly Art*. New York: The Macmillan Co., 1968.

Hill, Draper. *Mr. Gillray: The Caricaturist*. London: Phaidon, 1965.

———. *Fashionable Contrasts: Caricatures by James Gillray*. London: Phaidon, 1966.

Hillier, Bevis. *Cartoons and Caricatures*. New York: E. P. Dutton & Co., 1970.

Hirschfeld, Al. *Show Business Is No Business*. New York: Simon & Schuster, 1951. (Caricatures.)

———. *The American Theater*. New York: George Braziller, 1961.

———. *The World of Hirschfeld*. New York: Harry N. Abrams, 1970.

Hirsh, Michael, and Loubert, Patrick. *The Great Canadian Comic Books*. Toronto, Canada: Peter Martin Associates Ltd., 1971.

Hoff, Syd. *The Art of Cartooning*. New York: Stravon Educational Press, 1973.

Hofmann, Werner. *Caricature from Leonardo to Picasso*. New York: Crown Publishers, 1957.

Hogarth, Burne. *Tarzan*. New York: Watson-Guptill Publications, 1972.

Hokinson, Helen E. *So You're Going to Buy a Book!* New York: Minton Balch & Co., 1931.

———. *My Best Girls*. New York: E. P. Dutton & Co., 1941.

———. *"When Were You Built?"* New York: E. P. Dutton & Co., 1948.

———. *The Ladies, God Bless 'em!* New York: E. P. Dutton & Co., 1950.

Holme, Geoffrey, ed. *Caricature of To-day*. New York: Albert & Charles Boni, 1928.

Horn, George F. *Cartooning.* Worcester, Mass.: Davis Publications, 1965.

Horn, Maurice. *75 Years of the Comics,* Boston: Boston Book & Art, 1971.

Horn, Maurice, ed. *World Encyclopedia of Comic Art.* New York: Chelsea House, 1975.

Huot, Leland, and Powers, Alfred. *Homer Davenport of Silverton: Life of a Great Cartoonist.* Bingen, Wash.: West Shore Press, 1973.

Ivey, Jim, and Campbell, Gordon, compilers. *Wash Tubbs by Roy Crane.* Brooklyn, N.Y.: Luna Press, 1974. (Strips from 1924 and 1927–30.)

Jacobs, Frank. *The Mad World of William M. Gaines.* New York: Lyle Stuart, 1973.

Johnson, Crockett. *Barnaby.* New York: Dover Publications, 1967. (From *PM,* a newspaper of the 1940s.)

Johnson, Gerald W. *The Lines Are Drawn.* Philadelphia: J. B. Lippincott Co., 1958.

Johnson, Herbert. *Cartoons by Herbert Johnson.* Philadelphia: J. B. Lippincott Co., 1936.

Johnson, Lucy Black, and Johnson, Pyke, Jr. *Cartoon Treasury,* Garden City, N.Y.: Doubleday & Co., 1955.

Jones, Michael Wynn. *The Cartoon History of Britain.* New York: The Macmillan Company, 1971.

Josten, Josef, ed. *The Great Challenge.* London: International Federation of Free Journalists (Hulton House, Fleet Street), 1958.

Justus, Roy. *The Best of Justus.* Minneapolis: Minneapolis Star and Tribune Company, 1975.

Kane, Bob, and Infantino, Carmineintro. *Batman: From the Thirties to the Seventies.* New York: Crown Publishers, 1971.

Kaplan, Martin, ed. *The Harvard Lampoon Centennial Celebration, 1876–1973.* Boston: Little, Brown and Co. 1973.

Keller, Morton. *The Art and Politics of Thomas Nast.* New York: Oxford University Press, 1968.

Kelly, Walt. *The Incompleat Pogo.* New York: Simon & Schuster, 1954.

———. *Ten Ever-Lovin' Blue-Eyed Years with Pogo.* New York: Simon & Schuster, 1959.

———. *Walt Kelly's Pogo Revisited.* New York: Simon & Schuster, 1974. (Reprints *Instant Pogo, The Jack Acid Society Black Book,* and *The Pogo Poop Book.*)

Kempkes, Wolfgang. *The International Bibliography of Comics Literature.* New York: R. R. Bowker Co., 1971.

Ketchum, Alton. *Uncle Sam: The Man and the Legend.* New York: Hill and Wang, 1959.

Key, Ted. *If You Like Hazel.* New York: E. P. Dutton & Co., 1952.

Kinnaird, Clark, ed. *Rube Goldberg vs. the Machine Age.* New York: Hastings House, 1968.

Kirby, Rollin. *Highlights: A Cartoon History of the Nineteen Twenties.* New York: William Farquhar Payson, 1931.

Klingender, Francis Donald, ed. *Hogarth and English Caricature.* London: Transatlantic Arts Ltd., 1944.

Kurtzman, Harvey. *Inside Mad.* New York: Ballantine Books, 1955.

Landin, Leslie. *Blackboard Matinee: A Handbook of Blackboard Cartooning, Games and Ideas for Teachers.* Published by the author, Saratoga, Calif., 1955.

Lariar, Lawrence. *The Easy Way to Cartooning.* New York: Crown Publishers, 1950.

———. *Careers in Cartooning.* New York: Dodd, Mead & Co., 1949.

Lariar, Lawrence, ed. *Best Cartoons of the Year.* New York: Crown Publishers. (A series.)

Lee, Stan. *The Origins of Marvel Comics.* New York: Simon & Schuster, 1974.

Letheve, Jacques. *La Caricature et La Presse Sous La III Republique.* Paris: A. Colin, 1961.

Levine, David.. *The Man from M.A.L.I.C.E.* New York: E. P. Dutton & Co., 1966.

———. *Pens and Needles.* Boston: Gambit, 1969. (Caricatures of writers.)

———. *No Known Survivors: David Levine's Political Prank.* Boston: Gambit, 1970.

Lewis, Beth Irwin. *George Grosz: Art and Politics in the Weimar Republic.* Madison: University of Wisconsin Press, 1971.

Lichty, George. *"Is Party Line, Comrade!"* Washington, D.C.: Public Affairs Press, 1965.

Lockwood, George, ed. *The Cartoons of R. A. Lewis.* Milwaukee: The Journal Co., 1968.

Long, Scott. *Hey! Hey! LBJ!* Minneapolis, Minn.: Ken Sorenson Printing, 1970.

Loomis, Andrew. *Fun with a Pencil.* New York: Viking Press, 1939.

Loria, Jeffrey H. *What's It All About, Charlie Brown? Peanuts Kids Look at America Today.* New York: Holt, Rinehart & Winston, 1969.

Low, David. *The Best of Low.* London: Jonathan Cape, 1928.

————. *Low's Political Parade with Colonel Blimp.* London: Cresset Press, 1936.

————. *Years of Wrath: A Cartoon History, 1931–1945.* New York: Simon & Schuster, 1946.

————. *Low's Cartoon History, 1945–1953.* New York: Simon & Schuster, 1953.

————. *Low's Autobiography.* New York: Simon & Schuster, 1957.

————. *The Fearful Fifties.* New York: Simon & Schuster, 1960.

Lupoff, Dick, and Thompson, Don, eds. *All in Color for a Dime.* New Rochelle, New York: Arlington House, 1970.

Lurie, Ranan R. *Nixon Rated Cartoons.* New York: Quadrangle, 1973.

————. *Pardon Me, Mr. President!* New York: Quadrangle, 1975.

Lynch, Bohun. *A History of Caricature.* Boston: Little, Brown, and Co., 1927. (Mostly foreign.)

Lynx, J. J., ed. *The Pen Is Mightier: The Story of the War in Cartoons.* London: L. Drummond Limited, 1946.

McCay, Winsor. *Little Nemo.* New York: Nostalgia Press, 1972.

McCutcheon, John T. *The Mysterious Stranger and Other Cartoons.* New York: McClure, Phillips & Co., 1905.

————. *Drawn from Memory.* Indianapolis: The Bobbs-Merrill Co., 1950.

McDougall, Walt. *This Is the Life!* New York: Alfred A. Knopf, 1926.

McGeachy, D. P., III. *The Gospel According to Andy Capp.* Richmond, Va.: John Knox, 1973.

McManus, George, *Bringing Up Father.* Edited by Herb Galewitz. New York: Charles Scribner's Sons, 1973.

MacNelly, Jeff. *MacNelly, the Pulitzer Prize Winning Cartoonist.* Richmond, Va.: Westover, 1972.

Macpherson, Duncan. A series published by the *Toronto Star.*

Malton, Leonard. *The Disney Films.* New York: Crown Publishers, 1973.

Markey, Gene. *Literary Lights; A Book of Caricatures.* New York: Alfred A. Knopf, 1923.

Markow, Jack. *Drawing and Selling Cartoons.* 2d ed. New York: Pitman Publishing Corporation, 1964.

————. *Cartoonist's and Gag Writer's Handbook.* Cincinnati: Writer's Digest, 1967.

Marston, William M. *Wonder Woman.* New York: Holt, Rinehart & Winston, 1972.

Marzio, Peter C. *Rube Goldberg.* New York: Harper & Row, 1973.

Matthews, E. C. *How to Draw Funny Pictures.* Chicago: Frederick J. Drake & Co., 1928. (200 illustrations by Zim.)

Mauldin, Bill. *Up Front.* New York: Henry Holt & Co., 1945.

———. *Back Home.* New York: William Sloan Associates, 1947.

———. *What's Got Your Back Up?* New York: Harper & Brothers, 1961.

———. *"I've Decided I Want My Seat Back."* New York: Harper & Row, 1965.

———. *"Some Day, My Boy, This Will All Be Yours."* New York: W. W. Norton & Co., 1968.

———. *The Brass Ring: A Sort of Memoir.* New York: W. W. Norton & Co., 1971.

Maurice, Arthur Bartlett, and Cooper, Frederic Taber. *The History of the Nineteenth Century in Caricature.* New York: Dodd, Mead & Co., 1904.

Maurice, Arthur Bartlett. *How They Draw Prohibition.* New York: The Association Against the Prohibition Amendment, 1930.

Meglin, Nick. *The Art of Humorous Illustration.* New York: Watson-Guptill Publications, 1953.

Mendelson, Lee, in association with Charles Schulz. *Charlie Brown and Charlie Schulz.* New York: World Publishing, 1970.

Milenkovitch, Michael M. *The View from Red Square: A Critique of Cartoons from Pravda and Izvestia, 1947–1964.* New York: Hobbs, Dorman & Company, 1966.

Miller, Diane Disney. *The Story of Walt Disney.* New York: Henry Holt, 1957.

Murrell, William. *A History of American Graphic Humor.* 2 vols. Published for the Whitney Museum of American Art. New York: The Macmillan Co., 1938.

National Cartoonists Society. *President Eisenhower's Cartoon Book by 95 of America's Leading Cartoonists.* New York: Frederick Fell, 1956.

Nelson, Roy Paul. *Fell's Guide to the Art of Cartooning.* New York: Frederick Fell, 1962.

Nelson, William, ed. *Out of the Crocodile's Mouth: Russian Cartoons About the United States From "Krokodil," Moscow's Humor Magazine.* Washington, D.C.: Public Affairs Press, 1949.

Nevins, Allan, and Weitenkampf, Frank. *A Century of Political Cartoons.* New York: Charles Scribner's Sons, 1944.

Newell, Peter. *Topsys & Turvys.* New York: Dover Publications, 1974.

The New Yorker Album, 1955–1965. New York: Harper & Row, 1965.

The New Yorker Album of Art and Artists. Greenwich, Conn.: New York Graphic Society Ltd., 1970.

The New Yorker Album of Sports and Games. New York: Harper & Brothers, 1958.

The New Yorker 1950–55 Album. New York: Harper & Brothers, 1955.

The New Yorker Twenty-Fifth Anniversary Album. New York: Harper & Brothers, 1951.

Nickles, Marione R., ed. *After Hours: Cartoons from the Saturday Evening Post.* New York: E. P. Dutton & Co., 1960.

Norris, Len. A series published by the *Vancouver Sun.*

North, Joseph. *Robert Minor: Artist and Crusader.* New York: International Publishers, 1956.

Oliphant, Pat. *The Oliphant Book.* New York: Simon & Schuster, 1969.

———. *Four More Years.* New York: Simon & Schuster, 1973.

Opper, Frederick. *Willy and His Poppa.* New York: Grosset & Dunlap, 1901.

Osborn, Robert. *Low and Inside.* New York: Farrar, Straus & Young, 1953.

Outcault, Richard Fulton. *Buster Brown.* New York: Dover Publications, 1974.

Paine, Albert Bigelow. *Th. Nast: His Period and His Pictures.* New York: Harper & Brothers, 1904.

Parton, James. *Caricature and Other Comic Art in All Times and Many Lands.* New York: Harper & Brothers, 1878.

Petty, George, and Aldridge, Alan. *The Penguin Book of Comics.* Rev. ed. Baltimore: Penguin Books, 1971.

Price, George. *Geo. Price's Ice Cold War.* New York: Henry Schuman, 1951.

———. *We Buy Old Gold.* New York: Henry Schuman, 1951.

———. *My Dear 500 Friends.* New York: Simon & Schuster, 1963.

Raemaekers, Louis. *Raemaekers' Cartoons.* Garden City, N.Y.: Doubleday, Page, 1917.

———. *Raemaekers' Cartoon History of the War.* New York: The Century Co., 1918–19.

Rajski, Raymond B., ed. *A Nation Grieved: the Kennedy Assassination in Editorial Cartoons.* Rutland, Vermont: Charles E. Tuttle Co., 1967.

Raymond, Alex. *Flash Gordon: Into the Water World of Mongo.* New York: Nostalgia Press, 1971.

Reitberger, Reinhold, and Fuchs, Wolfgang. *Comics: Anatomy of a Mass Medium.* Boston: Little, Brown & Co., 1972.

Reynolds, E. S. *Fifty Cartoons by "Tige" Reynolds.* Portland: Metropolitan Press, 1931.

Robinson, Boardman. *Cartoons on the War.* New York: E. P. Dutton Co., 1915.

Robinson, Jerry. *The Comics.* New York: G. P. Putnam's Sons, 1974.

Rogers, W. G. *Mightier Than The Sword.* New York: Harcourt, Brace & World, Inc., 1969.

Rogers, William A. *Hits at Politics.* New York: Russell, 1896.

——. *America's Black and White Book.* New York: Cupples & Leon, 1917.

——. *A World Worth While.* New York: Harper & Brothers, 1922.

Rosenberg, Manuel. *The Manuel Rosenberg Course in Newspaper Art.* Published by the author, Cincinnati, 1922.

Rosenberg, Marvin, and Cole, William, eds. *The Best Cartoons from Punch,* Simon & Schuster, New York, 1952.

Rosenthal, Lois, ed. *The Writer's Cartoon Book.* Cincinnati: Writer's Digest, 1970.

Rosenthal, Richard, ed. *Cartoonist's Market.* Cincinnati: Writer's Digest, 1971.

Roth, Eugen. *Simplicissimus.* Hanover, Germany: Fackeltrager-Verlag, Schmidt-Küster GMBH, 1954.

St. Hill, Thomas Nast. *The Life and Death of Thomas Nast.* New York: Harper & Row, 1971.

——. *Thomas Nast: Cartoons and Illustrations.* New York: Dover Publications, 1974.

Sanders, Bill. *Run for the Oval Room, They Can't Corner Us There.* Milwaukee: Alpha Press, 1974.

Sanderson, William. *The Acid Test.* William Sanderson, P.O. Box 12012, Portland, Oregon, 1973.

Scarfe, Gerald. *Gerald Scarfe's People.* New York: David White Co., 1966.

Scheyer, Ernst. *Lyonel Feininger: Caricature and Fantasy.* Detroit: Wayne State University Press, 1964.

Schickel, Richard. *The Disney Version.* New York: Simon & Schuster, 1968.

Schulz, Charles. *Peanuts Treasury.* New York: Holt Rinehart & Winston, 1968.

——. *The Snoopy Festival.* New York: Holt, Rinehart & Winston, 1974.

————. *Peanuts Jubilee: My Life and Art with Charlie Brown and Others.* New York: Holt, Rinehart & Winston, 1975.

Segar, E. C. *Thimble Theater, Starring Popeye the Sailor.* New York: Nostalgia Press, 1971.

Seligman, Janet. *Figures of Fun.* New York: Oxford University Press, 1957.

Sempé, Jean-Jacques. *Des Hauts et des Bas* [*The Highs and the Lows*]. Paris, France: Editions Denoël, 1971.

Shaffer, Laurence F. *Children's Interpretations of Cartoons.* New York: Teachers College, Columbia University, 1930.

Sheridan, Martin. *Classic Comics and Their Creators.* Arcadia, Calif.: Post-Era Books, 1973. (Reprint of the 1942 book.)

Shikes, Ralph E. *The Indignant Eye.* Boston: Beacon Press, 1969. (About caricature.)

Short, Robert L. *The Gospel According to Peanuts.* Richmond, Va.: John Knox Press, 1965.

————. *The Parables of Peanuts.* New York: Harper & Row, 1968.

Siegfried, Joan C., ed. *The Spirit of the Comics.* New York: American Federation of Arts, 1970.

Simplicissimus: 180 Satirical Drawings from the Famous German Weekly. New York: Dover Publications, 1975.

Sloan, John. *Gist of Art: Principles and Practice Expounded in the Classroom and Studio.* New York: American Artists Group, 1939.

Smith, Mitchell. *The Art of Caricaturing.* Chicago: Frederick J. Drake & Co., 1941.

Smith, Sidney. *The Gumps.* Edited by Herb Galewitz. New York: Charles Scribner's Sons, 1974.

Spencer, Dick, III. *Editorial Cartooning.* Ames, Iowa: The Iowa State College Press, 1949.

————. *Pulitzer Prize Cartoons.* Ames, Iowa: Iowa State College Press, 1953.

Steadman, Ralph. *America.* San Francisco: Straight Arrow, 1974.

Steig, William. *The Steig Album.* New York: Duell, Sloan & Pearce, 1953.

————. *Dreams of Glory.* New York: Alfred A. Knopf, 1953.

————. *Man About Town.* New York: Ray Long and Richard R. Smith, 1970.

————. *Male-Female,* New York: Farrar, Straus & Giroux, 1971.

————. *The Rejected Lovers.* Rev. ed. New York: Dover Publications, 1973.

Steinberg, Saul. *The Art of Living*. New York: Harper & Brothers, 1949.
———. *The New World*. New York: Harper and Row Publishers, 1965.
———. *The Inspector*. New York: The Viking Press, 1973.
Steranko, James. *The Steranko History of Comics*. Reading, Pa.: Supergraphics, 1970. (A projected series of six volumes.)
Superman: From the Thirties to the Seventies. New York: Crown Publishers, 1971.
Syverson, Henry. *Lovingly Yours*. New York: E. P. Dutton & Co., 1957.
Szep, Paul. A series published by the *Boston Globe*.
Tarbell, Harlan. *The Chalk Talk Manual*. Minneapolis, Minn.: T. S. Denison & Co., 1962.
Taylor, Richard. *Introduction to Cartooning*. New York: Watson-Guptill Publications, 1947.
———. *R. Taylor's Wrong Bag*. New York: Simon & Schuster, 1961.
Thelwell, Norman. *Thelwell's Book of Leisure*. New York: E. P. Dutton & Co., 1969.
The Third New Yorker Album. Garden City, N.Y.: Doubleday, Doran & Co., 1930.
Thomas, Bob. *Walt Disney, The Art of Animation: The Story of the Disney Studio Contribution to a New Art*. New York: Golden Press, 1958.
Thomas, W. H., ed. *The Road to Syndication: The Complete Guide to Newspaper Syndication for Writers and Artists*. New York: Fleet Press Corporation, 1967.
Thompson, Don, and Lupoff, Dick. *The Comic-Book Book*. New Rochelle, N.Y.: Arlington House, 1973.
Thorndike, Chuck. *The Business of Cartooning: The Success Stories of the World's Greatest Cartoonists*. New York: The House of Little Books, 1939.
Thurber, James. *Men, Women and Dogs*. New York: Harcourt, Brace and Company, 1943.
———. *Thurber & Company*. New York: Harper and Row, Publishers, 1966.
Trim, Hal. *Trim's Arena*. New York: Sheed & Ward, 1974.
Trudeau, G. B. *Doonesbury*. New York: American Heritage Press, 1971. (Cartoons about college life. Other *Doonesbury* books are published by Holt, Rinehart & Winston.)
Ungerer, Tomi. *Horrible*. New York: Atheneum Publishers, 1960.
———. *The Underground Sketchbook of Tomi Ungerer*. New York: Dover Publications, 1964.

———. *Tomi Ungerer's Compromises*. New York: Farrar, Straus & Giroux, 1970.

Verbeek, Gustave. *The Incredible Up-Side-Downs*. Rajah Press, Box 23, Summit, N.J. 1969. (From the *New York Herald* at the turn of the century.)

Vinson, J. Chal. *Thomas Nast: Political Cartoonist*. Athens, Ga.: University of Georgia Press, 1967.

Walker, Mort. *Beetle Bailey*. New York: Grosset & Dunlap, 1968.

———. *Backstage at the Strips*. New York: Mason-Charter, 1976.

Walker, Mort, compiler. *The National Cartoonists Society Album*. 1972–77 ed. National Cartoonists Society, 9 Ebony Court, Brooklyn, N.Y. 11229.

Waltner, Elma. *Carving Animal Caricatures*. Gloucester, Mass.: Peter Smith Publisher, 1975.

Waugh, Coulton. *The Comics*. New York: The Macmillan Co., 1947.

Webster, H. T. *The Best of H. T. Webster*. Edited by Robert Sherwood and Philo Calhoun. New York: Simon & Schuster, 1953.

Weitenkampf, F. *American Graphic Art*. New York: Henry Holt & Co., 1912.

Wertham, Frederic. *Seduction of the Innocent*. New York: Rinehart, 1954.

———. *Fanzines: A Special Form of Communications*. Carbondale, Ill.: Southern Illinois University Press, 1973.

Westwood, H. R. *Modern Caricaturists*. London: Lovat Dickson Limited, 1932. (Mostly foreign, but covering Kirby and Fitzpatrick.)

White, David Manning. *From Dogpatch to Slobbovia: The World of Li'l Abner*. Boston: Beacon Press, 1964.

White, David Manning, and Abel, Robert H. eds. *The Funnies: An American Idiom*. New York: The Macmillan Co., 1963.

Whitman, Bert. *Here's How . . . About the Newspaper Editorial Cartoon*. Lodi, Calif.: Lodi Publishing Co., 1968.

Who's Who of American Comic Books. 4 vols. 487 Lakewood Blvd., Detroit, Mich., 48215. (Biographies of comic-book artists.)

Wilkenson, Endymion P. *The People's Comic Book*. Garden City, N.Y.: Doubleday & Co., 1973.

Willette, Allen, comp. *These Top Cartoonists Tell How They Create America's Favorite Comics*. Fort Lauderdale, Fla.: Allied Publications, 1964.

Williams, Gluyas. *The Gluyas Williams Gallery*. New York: Harper & Brothers, 1957.

――――. *The Best of Gluyas Williams,* New York: Dover Publications, 1971.

Williams, Gurney, ed. *Collier's Collects Its Wits,* New York: Harcourt, Brace & Co., 1941. (About 340 cartoons along with 66 self-caricatures.)

――――. *Look on the Light Side.* Englewood Cliffs, N.J.: Prentice-Hall, Inc., 1957. (Cartoons from *Look.*)

Williams, J. R. *Cowboys Out Our Way.* New York: Charles Scribner's Sons, 1951.

Williams, R. E., ed. *A Century of Punch Cartoons.* New York: Simon & Schuster, 1955.

Wilson, Gahan. *I Paint What I See.* New York: Simon & Schuster, 1971.

――――. *Playboy's Gahan Wilson.* Chicago: Playboy Press, 1972.

Wilson, Rowland B. *The Whites of Their Eyes.* New York: E. P. Dutton & Co., 1962.

Wilson, Roy. *Cartooning in the USA.* Cheshire Productions, P.O. Box 494, Torrington, Conn., 1974.

Wright, Don. *Wright On! A Collection of Political Cartoons.* New York: Simon & Schuster, 1971.

Wynn Jones, Michael. *The Cartoon History of Britain.* New York: The Macmillan Co., 1971.

Young, Art. *Art Young: His Life and Times.* New York: Sheridan House, 1939.

――――. *Best of Art Young.* New York: Vanguard Press, 1936.

――――. *On My Way: Being the Book of Art Young in Text and Picture.* New York: Horace Liveright, 1928.

Zaidenberg, Arthur. *Illustrating and Cartooning.* Garden City, New York: Doubleday & Co., 1959.

Periodicals

Cartoon Club Newsletter. 330 Myrtle Street, Redwood City, Calif. 94062. (Monthly.)

The Cartoonist. National Cartoonists Society, 9 Ebony Court, Brooklyn, N.Y. 11229. (Annual.)

Cartoonist Profiles. P.O. Box 325, Fairfield, Conn. 06430. (Quarterly.)

Cartoon World. P.O. Box 30367, Lincoln, Neb. 68510. (Monthly.)

The Gag Re-Cap. Box 86, East Meadow, N.Y. 11554. (Monthly.)

Graphic Story Magazine. 4878 Granada St., Los Angeles, Calif. 90042. (Quarterly.)

The Harvard Journal of Pictorial Fiction. Box 21 Memorial Hall, Harvard University, Cambridge, Mass. 02138. (Semiannual.)

Inside Comics. Galaxy News Service, Inc., 11 West 17th Street, New York, N.Y. 10011. (Quarterly.)

The Menomonee Falls Gazette: America's Greatest Comic Weekly. Menomonee Falls, Wis. (Weekly.)

Olde Time Comics. Box 428H, Seabrook, N.H. (Quarterly.)

The Press. The Greater Buffalo Press, Inc., 302 Grote Street, Buffalo, N.Y. 14207 ("Published almost every other month for the friends of the funnies.")

Index of Cartoonists

Numbers in italics indicate pages containing examples of cartoons.